THE HISTORY OF BRITISH MILITARY BANDS

VOLUME TWO

GUARDS & INFANTRY

THE HISTORY OF BRITISH MILITARY BANDS

VOLUME TWO

GUARDS & INFANTRY

INCLUDING
THE GUARDS DIVISION
THE SCOTTISH DIVISION
THE QUEEN'S DIVISION

THE HISTORY OF BRITISH MILITARY BANDS

VOLUME TWO

GUARDS & INFANTRY

INCLUDING
THE GUARDS DIVISION
THE SCOTTISH DIVISION
THE QUEEN'S DIVISION

MAJOR (Retd)
GORDON TURNER
MBE BA ARCM LGSM FTCL FLCM

& ALWYN W TURNER BA

SPELLMOUNT
PUBLISHERS
STAPLEHURST

Also available:

Volume I
Cavalry and Corps
(including The Parachute Regiment,
The Brigade of Gurkhas)

To be published

Volume III
Infantry and Irish
(King's Division, The Prince of Wales's
Division, The Light Division and the Irish
regiments)

Frontispiece:
Bugler, 2nd Battalion The Lincolnshire Regiment,
Tower of London 1905   (Eagles/Ogilby)
Left:
Band Sergeant Eustace Cox, Grenadier Guards   (M Cox)
Right:
Bass drummer, Scots Fusilier Guards   (Turner)

British Library Cataloguing in Publication Data
A catalogue record for this book is available from
the British Library.

Copyright © Gordon Turner and Alwyn W. Turner

ISBN 1-873376-08-1

First published in the UK in 1996 by
Spellmount Limited
The Old Rectory
Staplehurst
Kent TN12 0AZ

1 3 5 7 9 8 6 4 2

Design by Words & Images, Burwash, East Sussex
Printed in Great Britain by
Short Run Press Ltd, Exeter

CONTENTS

ACKNOWLEDGEMENTS

At the risk of repeating ourselves, we must thank again those we thanked in the first volume of this series. Messrs William Tanner, Reg Saunders and Stanley Eagles spent many years compiling lists of bandmasters, notes on regimental music and photographic archives respectively; we have drawn heavily on the work of all three, and again express our gratitude for their historical endeavours.

Similarly our thanks are due to the directors of music and bandmasters – both serving and retired – and to the librarians and curators of all the regimental museums who have assisted our research, including those of the National Army Museum in Chelsea, and the Royal Military School of Music at Kneller Hall. In particular we are indebted to Colonel Peter Walton of the Ogilby Trust in Winchester, who administers the Stanley Eagles collection of photographs, and to Mr Colin Dean: the courtesy and enthusiasm of both has been invaluable.

To these, we must add the contributions made by Mr Walter Babbs, Mr Bill Coughlan, Captain (retd) Bill Ewbank MC, Major James Falkner, Mr Charles Packer MM, Mr Tim Parkinson, Captain (retd) Cliff Pike, Mr Alan le Vicount, Lieutenant-Colonel (retd) Les Wilson MBE and the late Mr Jerome Gatehouse.

The most notable omissions from our earlier list of credits were those at Spellmount Publishers who have encouraged and shaped this project: Mr Ian Morley-Clarke, Mr Jamie Wilson, our editor Ms Elizabeth Imlay and the designer, Ms Diane Drummond.

Finally we would wish to record once more our appreciation of the support and assistance rendered by Ms Olive Turner.

The outlines of the regimental evolutions at the beginning of each chapter are taken from Mr David Ascoli's *A Companion to the British Army 1660-1983*, published by Harrap Ltd in 1983.

PICTURE CREDITS

We would like to thank the following museums, bands and individuals for providing photographs for this book: Army Museums Ogilby Trust, Royal Military School of Music (Kneller Hall), Stanley Eagles Collection, Grenadier Guards Bands, Coldstream Guards Band, Scots Guards Band, Irish Guards Band, Welsh Guards Band, Royal Scots Band, Queen's Own Highlanders Band, Gordon Highlanders Band, Argyll and Sutherland Highlanders Band, 3rd Battalion Royal Anglians Band, Rodney Bashford, Peter Clarke, Michael Cox, Brian Cunningham, Colin Dean, Peter Hannam, James Howe, Kevin Lamb, Wolfgang Luedecke, A Noble, Charles Packer, Tim Parkinson, Cliff Pike, Antony Richards, Robin Ridewood, Norman Rogerson, Ernest Trotter, Dick Tulip, Jean Walker, Vic Webster.

COMPACT DISC

All tracks on the compact disc were recorded by the Band of the Royal Corps of Signals conducted by Major D F Wall and Major G Turner, and are leased from Droit Music Ltd, 38 Pashley Road, Eastbourne, East Sussex, BN20 8DY.

Left: Bandmasters: L Stockham, KOSB; J H Howe, A&SH; C E Smith, RS; C H Pike, Cameronians (RMSM)

Above: Trumpeters, Royal Sussex Regiment, Lewes 1949

(Eagles/Ogilby)

INTRODUCTION

THE EVOLUTION OF THE INFANTRY

The first volume of this history of the bands of the British Army covered the cavalry and the corps. In this second volume we venture into the infantry with the Foot Guards, the Scottish infantry regiments and The Queen's Division, and at this point a word of warning is perhaps necessary. The evolution of the British Army is far from straightforward, with a seemingly endless series of re-namings, renumberings, amalgamations and disbandments; this is particularly true of the infantry of the line, where regimental histories can sometimes be of labyrinthine complexity.

The first key date is 1881, when the Army was restructured under the influence of Lord Cardwell. By the time the process was complete, there were fewer infantry regiments, and the numbering system indicating seniority, in operation since the Restoration, had been replaced by a series of county titles.

The senior infantry regiments – the 1st Foot through to the 25th – each consisted of two battalions by this stage, and the reforms had little effect on them, save for the formalizing of a county attachment that in most cases already existed: thus the 17th (Leicestershire) Foot became The Leicestershire Regiment. There were some new titles, so that the 20th (East Devonshire) Foot became The Lancashire Fusiliers, but generally the first and second battalions of the old formation simply changed their regimental titles and continued as the first and second battalions of the new unit.

For the majority of the infantry, however, 1881 also brought amalgamations: two regiments of a battalion apiece came together to form a single regiment comprising two battalions. In a typical example, The 49th (Princess of Wales's) Hertfordshire Foot became the 1st Battalion, and The 66th (Berkshire) Foot became the 2nd Battalion of the newly formed Berkshire Regiment (Princess Charlotte of Wales's). The old regimental connexions were thus honoured in the new title, but unofficially even the discarded numbers still retained their appeal; for more than half a century, many regiments continued to refer to the two battalions by the original numbers, keeping alive the pre-1881 traditions.

The organization of military music was less affected by 1881. The bands simply transferred to the new regimental allegiance – with, for instance, the Band of the 57th (West Middlesex) Foot being re-named the Band of the 1st Battalion, The Middlesex Regiment – and for the most part separate marches were retained to distinguish the battalions, but there was one major change.

The growing strength of Kneller Hall as the governing body of military music had begun to produce a more regular system of appointments and a more consistent standard of performance. This fact, combined with the growing demand for music in the Empire, was prompting a re-evaluation of the position of bands, and the 1881 reforms responded to their growing status by creating the rank of Warrant Officer (Bandmaster); prior to this, the leader of the band had been a Sergeant Bandmaster (not to be confused with the Band Sergeant).

When the rank of Warrant Officer was split into two classes in 1915, the bandmaster became a WO1 (BM). A year earlier, the title Director of Music had been introduced, to signify the status of commissioned leaders of bands.

Between 1881 and the end of the Second World War, the structure of the infantry remained largely intact. Several regiments raised short-lived 3rd and 4th Regular Battalions at the turn of the century, but the essential character was untouched. It was not until 1947/8 that a further blow was dealt to the old traditions: the post-war reduction in the Army saw the disbandment of the 2nd Battalions of the infantry of the line, and with them went the fiercely protected

Right: Bandmaster W Windram, 2 Gordons   (RMSM)

'The Raw Recruit' – oil painting by Miss Gloag, exhibited at the Royal Academy Summer Exhibition 1893   (Noble)

division between the component regiments from pre-1881 days.

Thereafter the evolution of the infantry lost all sense of organic development and became instead a series of cost-cutting exercises, in which logic was not always discernible. Between 1958 and 1960, for example, The East Anglian Regiment brought together six existing regiments (one of them from the Midland Brigade) into three battalions; in 1964 The Royal Leicestershire Regiment was added and The Royal Anglian Regiment was formed with four battalions, the fourth of which was disbanded in 1970 and the third in 1992.

For military bands, the creation of these large amalgamated regiments was not the end of the story. In 1984 the three surviving battalions of The Queen's Regiment opted to merge their music into two larger bands rather than the three small combinations then existing. Thus the Albuhera Band and the Quebec Band of The Queen's Regiment represented the result of a century of amalgamations: twelve bands had been reduced to just two. (Though even this was not to last: in 1992 The Queen's

Regiment amalgamated with the Hampshires, with just two bands surviving.)

In an attempt to make some sense of this maze of mergers, we have adopted the following structure.

As in *Volume One*, the chapters are based on the 1992 Army List, i.e. the regiments as they existed prior to the implementation of the Options for Change programme of cuts. Regiments that were amalgamated in 1881 are covered within their post-1881 formations, since for the bands at least there was no break in continuity. Thus – to return to the example cited above – the Bandmasters of the 57th Foot have been listed under the 1st Battalion, The Middlesex Regiment, though the career details of each give the regimental title appropriate to the era.

At the beginning of each of the groups of chapters, we have given a brief summary of the evolution of the regiments concerned, which we hope will provide a map through the maze.

Only the regular battalions of the regiments have been covered. Though occasional reference is made to territorial battalions, the pressures of space and the absence of sufficient records regrettably do not allow for a full treatment of the many fine bands that were not part of the regular standing army.

Finally, we must mention the role of pipes in the Scottish regiments and of the corps of drums in the infantry generally. These are not part of the military bands, and therefore technically fall outside the remit of this book. Nonetheless, we recognize that for most people Scottish military music is inextricably tied up with the sound of the pipes, and we have therefore felt free to mention their history and achievements in the text. Similarly, we have included references to the drums where it seemed appropriate to us so to do. We understand that, for some in the Army, this is an unpardonable confusion, but we trust the general reader will appreciate our decision.

Tidworth Tattoo 1934   (RMSM)

THE GUARDS DIVISION

Under Army Order 34, dated 1968, what had been known as the Brigade of Guards was retitled The Guards Division. It comprises the five foot guard regiments:

Grenadier Guards	raised 1660
Coldstream Guards	raised 1660
Scots Guards	raised 1660
Irish Guards	raised 1900
Welsh Guards	raised 1915

All five regiments still have bands.

BAND OF THE

GRENADIER GUARDS

GRENADIER GUARDS

1660	The King's Royal Regiment of Guards
1685	The First Regiment of Foot Guards
1815	The 1st, or Grenadier Regiment of Foot Guards

The Grenadier Guards trace back their origin to around 1656 during the exile of Charles II; when a new standing army was formed on the Restoration in 1660, it included the King's Royal Regiment of Foot Guards. From the outset, drummers were included in the establishment, the King's Company being allowed three drummers and the remaining companies two each. In October 1662 the position of drum-major was created with the pay of one shilling and sixpence per day; at the same time a single fifer was added to the establishment at one shilling a day.

In 1664, under the terms of a Royal Warrant, a musician by the name of Peter Vanhausen was engaged to instruct one man per company to play the fife. He was paid one shilling and sixpence per day, the fruits of his labour being the birth of the Grenadiers Band, generally considered to date from 1665.

A warrant signed by Charles II on 3 January 1685 authorized the maintenance of twelve hautbois in the King's Regiment of Foot Guards in London, though there seems to have been some confusion over the funding of these musicians. It was initially suggested that false names be added to the regimental roll so that the players could be given a better wage, but state papers from 1686 refer to payments being made to drummers and hautbois, implying that the crown took a direct interest in the music of the senior regiment of foot guards. Eighty years later, there is mention in official documents of the purchase of liveries, for the hautbois serving with a troop of mounted Grenadiers under the Duke of Monmouth.

Gradually the instrumentation was expanded; according to *St James's Evening Post* two French horns were added in 1725, whilst bugle horns costing £27 were purchased in 1772.

In the mid-18th century military music was dominated by Germany, probably due to the influence of the Duke of Cumberland, son of the Hanoverian George II and a man referred to by

Drummers, 1st Battalion Grenadier Guards c1874 (Eagles/Ogilby)

historian Fortescue as 'a soldier of the extremest German type'. From the *London Evening Post* of April 1749 we learn that:

> *On Sunday last the English Band of Music belonging to the First Regiment of Guards received their dismission to make room for a band of Germans.*

The success of this musical migration is apparent from Dr Burney's *Present State of Music in Germany* in which he writes of his visit to Mannheim in 1772:

> *The first music I have heard here is military. The retreat had only drums and fifes, and in the morning there was nothing worth listening to. If I had any inclination to describe in a pompous manner merely the effects of wind instruments in martial music, there had been no occasion for me to leave London, for in St James' and in the Park every morning there is an excellent band.*

By 1783 the instrumentation had settled down to that of the continental wind octet known as 'Harmonie Musik'. This comprised: 2 hautboys, 2 clarinets, 2 bassoons and 2 horns. The hautboys were the main melodic instruments, with clarinets taking a secondary role.

A decade later comes the first mention of a bandmaster. *The Musical Directory, London* of 1794 gives 34 Tufton Street, Westminster as the address of Mr Elrington, flute player and bandmaster of the 1st Foot Guards. The same source mentions sixteen other members of the band, five of whom had the same address. The instrumentation was one flute, six clarinets, three bassoons, three horns, one trumpet, two serpents and one drums. Another report from the era omits mention of drums but does talk of 'Turkish Music', referring to the contemporary fashion for flamboyant percussion instruments.

These instruments were played by black musicians, who, when it came to smaller items such as cymbals and tambourines, were often very young. The bass drummer, however, was invariably older with a formidable physique, as seen in the well known lithograph by E Hull showing the big drummer of the Grenadiers in 1829.

The first bandmaster to be named in the regimental records was Mr Blaney, who was almost certainly James Blaney, a clarinettist whose name appears in *The Musical Directory* along with Mr Elrington. He had joined the Regiment in 1784 at the age of ten, and when he was eventually discharged on medical grounds, he was awarded a pension because 'his conduct throughout his long service has been such as to entitle him to every consideration'. Mr Blaney took over in 1815 whilst the Band was with the British troops during the occupation of Paris.

By 1848 the instrumentation had expanded to: 2 flutes, 1 piccolo, 3 Eb clarinets, 8 Bb clarinets, 3 bassoons, 4 French horns, a family of trumpets, 1 althorn, 3 ophicleides, 3 tambourines and drums. Later additions were saxophones, cornets, flugel horn, euphonium and bass.

In 1856 Dan Godfrey, son of Charles Godfrey of the Coldstream Guards, was appointed bandmaster. Although only 25 years of age, he had studied at the Royal Academy of Music and had the reputation of being a first-class musician. He was to remain in his post for 40 years.

One of Dan Godfrey's major contributions was the bringing of ever-greater audiences to military concerts, particularly with his performances in Hyde Park. He later commented on this development:

The original proposal was that we should play on a Wednesday or Saturday. I urged that it would be better for us to play on a day when as many people as possible could come and hear us, and that Sunday would be best. I gained my point. I believe about 90,000 were present the first time we played, and I shall not easily forget the cheer I got when I went to my stand.

In the summer of 1872, the Band visited the United States to take part in the International Peace Jubilee, held in Boston. This was the first time that a British Army band had toured abroad in the absence of its regiment and it took a debate in parliament to sanction the visit. The other guest band was that of the German Grenadier Regiment.

On the occasion of Queen Victoria's Jubilee in 1887, the Queen had Dan Godfrey gazetted as Lieutenant, the first bandmaster in the British Army to be commissioned, albeit with an honorary title.

Sousa's Band and Grenadier Guards, USA, 1904, Bandmaster A Williams   (RMSM)

The following decade Lt Godfrey finally retired and was replaced by Mr Albert Williams of the Royal Marine Artillery Band.

Although very much a product of the Army, having joined as a boy knowing virtually nothing about music, Lieutenant Williams had already passed the examination of Bachelor of Music at Oxford University and was later to be awarded a Doctorate of Music. On this occasion, in 1906, the entire Grenadier Guards Band travelled to Oxford at their own expense to witness the ceremony of the conferring of the degree, and to hear the Vice-Chancellor comment, 'I understand that you are a pioneer in the Army in regard to the degree of Doctor of Music. I hope it will bear the fruit it deserves.'

Lt Williams was also a pioneer when it came to new music. When Richard Strauss wrote the opera *Elektra* in 1909, he quickly made an arrangement of it for the Band; unfortunately the first performance was to an audience that included George V, who had never been noted for his adventurous musical taste. A message was passed to Lt Williams which read, 'His Majesty does not know the name of the music played this morning, but it will not be played again.'

In 1904 the Band once more visited the United States, this time extending the tour to include Canada. In 1919 the Band was in Canada again for the Canadian National Exhibition, where a fellow visitor was the Prince of Wales.

After 44 years in the service, Dr Williams retired in 1921 in the rank of Captain. The King received him in audience and, graciously putting to one side their musical differences, conferred upon him the honour of the Royal Victorian Order. In 1922 the Worshipful Company of Musicians made a presentation at which Sir Dan Godfrey, son of the previous incumbent and conductor of the Bournemouth Symphony Orchestra, offered an even greater compliment: 'Dr Williams was a musician of such culture as had never before occupied the position of Director of Music of the British Army.'

His successor was George Miller, who had been bandmaster of the 1st Life Guards since 1908. He was the son of Major George Miller, formerly bandmaster of the Royal Marines, Portsmouth, and grandson of Bandmaster George Miller of the Manchester Regiment.

In 1931 the Band made an extremely successful tour of South Africa and Southern Rhodesia. The Band had prepared by learning several Boer folk songs, a gesture that won the South Africans' hearts.

Major G Miller (later Lt-Col), Grenadier Guards
(RMSM)

Up until the Second World War, the uniform of the Grenadiers Band had a distinctive feature commemorating King Charles II. A dark blue cloth went half round the arm and was a relic of the old mourning band worn for Charles II who, as mentioned had introduced the hautbois. A further distinctive feature of foot guards' uniforms which has survived is the grouping of the buttons on the front of their tunics: the Grenadiers being the senior are normally spaced, Coldstreamers grouped in twos, Scots in threes, Irish in fours and the Welsh in fives.

During the war years, the Band gave many

Grenadier Guards, New York, 1956, Director of Music Lt-Col F Harris   (RMSM)

concerts to boost morale and also to raise funds for the war effort. In 1944 the bandsmen entertained the troops in Europe and North Africa. It was in Italy in July of that year that they played for King George VI, an occasion described in a soldier's letter home:

> *We were lucky, as the Indians fought a good little battle about six miles away. He had a wonderful view, first from an OP [observation post] in Arezzo and then from his bath, while the Grenadier band played just behind his caravan. He was thrilled. Few Kings these days can have watched a battle from his bath to the strains of martial music by his own guards.*

> (Morris *Circles of Hell* p.358)

In 1947 the Band renewed its ties with North America, playing concerts in 52 Canadian and US cities over three months; Director of Music Fred Harris, now in his nineties, remembers that visit as a particularly punishing schedule, with the Band travelling across virtually the whole continent by coach.

Such is the popularity of the Grenadiers in the USA that, during a short tour in the autumn of 1971, Mayor Richard Martin of New London, Connecticut, designated 30 September as 'Grenadier Guards Band Day'. Six years later the Band, accompanied by the pipes, drums and dancers of the Scots Guards, covered another 18,000 miles touring the States, and ten years after that it returned yet again, this time with the pipes and drums of The Gordon Highlanders, on a 75-day, 64-city tour.

Though the practice of employing German band-masters and musicians in the British Army ceased a century ago, the Grenadiers in recent years have featured a curious throw-back to the old traditions. Karl Schauenberg joined the Regiment shortly after the war as a trumpet-player and cellist, retiring in the rank of Colour Sergeant in 1984.

1985 was the tercentenary of the Band and amongst the many engagements was a visit to the 2nd Battalion in Belize. The Band travelled to Punta Gorda to visit part of the Battalion at Salamanca, and then into the jungle to play to a tribe descended from the ancient Maya Indian civilization. At the beginning of March, it flew out to Australia for a six-week tour that was to encompass the Melbourne

Military Tattoo (which formed part of the celebrations for the 150th Anniversary of the State of Victoria) and concerts in Townsville, Rockhampton and Brisbane in Queensland. In October a Tercentenary Concert was given at the Royal Albert Hall. On this occasion, guest conductors were Lt-Col Fred Harris (who had retired in 1960 and was aged 85) and Lt-Col Rodney Bashford.

In 1989 the Band were in France and Spain, and in 1991 eighteen musicians toured Osaka, Bangkok, Hong Kong and Singapore. This latter tour featured a period ensemble, with musicians dressed in 18th-century costume – a highly popular item in the Band's performances in recent years.

Regimental Music

The quick march is the famous song 'The British Grenadiers':

Some talk of Alexander,
And some of Hercules,
Of Hector and Lysander,
And such great names as these.
But of all the world's great heroes,
There's none that can compare,
With a tow row row row row row
To the British Grenadiers.

Whene'er we are commanded
To storm the pallisades,
Our leaders march with fuses
And we with hand grenades.
We throw them from the glacis
About the enemy's ears,
With a tow row row row row row
For the British Grenadiers.

And when the siege is over,
We to the town repair
The Townsmen cry hurrah boys
Here comes a Grenadier,
Here comes a Grenadier, my boys
Who knows no doubt or fears,
Then sing tow row row row row row
To the British Grenadiers.

Then let us fill a bumper
And drink a health to those
Who carry caps and pouches
And wear the Louped Clothes,
May they and their Commanders
Live happily all their years,
With a tow row row row row row
For the British Grenadiers.

Capt (later Lt-Col) R Bashford, Grenadier Guards
(Bashford)

The origin of the tune is not known but it is extremely old and can be found in various forms. It first appeared in print in roughly the present version in 1740. As Grenadier companies were not introduced into the British Army until 1678, the words are unlikely to date from before then.

The tune was adopted as the regimental march in 1815 but prior to this had been used by all Grenadier companies in the British Army. The Grenadier companies were the right-hand companies of infantry

Left: Major F Harris (later Lt-Col), Grenadier Guards

Below: Captain A E Williams, Grenadier Guards

(RMSM)

battalions, and it is thought that this accounts for the usage of the tune in the Trooping of the Colour ceremony when the Escort, the right flank company, marches down to receive the colour.

The slow march is 'Scipio' composed by George Frederick Handel and used in the opera of that name, first performed in 1726. Some authorities consider that it was composed prior to that date and presented to the 1st Foot Guards before being introduced into the opera.

'The Grenadiers March' is used both in slow and quick time. As a slow march it is used throughout much of the Army when the colours are trooped, and as a quick march is always played as the final march into barracks when the full battalion of Grenadier Guards has been on parade. The tune dates back to about 1776.

Come, come, my brave boys, let's away to the town,
Where the drums they do beat, and the trumpets
* do sound,*
Our bridges shall be laid, in order to storm them;
If they'll not surrender, so bravely we'll warm
* them.*
Our bridges shall be laid, in order to storm them;
If they'll not surrender, so bravely we'll warm
* them.*

We'll warm them so bravely with powder and ball;
He that enters the town shall be landlord of all.
Come, brave grenadiers, let your grenades deliver,
And make these French dogs and their proud
* hearts to quiver.*
Come, brave grenadiers, let your grenades deliver,
And make these French dogs and their proud
* hearts to quiver.*

BANDMASTERS AND DIRECTORS OF MUSIC OF THE GRENADIER GUARDS

1664-16?? **VANHAUSEN**, Peter (also recorded as van Hausen and van Hansen; commencement also recorded as 1674).

1794-1815 **ELRINGTON**, E D (also recorded as James and surname as Elerington; dates also recorded as 1780-1801). MoB Gren Gds 1794; retd 1815.

1815-1822 **BLANEY**, James (also recorded as Blayney; dates also recorded as 1801-1830). Born 1774 died 18??. Enl Gren Gds 4/84; MoB (probably a Sgt) Gren Gds 1815; retd 1822.

1822-1830 Bandmaster(s) not known, though see James Blaney above.

1830-1838 **HARDY**, William. Civ BM (possibly a Sgt) Gren Gds 1822; transferred SG 1838; retd 1842.

1838-1844 **SIBOLD**, William J. Civ BM (possibly a Sgt) Gren Gds 1838; retd 1844.

1844-1856 **SCHOTT**, Adam J. For full details see Queen's Own Highlanders.

1856-1896 **GODFREY**, Daniel MVO FRAM. Born 1831 died 1903. Sgt (BM) Gren Gds 2/7/56; retd rank of Lt 31/12/96.

1897-1921 **WILLIAMS**, Albert Edward MVO Mus Doc. Born 1863 died 1926. Enl 61st (South Gloucestershire) Regiment 14/1/78; WO (BM) 10H 11/2/88; WO (BM) RM Artillery 1/4/92; WO (BM) Gren Gds 1/1/97; 2 Lt (BM) 2/1/07; retd 28/7/21 rank Capt.

1921-1942 **MILLER**, George John MVO MBE LRAM psm. Born 1877 died 1960. Enl 4 KRRC 20/1/96; WO (BM) 1 DCLI 22/11/98; WO (BM) RA (Port) 1/4/03; WO (BM) 1 LG 16/10/07; Lt (DoM) 1/3/19; Lt (DoM) Gren Gds 4/10/21; Snr DoM Bde Gds 1937; retd 19/1/42 rank of Lt-Col.

1942-1960 **HARRIS**, Frederick John OBE (MBE) ARCM psm. Born 1900. Enl 1 Wilts R 22/6/16; WO1 (BM) 2 E York R 22/3/30; WO1 (BM) RA (Sal Pl) 9/4/38; Lt (DoM) Gren Gds 20/1/42; Snr DoM Bde Gds 1959; retd 15/7/60 rank of Lt-Col.

1960-1970 **BASHFORD**, Rodney Bowman OBE LRAM ARCM psm. Born 1917. Enl 2 KRRC 2/8/32; WO1 (BM) 17/21L 5/2/50; WO1 (BM) RMSM 27/10/54; Lt (DoM) RAC JLR (badged 17/21L) 1/9/59; Lt (DoM) Gren Gds 16/7/60; Snr DoM Household Div 1968; Lt-Col RMSM 19/10/70; retd 17/6/74; RO2 (Ass DoM) RMSM 18/6/74.

1970-1977 **PARKES**, Peter William LRAM ARCM psm. Born 1928. Enl 1 Leicester R 20/9/45; WO1 (BM) 1 DCLI 2/2/54; WO1 (BM) SCLI 6/10/59; Lt (DoM) RTR (Alamein) 22/5/62; Capt (DoM) RE (Chat) 9/5/64; Capt (DoM) Gren Gds 19/10/70; Maj (DoM) RAMC 1977; retd 7/5/79.

1977-1987 **KIMBERLEY**, Derek Richard MBE FTCL LRAM LGSM LTCL ARCM psm. Born 1931. For full details see Royal Warwickshire Fusiliers.

1987-1988 **PARKER**, Rodney James FTCL ARCM psm. Born 1941. For full details see RRF.

1988-1992 **WATTS**, Stuart Alastair LRAM psm. Born 1945. For full details see 3 R Anglian.

1992 **HILLS**, Phillip Elvin FLCM psm. Born 1947. For full details see Albuhera Band, The Queen's Regiment.

Bandmaster (Training Officer)

1994 **WHITTINGHAM**, Terence W, LTCL. Born 1956. For full details see QO Hldrs 7/12/87.

BAND OF THE

COLDSTREAM GUARDS

COLDSTREAM GUARDS

1660	General Monk's Regiment of Foot (also 'The Coldstreamers')
1661	The Lord General's Regiment of Foot
1662	The Lord General's Regiment of Foot Guards
1670	The Coldstream Regiment of Footguards (also 2nd Foot Guards)
1817	The Coldstream Guards

The Coldstream Guards claim a double distinction in the British Army: first that it is the oldest regiment in continuous existence, and second that it is the sole representative by direct descent of the New Model Army, the first regular army in Britain. Raised in 1650 by General George Monck (sometimes spelt Monk), it transferred to the new standards in 1661 in a ceremony that consisted of laying down its arms and taking them up again in the service of the King. Charles II conferred the titles of Duke of Albemarle and Lord General upon Monck, and the Regiment retained its connexion with him until his death in 1670.

The Coldstream regimental motto is 'Nulli Secundus' (Second to None) partially in recognition of its claim to be the oldest regiment. In keeping with this, the Regiment has always insisted that if it cannot march at the head of the Household Division then it will march at the end.

The aforementioned Royal Warrant of 1685 that entitled the Grenadiers to add hautbois to their establishment applied also to the Coldstream.

As can be seen from pictures in the possession of the Regiment, there was, in addition to a Corps of Drums, a band of eight musicians as early as 1742. By 1768 the Coldstream Guards had what was described as 'a fine Band of Musik', comprised of civilians who were hired by the month. Their only military duty was to march the guard from St James' Park to the Palace and back.

An inherent conflict between musical and military roles was exposed in 1783, when Lord Cathcart, an officer of the Regiment, asked the Band to play during an aquatic excursion to Greenwich; the musicians refused on the grounds that such an engagement was 'incompatible with their several respectable and private engagements'. The officers petitioned their Colonel-in-Chief, the Duke of York,

Lt-Col J Mackenzie Rogan, Coldstream Guards
(RMSM)

then in Hannover, for leave to have a band that they could command at all times. The Duke enlisted twelve German musicians – two oboes, four clarinets, two bassoons, one trumpet, two horns and a serpent – and sent them to London. They were led by Music-Master Eley, remembered today for his slow march, 'Duke of York'. Reporting on the change, *The Times* of 20 May 1785 spared a thought for the dismissed musicians:

This day the new musical band belonging to the Coldstream Regiment of Guards will mount guard for the first time on the parade in St James's Park. They are young lads from Germany, with a captain who is their master of music, making eleven in number. They have enlisted for eight years and are to be under the same martial law as a private man; their pay is nine shillings per week per man, and one guinea for the captain.

In all probability we never shall hear a regimental band equal to that which is dismissed, they have for many years been a treat to those persons who have attended the courtyard at St James's, and we sincerely hope, after so long and faithful service, they will at least be entitled to half pay for the remainder of their lives.

Mr Eley was succeeded in turn by John Weyrauch in 1800 and by James Denman in 1815. By this time the band had been augmented by flutes, key bugles and trombones and now numbered 20 performers. With this combination, the Coldstream Guards were ordered to Paris during the occupation following Waterloo.

For several years the Coldstream Band, in keeping with those of other regiments, had three black musicians playing tambourines and a 'Jingling Johnny'. The practice was discontinued in 1837.

In 1818 Thomas Lindsay Willman was appointed bandmaster. One of the best and most popular clarinettists of his day, holding appointments with the Philharmonic and Opera orchestras as well as with the Band, he employed the curious technique of playing with the reed against his upper lip. Under his guidance the Coldstream became renowned for its woodwind section, producing most famously Henry Lazarus, who took over from Mr Willman as principal clarinettist with the Opera orchestra in 1840. Mr Lazarus was later to become Professor of Clarinet at the Royal Academy of Music, at Kneller Hall and at the Royal College of Music.

When Mr Willman retired in 1825, Charles Godfrey, who had joined the Band from the Surrey Militia, was appointed bandmaster. Charles was the founder of the dynasty that was to have such a marked influence on military music. (See 'Musical Families' in *Volume One*). When he completed his military service in 1834, the officers of the Regiment retained him as a civilian bandmaster until his death at the age of 73.

His second son, Frederick Adolphus, joined the Coldstream Guards in 1856 and took over the baton when his father died in 1863. Frederick Godfrey was renowned in his day as an arranger and, although his works are now a little dated in style and content, some of his transcriptions of the classics are still played.

The Coldstream tradition of exceptional musicians was continued during Charles Godfrey's era by Bandsman Phasey, a virtuoso who did much to popularize the euphonium in Britain. Indeed, although the instrument had been invented in 1790, Mr Phasey's contribution to its technical develop-

Coldstream Guards, 1921, Director of Music Lt R Evans   (RMSM)

ment was such that it was almost named the Phasey-phone; wisely rejecting the honour, he instead gave it the name of euphonium. In 1859 he became the first professor of euphonium at Kneller Hall.

After more than half a century of Godfreys, Mr Cadwallader Thomas, who had joined the Cold-stream Guards Band in 1853, took up the position of bandmaster. He was another outstanding clarinet-tist and had been bandmaster at the Duke of York's School for ten years prior to returning to his old regiment. He had the misfortune, however, to serve between, and thus be overshadowed by, the two Godfreys and the next incumbent, John Mackenzie Rogan.

The Coldstream Guards Band under Mr Rogan was the first British Army band to visit one of the Dominions, when they toured Canada in 1896; they were also, in 1907, the first Guards band to visit France at the invitation of the French Government, having gained the approval of King Edward VII. Mr Rogan was the first bandmaster in the Brigade of Guards to be granted a substantive commission, being promoted to the rank of 2nd Lieutenant in 1904; after passing through all the various ranks he retired as a Lieutenant-Colonel. Never before had a serving bandmaster or director of music attained this rank.

The Coldstream Guards lay claim to having introduced Tchaikovsky's *1812 Overture* to Britain. In 1896 a Coldstream officer heard the work in St Petersburg, and brought back a copy of the score for the director of music. Mr Rogan played it at concerts throughout the country and brought it to the attention of Henry Wood. It remains a firm favourite at concerts to this day, its martial themes being supremely well suited to the military band.

For 20 years Lt-Col Rogan was the senior direc-tor of music of the Brigade of Guards, and he was responsible for the massed bands of the Brigade at the funeral of Queen Victoria, the coronation and funeral of King Edward VII and the coronation of King George V. Amongst the many decorations and awards that he received were the Commander of the Royal Victorian Order, Officer (Knight) of the Order of the Crown of Belgium, Cavaliere of the Order of the Crown of Italy and Officer of the Black Star of Benin (France). His service medals consisted of the Silver Medal Queen Victoria's Jubilee, Silver Medal Royal Victorian Order, Long Service Medal, Burmah Medal and two clasps (1885-87 and 1887-1889), Victory Medal, General Services Medal and Coronation Medal (1911). In October 1904 he was elected Honorary Member of the Royal Academy of Music, and in 1907 the Senate of the University of

Toronto conferred an honorary Doctor of Music degree on him. He retired in 1920 and was succeeded by Lieutenant Robert Evans.

Robert Evans' career was unusual. He had served in both the Royal Artillery and the Coldstream Guards as a musician and, after a spell as bandmaster with the Highland Light Infantry, he became bandmaster of the Royal Garrison Artillery at Plymouth before returning to the Coldstream. It was under the command of Lieutenant Evans that in 1927 the Band once more visited Canada.

The next director of music, James Causley Windram, came from a military background; his father had been bandmaster of the Highland Light Infantry and then a commissioned bandmaster with the Royal Marines. The Band made two visits to France and also journeyed to New York for the World Fair in the spring of 1939. In January 1942, Major Williams was appointed Senior Director of Music of the Household Division, but it was to be a tragically short-lived appointment.

On 18 June 1944 a section of the Band conducted by Major Windram was playing for the service in the Guards Chapel, Wellington Barracks, when a German V-1 rocket crashed through the roof and exploded, wrecking the Chapel. Amongst the 120 fatalities were Major Windram and five of the musicians; a further twelve members of the Band were injured, and all the instruments destroyed beyond repair. As a memorial to Major Windram and those killed, fellow musicians presented a beautiful conductor's stand, which can be found in the Guards Chapel, whilst a plaque was placed in the Chapel at Kneller Hall.

Douglas A Pope, bandmaster of the Royal Army Service Corps, was immediately flown home from Italy where he was on tour playing to the Allied troops. In being appointed to the Coldstream Guards he achieved the unique record of four cap badges within a year, moving from the 1st Bn The Queen's Own Cameron Highlanders to the Royal Military College (Sandhurst) as bandmaster on 8 September 1943, to the RASC on 1 February 1944 and then to the Coldstream on 5 September of that year. Under his leadership, the Band visited France, Holland, Belgium, Austria and Northern Italy, playing to the troops. In June 1946, whilst in Vienna, Lieutenant Pope organised a Searchlight Tattoo at the Schönbrunn Palace and raised over £10,000 for local charities. Other bands taking part were those of the Royal Dragoons and the Royal Warwickshire Regiment.

In 1960 the Band, with the pipes, drums and dancers of Major Pope's previous regiment, The Queen's Own Cameron Highlanders, toured America, playing to capacity crowds.

Lieutenant-Colonel Pope was appointed Senior Director of Music, the Brigade of Guards in 1960. On his retirement in 1963, he held the retired officer appointment of Director of Music, Junior

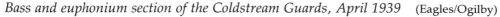

Bass and euphonium section of the Coldstream Guards, April 1939 (Eagles/Ogilby)

Musicians Wing, Guards Depot, Pirbright as well as that of Professor of Instrumentation at Kneller Hall.

On Colonel Pope's retirement, Captain Trevor Sharpe was transferred from the Junior Leaders Regiment, Royal Armoured Corps to the Coldstream Band. Apart from his numerous appearances at state functions, tattoos and massed bands, Captain Sharpe achieved a degree of fame when he secured the contract for the Band to play the signature tune for the popular television series *Dad's Army*, with his name appearing in the closing credits.

In 1972, this time with the pipes and drums of The Black Watch, the Coldstreamers visited the USA and Canada.

Major Sharpe was promoted to Lieutenant-Colonel in 1972 on his appointment as Director of Music at Kneller Hall. Retiring in 1978, he took up the position of Professor of Instrumentation, Kneller Hall.

Subsequent directors of music have been Lieutenant-Colonel 'Dick' Ridings, Major Roger Swift and Major David Marshall, with the international commitments of the Band continuing throughout. With Colonel Ridings, the Band toured Australia and New Zealand in 1984, returning there with Major Swift in 1988 to play at the bicentenary celebrations. It has also toured Japan twice as the guests of the Japan Orchestral Society.

On his retirement from the Guards, Major Swift was appointed Professor of Conducting at Kneller Hall and also became Director of Music of the Honourable Artillery Company. Major Swift has appeared at several massed bands concerts as a solo pianist, most famously playing 'Rhapsody in Blue'.

Thirty-one years after Major Pope's American tour, the Band again toured North America with the pipes and drums of The Queen's Own Highlanders (the successors to the Camerons), playing for three months. During this tour, Captain Marshall was promoted to Major.

A visit to war-wracked Bosnia in 1994 to play at a football match won rapturous acclaim in the international media, television pictures of the symbolic event being shown around the world.

Regimental Music

The regimental quick march is 'Milanollo', composed by Johann Valentine Hamm, director of music of a theatre in Würzburg, Germany. It was written for Teresa and Maria Milanollo, two Italian violinists who toured all over Europe to great acclaim in

Coldstream Guards in the ruins of Coventry Cathedral, 1946, Director of Music Maj D Pope   (RMSM)

the 1840s, until the untimely death of Maria of consumption at the age of 16. The official arrangement as a march was authorized in 1882 under the title 'Milanollo' and was re-published in 1925, rearranged by Mackenzie Rogan.

The slow march is 'Figaro' based on the air 'Non Piu Andrai' from Mozart's opera *The Marriage of Figaro*. It was adopted by the Regiment in 1805.

Major R G Swift, Coldstream Guards   (Swift)

BANDMASTERS AND DIRECTORS OF MUSIC OF THE COLDSTREAM GUARDS

1785-1800? **ELEY**, Chistopher Frederick. Born 1756 died 1832. Music Major Coldm Gds 1785; retirement date not confirmed but thought to be 1800.

1800-1815? **WEYRAUCH**, John (sometimes given as Weybranch). MoB Coldm Gds 1800; retd 1815 (possibly 1814).

1815-1818 **DENMAN**, James. MoB Coldm Gds 1815; retd 1818.

1818-1825 **WILLMAN**, Thomas Lindsay. Born 1784 died 1840. MoB Coldm Gds 1818; retd 4/2/25.

1825-1863 **GODFREY**, Charles. Born 1790 died 1863. Enl Coldm Gds 1813; Sgt (BM) Coldm Gds 5/2/25; retd 12/12/63.

1863-1880 **GODFREY**, Frederick Adolphus. Born 1837 died 1882. Enl Coldm Gds 2/9/56; Sgt (BM) Coldm Gds 14/12/63; retd 31/8/80.

1880-1896 **THOMAS**, Cadwallader. Born 1838 died 19??. Enl CG 26/8/56; Sgt (BM) Duke of York's Royal Military School 1870; WO (BM) Coldm Gds 1/9/80; retd 9/4/96.

1896-1920 **ROGAN**, John Mackenzie (also known as Mackenzie-Rogan) CVO Mus Doc Hon RAM. Born 1851 died 1932. For full details see The Queen's Royal Regiment (West Surrey).

1920-1930 **EVANS**, Robert George psm. Born 1868 died 1946. For full details see Highland Light Infantry.

1930-1944 **WINDRAM**, James Causley LRAM psm. Born 1886 died 1944. For full details see Northumberland Fusiliers.

1944-1963 **POPE**, Douglas Alexander OBE FRCM psm. Born 1903 died 1984. For full details see Cameron Highlanders.

1963-1974 **SHARPE**, Trevor Le Mare LVO OBE (MBE) LRAM ARCM psm. Born 1921. For full details see The Buffs.

1974-1985 **RIDINGS**, Richard Annison OBE ARCM psm. Born 1929. Enl 1st Bn Foresters 30/5/44; WO1 (BM) KSLI 24/5/57; WO1 (BM) Lowland Bde (R Scots) 8/1/67; Capt (DoM) RE (Ald) 17/6/68; Capt (DoM) RE (Chat) 19/10/70; Capt (DoM) Coldm Gds 4/3/74; Lt Col Snr DoM Household Div 1977; retd 28/1/86.

1985-1990 **SWIFT**, Roger Graham LRAM LTCL ARCM psm. Born 1938. Enl RE (Ald) 20/1/60; WO1 (BM) QRIH 4/11/74; WO1 (BM) RMSM 4/79; Capt (DoM) HQ Light Div (badged LI) 11/2/81; Capt (DoM) RAOC 1/11/83; Capt (DoM) Coldm Gds 4/11/85; retd 3/9/90 rank of Maj (DoM) HAC 1/10/92.

1990 **MARSHALL**, David John ARCM LTCL BBCM psm. Born 1944. Enl SCLI 12/1/60; WO1 (BM) WFR 11/11/75; WO1 (BM) RMSM 8/9/81; Capt DoM RAC (badged RTR) 15/8/85; Capt (DoM) RCT 18/8/87; Capt (DoM) Coldm Gds 4/9/90; Major (DoM) 30/9/91.

Bandmaster (Training Officer)

1994 **BRIGHT**, Geoffrey John MBE LRAM LTCL ARCM ALCM. Born 1959. Enl RGJ 14/9/76; WO1 (BM) 9/12L 24/11/89; WO1 (BM) Coldm Gds 2/7/94.

BAND OF THE

SCOTS GUARDS

SCOTS GUARDS

1660	The Scots Regiment of Guards
1712	3rd Foot Guards
1831	Scots Fusilier Guards
1877	Scots Guards

The Royal Warrant of 1685 authorizing the maintenance of hautbois in the Foot Guards in London did not apply to the Scots Regiment of Guards, which was at the time on the Scottish Establishment. Soon after, however, the Scots Guards moved to London, becoming part of the Household troops in 1707, and by 1716 they too had six hautbois together with three drummers. These drummers were employed as musicians – as distinct from the regimental drummers, who had a military role – and were sometimes referred to as drum-majors.

The uniform of the hautbois and drums on state occasions comprised elaborate gold-braided coats with plush caps, similar to those used by the drum-majors of the Foot Guards and the Household Cavalry today. The records from 1716 give the cost of these uniforms for drummers and hautbois as £54 and £30 respectively, with the cost being borne by the King's Wardrobe.

About this period the 'Musik' of the 3rd Foot Guards consisted of two hautbois, two horns/trumpets and two bassoons. Later two clarinets were added.

How effective this band was is not known, but soon after the Grenadiers replaced their band with German musicians, the *Morning Advertiser* of 29 March 1749 reported that The Scots Guards too had changed their band.

Following the defeat of Napoleon in 1815, the three foot guards bands travelled to Paris. Just prior to their departure, the key bugle, known as the 'Kent Bugle', was introduced into the Scots Band. It proved to be a sensation in Paris and inspired M. Halany, the French instrument maker, to bring out a whole family of keyed bugles: the claritube (key bugle), the quintitube (alto ophicleide) and the ophicleide.

On their return to London from Paris, the hired professional musicians then serving were dismissed and replaced by enlisted men. The new band consisted of 22 performers and, like the hautbois of old, they wore the state uniform on special occasions, though this custom was discontinued in 1832 for all save the drum major, who still wears it when a member of the royal family is present. The cost of the uniforms for the Band in 1815 was £1170.

In 1839 Charles Noble enlisted into the Regiment. Though not a musician himself, he founded a dynasty that was ultimately to produce a noted Bandmaster. Both Charles Noble's sons, Richard and Albert, joined the Corps of Drums of the Scots Guards, enlisting in 1856 and 1862 respectively, and Albert contributed three sons himself as drummers to the Regiment. Amongst them was Albert Ernest Noble, who became Drum Major of the 3rd Battalion prior to taking the bandmasters' course at Kneller Hall. In 1908 he was appointed Bandmaster of the 1st Battalion, The Cheshire Regiment, one of the very few drum majors to take command of a British Army band.

The first two bandmasters of the Regiment were clarinettists, playing – as was the fashion prior to the Crimean War – along with the band and signifying changes in tempo by gesturing with the instrument. Their successor, William Hardy, was a virtuoso on the cornopean and similarly when on parade he marched on the flank of the front rank. Mr Hardy had the reputation of being an outstanding arranger, but little was published and less has survived, save his 'Spanish Chant' (1891), which probably does not reflect his true ability. Indeed, the title itself is unrepresentative, since the tune is actually 'Old Hundredth'!

The next bandmaster, Carl Boosé, was one of the most influential military musicians of the century. Born in Hesse-Darmstadt, he had enlisted in a German band in 1830 and later found his way to Britain, where he established a reputation as a fine clarinettist. He moved from the 9th (East Norfolk) Regiment in 1842, and in 1845 made his greatest contribution, with the founding of *Boosé's Military Band Journal*. The arrangements he published in this periodical achieved such wide circulation that they helped standardize the instrumentation of military bands in Britain. He was decorated with the Order of Merit by the Grand Duke of Hesse-Darmstadt.

On Boosé's departure in 1859, a competition was held to chose the new bandmaster; the winner was Charles Godfrey junior. Though only 20 years old, he was already an accomplished musician, having received tuition from his father, from Henry Lazarus on the clarinet and from Sir George MacFarren. He had also played at various London theatres and in Louis Jullien's orchestra. After ten years with the Regiment, he transferred to the Royal Horse Guards

Drum Major A C Noble, 2nd Battalion Scots Guards c1880 (Noble)

where he remained for almost 34 years. He was the founder and editor of the *Orpheus Military Band Journal* published by Lafleur, and later of the *Army Band Journal*.

His successor, J C van Maanen, was born in Nijmegen, Holland and received his musical training at the Royal Conservatory of Music at The Hague. He came to London in 1843 to join the orchestra of Her Majesty's Theatre conducted by (Sir) Michael Costa. On Mr Costa's recommendation, he was appointed bandmaster of the 52nd (Oxfordshire Light Infantry) Regiment in 1845 and, after various moves, became bandmaster of the Scots Guards in 1868. In 1875 he exchanged appointments with John Power Clarke to become bandmaster of the Royal Irish Constabulary.

Drummer, piper, bugler (drummer) of 1st Battalion and bandsman of the regimental band, Scots Guards c1891 (Eagles/Ogilby)

Mr Clarke had served with the 61st (South Gloucestershire) Regiment and the 7th Hussars as a bandsman but purchased his discharge in order to obtain a more thorough training. Between 1844 and 1875, when he became bandmaster of the Scots, he had served with seven regiments in addition to the Constabulary.

The first Kneller Hall trained bandmaster was Edward Holland, whose father had been Bandmaster of the 24th (2nd Warwickshire) Regiment. Subsequent bandmasters were Henry Dunkerton and Frederick Wood. Under the latter the Band, by now 40 strong, visited Canada in 1912 to perform at the Toronto Exhibition and in adjoining towns.

During the Great War it carried out its tour of duty with the Brigade of Guards in France and Belgium – at Ypres and the Somme in 1916, at Ypres again in 1917 and at Cologne in 1918 – returning to London with the Brigade in 1919. In 1916 it was the only British band at the review of the Allied International Troops held in Paris on 14 July, playing

with the Regiment's pipers. It formed part of the massed bands of the Brigade of Guards who played in Paris in 1917, and the following year the string band was chosen to play at the reception given by King George V at the British Embassy in Paris. Later in 1918 it went to Italy with the massed bands, playing in Rome and Milan.

Bandmaster Wood was commissioned as Lieutenant in 1919 and appointed Senior Director of Music, the Brigade of Guards in 1921. The following year the Band visited Canada, playing in most of the principal towns of the Dominion, from Quebec to Victoria. In all, 56 concerts were given in 28 towns.

In 1927 Lt Wood was promoted to Captain and was decorated by King George V with the Royal Victorian Order the following year. He retired in 1929.

Horace Dowell served as director of music until 1938 when he retired in the rank of Captain. He later formed a voluntary band for the Royal Army Pay Corps during the war (for details see *Volume*

One).

He was followed by Sam Rhodes, one of the finest musicians produced by the army. As Senior Director of Music, the Brigade of Guards from 1949 to 1959, he was promoted Lieutenant-Colonel in 1955 and awarded the MVO and the MBE. He is remembered mainly for the slow march 'Golden Spurs'.

Perhaps the most moving and symbolic performance of the period came at Rotenburg Airfield in Germany on 9 June 1945 for the final parade of the Guards Armoured Division, the Division that had played such a central part in the Allied war effort. When Field-Marshal Montgomery had inspected and taken the salute of the armoured battalions for the last time, the tanks were driven off the parade ground and over the hills behind to the sounds of the Scots and Welsh Guards Bands playing 'Auld Lang Syne'. After a few moments, the men came back over the hill, footguards once more, as the Bands struck up the regimental marches.

The next director of music was James Howe, who had served in the Royal Scots under Lt-Col Rhodes when the latter had been the bandmaster. (For details of his early career see The Argyll and Sutherland Highlanders).

In January 1964 the Band, together with the pipes and drums, proceeded on a three-month tour of New Zealand and Australia, spending three days in Hong Kong en route. The Bands arrived back in London on 19 April, having travelled nearly 40,000 miles and given 147 concerts.

A trip to Paris at the end of 1970 was made to receive an award for the best recorded disc during the year – the hit album *Band of the Scots Guards* – and several concerts were given there. This was followed by a visit to the Persian Gulf to play to the troops.

Major Howe was appointed Senior Director of Music, the Household Division in 1970 and awarded the MBE in 1971. In December 1971 he represented the British Army at the 10th Military Music Festival in Belgrade along with directors of music from around the world.

In 1972 the Band made an extremely successful tour of America and Canada lasting three months. Whilst there it took part in the Canadian National Exhibition.

Major Howe retired on 10 November 1974. His last major appearance should have been at the Edinburgh Tattoo earlier that year, but he returned from leave to make a final broadcast on the Radio 3 *Bandstand* programme the day before his retirement,

and on the day itself he took a final bow at the Cenotaph service as Senior Director of Music. Also present that day was his successor, Captain Duncan Beat; this is believed to be the only time that two directors of music of the same band have paraded together.

Captain Beat was an ideal choice for the Scots Guards, his father having been bandmaster of The Argyll and Sutherland Highlanders, while he himself had previously been bandmaster to The Black Watch.

The Band visited America as part of what was effectively a touring version of the Edinburgh Tattoo, playing at the Wolf Trap in New York State to capacity audiences for fifteen days. The director of music for the Tattoo was Lieutenant-Colonel Sharpe.

Bandsmen of the Scots Guards showing uniforms worn pre (left) and post-Second World War (Eagles/Ogilby)

Scots Guards, 1991 Director of Music Major D Price   (Scots Guards)

Further overseas trips were undertaken in 1979, to Western Australia and to Canada for the National Exhibition in Toronto.

In 1980 Major Beat was responsible for the music at the ceremonies in Scotland to mark the 80th Birthday of HM Queen Elizabeth, the Queen Mother. As a result he was appointed a Member (4th Class) of the Royal Victorian Order; this was later re-designated Lieutenant (LVO). At the end of 1982 he was appointed Chief Instructor, Kneller Hall; he was replaced by Major Brian Hicks.

The Band, accompanied by the pipes and drums of The Black Watch, made a very successful three-month tour of North America in 1983. Soon after the return to England, however, Major Hicks was forced to retire due to ill-health.

Major Don Carson assumed command and in 1984 was musical director of the Edinburgh Tattoo. In 1986 he took the Band to Australia, playing at tattoos in Adelaide and Sydney. The same year he directed the massed bands of all three services at the opening ceremony of the Commonwealth Games in Edinburgh. He retired prematurely in 1988 to become head of woodwind and brass at Dulwich College in London.

Captain David Price moved to the Scots in December 1987, and the following April was promoted to Major.

In 1990 a section of the Band flew out to Trieste to play for P&O and later the complete Band flew to New York for the same sponsors. It was on the return flight that they heard that they were to go to the Gulf as medical orderlies. On 3 November 1990, Major Price and the Band arrived in the Gulf to fulfil their secondary role. This was the first time that a Guards band had been so deployed in war conditions.

In October 1991 the men played alongside the Welsh Guards Band in Paris for the Prix de L'Arc de Triomphe. More recently they have been to Monte Carlo, to support Manchester's ill-fated bid for the Olympic Games, and to China in 1994, where they played for the naming ceremony of a P&O container vessel at Shenzhen Bay.

Major Price became Senior Director of Music, the Household Division in March 1993, and shortly afterwards was promoted to Lieutenant-Colonel.

Regimental Music

The quick march is 'Hielan' Laddie'. Versions of this tune appear in manuscript form dating back to

1692, sometimes under the title 'Cockle Shells' or 'Wilt Thou Play Me Fair Play?', though it may well be older even than that. The composer of the tune is unknown. (Though the Scots Guards call the piece 'Hielan' Laddie', all other regiments use a variant title 'Highland Laddie'.)

The slow march is 'The Garb of Old Gaul'. The music was composed in 1770 by General John Reid, a former Black Watch officer who had commanded the Connaught Rangers, and the words were written by Lieutenant-General Sir Henry Erskine:

In the Garb of Old Gaul, with the fire of old Rome,
From the heath-covered mountain of Scotia we
* come;*
Where the Romans endeavoured our country to
* gain;*

But our ancestors fought, and they fought not in
vain.

No effeminate customs our sinews unbrace,
No luxurious tables enervate our race;
Our loud sounding pipe bears the true martial
* strain,*
So do we the old Scottish valour retain.

From the late 18th century through to the 1840s, another slow march was also used, known as 'Kellman's March'. This is assumed to be a piece written around 1795 by the organist of His Majesty's Chapel at St James's, A F C Kellman, with the full title 'A Characteristic March with the sentiments as expressed in it, as performed by the Third Regiment of Guards'.

BANDMASTERS AND DIRECTORS OF MUSIC OF THE SCOTS GUARDS

178?-179? **MAHON**, John. Born 1755 died 1834. MoB Scots Fus Gds sometime during the 1780s & 90s.

1797-1838 **HOPKINS**, Edward. Born c.1778 died 1860. MoB Scots Fus Gds (possibly a Sgt) 1797; retd 1838.

1838-1842 **HARDY**, William. Died 1842. Civ BM (or possibly a Sgt) Gren Gds 1822; transferred Scots Fus Gds 1838; retd 1842.

1842-1859 **BOOSÉ**, Carl. Born 1815 died 1868. Bdmn 1st Regiment German army; Sgt (BM) 9L 1841; Sgt (BM) Scots Fus Gds 1842; Sgt (BM) RHG 1859; retd 1868.

1859-1868 **GODFREY**, Charles MVO FRAM. Born 1839 died 1919. Sgt (BM) Scots Fus Gds 1859; Sgt (BM) RHG 1868; retd 6/1/04 rank of Capt.

1869-1875 **MAANEN**, Van J C. Born 1827 died 1899. For full details see Royal Scots.

1875-1887 **CLARKE**, John Power. Born 1816 died 1889. Served as Bdmn 61 Ft & 7H; BM 47 Ft 1844; BM 7H 1846; BM 11H 1853; BM 36 Ft 1861; BM 83 Ft 1862; BM 54 Ft 1/6/67-9/12/68; BM 43 Ft 1/6/68-29/7/72; BM R Ir Constab 1873; BM Scots Fus Gds 1875; retd 7/2/87.

1887-1893 **HOLLAND**, Edward. Born 1850 died 1933. Enl 1 Rifle Bde 17/9/65; Sgt (BM) 48 Ft 8/2/78; WO (BM) SG 29/6/87; retd 26/8/93; BM Norfolk Artillery (TA).

1893-1900 **DUNKERTON**, Henry Thomas. Born 1843 died 1919. Enl 2 Essex R 20/10/57; WO (BM) 1 R Mun Fus 3/10/84; WO (BM) SG 26/8/93; retd 4/1/1900.

1900-1929 **WOOD**, Frederick William MVO. Born 1864 died 1944. Enl 5L 21/6/78; WO (BM) 1 York & Lanc R 16/11/90; WO (BM) SG 5/1/1900; Lt (DoM) SG 1/3/19; retd 20/6/29 rank of Capt; DoM Bristol City Police 1929-1944.

1929-1938 **DOWELL**, Horace Edwin LRAM psm. Born 1874 died 1945. For full details see Cameronians.

1938-1959 **RHODES**, Sam MVO MBE Mus Bac ARCM psm. Born 1900 died 1977. For full details see Royal Scots.

1959-1974 **HOWE**, James Hakin MBE LRAM ARCM psm. Born 1917. For full details see Argyll & Sutherland Highlanders.

1974-1982 **BEAT**, Duncan Richie LVO ARCM psm. Born 1931. For full details see Black Watch.

1982-1984 **HICKS**, Brian Erwin FVCM LRAM ARCM psm. Born 1935. For full details see The Royal Fusiliers.

1984-1987 **CARSON**, Donald MBE LTCL psm. Born 1934. Enl 1 Midd'x R 1/12/50; WO1 (BM) Glosters 31/12/63; WO1 (BM) Highland Bde (badged BW) 9/3/69; WO1 (BM) PoW Depot (Wessex) (badged Glosters) 1/2/73; Capt (DoM) King's Div (badged PWO) 20/2/75; Capt (DoM) RAMC 7/5/79; Maj (DoM) SG 11/4/84; retd 1988.

1987- **PRICE**, David Evan psm. Born 1945. Enl KRRC 22/8/60; WO1 (BM) Cheshire 5/3/73; WO1 (BM) Queen's Div (badged Queens) 21/10/77; Capt (DoM) HQ Scottish Div (badged RS) 14/4/80; Capt (DoM) RAOC 30/9/85; Capt (DoM) SG 4/12/87; L/Lt-Col Snr DoM Household Division 1993; Lt-Col (sub) 29/4/95.

Bandmaster (Training Officer)

1994 **MILGATE**, David J. Born 1962. Enl R Anglian 31/5/78; WO1 (BM) King's Own Border 25/5/93; WO1 (BM) SG 1/8/94.

BAND OF THE

IRISH GUARDS

IRISH GUARDS

1900	Irish Guards

The Irish Regiment of Foot Guards was raised by Army Order 77, 1900 'to commemorate the bravery shown by the Irish regiments in the recent operations in South Africa'. Mr Charles Hassell, then Bandmaster of the 4th Battalion, The King's Royal Rifle Corps, was appointed to form a band for the new regiment.

Following the example of the established Guards bands, it was not long before the Band of the Irish Guards was undertaking overseas trips, visiting Canada in 1906 and again in 1913 to perform at the Canadian National Exhibition, Toronto. It also took part in the opening ceremony of the 1st Dominion Fair, on the west coast in British Columbia.

During the Great War, the Band was attached to the Guards Division and made tours of France in 1916, 1917 and 1918. Whilst stationed in Arras in 1918, it had the honour of being invited by the Italian Government to pay a visit to Rome where it was received by Her Majesty, Queen Elenor. It also performed in Italy with the massed bands of the Brigade of Guards.

Amongst other distinctions, the Irish Guards Band is the only band in the British Army to have taken part in three victory parades at the end of the war, in Paris, London and Belfast.

Mr Hassell was commissioned as Lieutenant on 1 March 1919 and retired in the rank of Captain in 1929. He was succeeded by Lieutenant (later Major) James Hurd and then in 1938 by Lieutenant George Willcocks.

'Polly' Willcocks, as he was known throughout the musical world, was a talented musician and a stylish conductor. He was also a military musician who between the years 1915 and 1921 had seen service in France, Germany, Iraq, Persia, India and Italy. In October 1943 the full band of over 60 musicians departed for a tour of various theatres of war to entertain the troops, returning in the spring of 1944. During the tour, which extended to Italy and South Africa, the Band travelled 13,000 miles and gave more than 300 concerts, playing to over 150,000 troops. There followed a tour of Northern Ireland and Scotland.

Major Willcocks left the Irish Guards in April

Above: Irish Guards c1921, Director of Music Capt C Hassell   (RMSM)
Below: Irish Guards c1950   (Eagles/Ogilby)

Irish Guards Italy c1961, Director of Music Major C Jaeger   (RMSM)

1949, initially to take up a civilian post in Southern Rhodesia, though he was later to return to Britain to become Director of Music to the Ford Motor Works Company. He was relieved by Lieutenant Cecil Jaeger who, at the age of 35, was the youngest director of music that the Guards had ever had.

'Jiggs' Jaeger was one of the great characters in army music, known for being both a witty raconteur and a skilled musician. As a young bandmaster with the 4th Hussars in Vienna at the end of the war, his talent had been acknowledged in an invitation to conduct the Vienna Symphony Orchestra for a series of five concerts.

In 1954 the Band visited Canada once more to play at the National Exhibition, and the tour was extended to include several cities in New England. Amongst the most prestigious concerts was one in the Boston Symphony Hall, where the Band was given a standing ovation on its debut. Between August and December 1957 the Band, accompanied by the pipes and drums of the 1st Battalion, travelled some 35,000 miles by air, visiting Canada, the United States, Honolulu and Australia.

One of the Band's greatest successes internationally was a ten-day visit to Turin to play for the Italia 1961 celebrations. At the International Military Band Week, it faced competition from some of the finest bands of the world, including the Garde Républicaine from France, the Carabinieri of Italy, the Belgian Guides, the Swedish Life Guards and the American No 4 Army Field Band. The Irish Guards was one of the smallest of these bands, at just one third of the size of the world-renowned Garde Républicaine, but it was the Irish who stole the show.

Together with the pipes and drums of The Royal Scots, they flew to Buenos Aires in November 1963 for a month's tour of South America, visiting Argentina, Uraguay and Chile. No fewer than 130,000 people, including the President of the Republic of Chile, attended the two concerts given in the World Cup Stadium, Santiago, whilst the English language edition of the *Buenos Aires Times* of 13 November reported:

Sixty men in bright scarlet and a score of skirling bagpipers were the sensation of Buenos Aires yesterday . . .

Their mission was the normally staid and solemn one of placing a wreath before the monu-

ment to General San Martin. But they turned it into a holiday occasion.

There were cheers, applause and showers of confetti as the guards quick marched through throngs of people from Plaza Vincente Lopez to Plaza San Martin.

There was a moment's silence as their commander Major C H Jaeger laid a wreath. By this time the crowds there numbered by the thousands.

Back home the Band responded to the changing cultural climate of the '60s with the classic *Marching With The Beatles* album, for which Lennon and McCartney's songs were arranged by Arthur Wilkinson. It also appeared in two of the most successful and significant British films of the decade: *The Ipcress File*, in which 'Jiggs' can be seen announcing the overture to *The Marriage of Figaro*, and *Oh What A Lovely War*, in which he appeared complete with false moustache.

In 1963 Lieutenant-Colonel Jaeger was appointed Senior Director of Music, the Household Division, and was later responsible for the music arrangements at the State Funeral of Winston Churchill.

After a tour of Canada in 1968, he relinquished the reins and took a sabbatical period prior to taking up the appointment as Director of Music, Kneller Hall. In June 1969, in a typically high-profile engagement, he conducted the trumpeters from a lofty perch on one of the towers at Caernavon Castle at the Investiture of Prince Charles as Prince of Wales. In September the following year, he conducted the Bands of the Grenadier and Welsh Guards, together with the antiphonal trumpeters in the music of the Investiture in the Lower Ward of Windsor Castle as part of the Windsor Festival. It was to be his last performance, for the next day he died at his home in Whitton. His ashes were placed behind a memorial plaque in the chapel at Kneller Hall.

To choose a replacement for 'Jiggs', who had been with the Irish Guards for 21 years, was an unenviable task but the selection of Gerry Horabin was excellent. Captain Horabin was without doubt one of the finest natural musicians to have graduated at Kneller Hall since the War and was also an extremely charismatic character. Within a short time he had put his own stamp on the Band.

Captain Horabin was promoted to Major on 17 March 1972 (St Patrick's Day) and appointed Senior Director of Music, The Household Division

on 12 November 1974. He retired prematurely in 1977 due to ill-health.

The new director of music, Captain Michael Lane, was a gifted musician, playing violin, French horn, piano and organ. He was also a great teller of jokes, and there was an endless stream of Irish stories at his concerts. A devout Christian, he was reputed to know every hymn and tune in the *Ancient and Modern* hymnal. He was appointed Senior Director of Music, the Household Division in 1987 and promoted to Lieutenant-Colonel.

It was not to be a long incumbency; whilst visiting Kneller Hall on 19 September 1989, he suffered a heart attack, went into a coma and died at the Cambridge Military Hospital on 7 November.

With the untimely death of Colonel Mick Lane, Captain Michael Henderson was transferred from the Royal Army Ordnance Corps to become the Band's seventh director of music.

Regimental Music

The quick march is 'St Patrick's Day'. Its first appearance in print was probably in a collection compiled by Rutherford, *Country Dances*, in 1749, although it is known to have been popular as early as 1615, sometimes under the names 'Barbary Bell' and 'Bacon and Greens'. The version used is an arrangement by Jacob Adam Kappey and was the regimental march of The Connaught Rangers.

The slow march is 'Let Erin Remember'. The tune first appeared in print in Bunting's *Ancient Music of Ireland* under the title 'The Little Bold Fox'. The words 'Let Erin Remember' were written by Thomas Moore to be sung with his collection of traditional Irish melodies. The first verse is:

Let Erin remember the days of old,
Ere her faithless sons betrayed her,
When Malachio wore the collar of gold
Which he won from the proud invader;
When her Kings, with standard of green unfurl'd,
Led the Red-Branch Knights to danger,
Ere the em'rald gem of the western world
Was set in the crown of the stranger.

Lieutenant-Colonel Jaeger left behind two marches specifically written for the Regiment: 'Blue Plume', referring to the colour of the plume worn in the Irish Guards' bearskins, and 'Paddy's Day'.

BANDMASTERS AND DIRECTORS OF MUSIC OF THE IRISH GUARDS

1900-1929 **HASSELL**, Charles Hazard, OBE. Born 1864 died 1934. Enl 2 Foresters 18/5/78; WO (BM) 4 KRRC 2/11/92; WO (BM) IG 21/11/1900; Lt (DoM) IG 1/3/19; retd 18/3/29 rank of Capt; DoM Metropolitan Police 1929-1934.

1929-1938 **HURD**, James Lyne Thorne LRAM psm. Born 1878 died 1968. Enl 1 A and SH 9/5/93; WO (BM) 2 E York R 13/5/05; WO1 (BM) 1 E York R 25/4/19; WO1 (BM) RA (Gib) 3/6/20; WO1 (BM) RA (Sal Pl) 12/1/22; WO1 (BM) RA (Port) 1922; Lt (DoM) IG 18/3/29; retd 8/4/38 rank of Capt.

1938-1949 **WILLCOCKS**, George Henry MVO MBE ARCM psm. Born 1899 died 1962. Enl R Fus (served with 1st & 4th Bns) 25/1/15; WO1 (BM) 2 S Wales Bord 11/9/26; WO1 (BM) RA (Sal Pl) 20/1/37; Lt (DoM) IG 9/4/38; Snr DoM Bde Gds 1948; retd 8/4/49 rank of Maj.

1949-1968 **JAEGER**, Cecil Harry OBE Mus Bac LRAM ARCM psm. Born 1913 died 1970. Enl 1 KOYLI 6/10/27; WO1 (BM) 4H 21/7/42; Lt (DoM) RMA (Sand) 6/3/48; Lt (DoM) IG 9/4/49; Snr DoM Bde Gds 1963; Lt-Col (DoM) RMSM 2/12/68; died whilst serving 27/9/70.

1968-1977 **HORABIN**, Edmund Gerald LRAM ARCM psm. Born 1925. Enl S Lan R (served with 1st & 2nd) 24/8/40; WO1 (BM) 7H 21/5/54; WO1 (BM) QOH 3/11/58; Lt (DoM) RE (Ald) 12/10/62; Capt (DoM) IG 14/8/68; Snr DoM Household Div 1974; retd 31/3/77 rank of Maj.

1977-1989 **LANE**, Michael Gerald ARCM psm. Born 1933 died 1989. Enl RAMC 8/9/50; WO1 (BM) 10H 20/3/64; WO1 (BM) Depot RGJ 29/10/69; Capt (DoM) WRAC (badged RH) 22/12/71; Capt (DoM) RMA 13/8/74; Capt (DoM) IG 31/3/77; Lt-Col Snr DoM Household Division 1987; died whilst serving 7/11/89.

1990- **HENDERSON**, Michael John psm. Born 1944. Enl Gordons 11/10/65; WO1 (BM) 5 Innis DG 20/12/76; Capt (DoM) (badged D&D) Infantry (South) 6/1/86; Capt (DoM) RAOC 23/11/87; Capt (DoM) IG 22/1/90; Maj (DoM) 30/9/92.

Bandmaster (Training Officer)

1994 **BARNWELL**, Stephen Clifford BBCM. Born 1959. Enl RA (Wool) 18/8/75; WO1 (BM) QLR 21/3/88; WO1 (BM) IG 3/10/94.

Top: Lt-Col C Jaeger, Irish Guards (RMSM)
Right: Major G. H. Willcocks, Irish Guards (RMSM)

WELSH GUARDS

1915   Welsh Guards

The Welsh are the youngest of the foot guards, being raised in 1915. On 8 September of that year, Mr Andrew Harris, of the Royal Artillery (Gibraltar) was appointed to be the first bandmaster, and in November the Band itself was formed. The regimental history tells us that the funds to buy the instruments were provided by the City of Cardiff.

With the prospect of having to live up to the high standards set by the existing guards bands, the Welsh Guards faced a tough challenge. Their first appearances on 1 March 1916, St David's Day, however, dispelled any doubts that may have been harboured; a guard mounting at Buckingham Palace, followed by a performance at a Welsh Patriotic Meeting at the London Opera House with Lord Harlech and Major-General Sir Francis Lloyd in attendance, demonstrated clearly the musical quality of the new band.

Coming together in the midst of the Great War, it was not long before the bandsmen were sent overseas. On 28 October 1916 they proceeded to France for duty with the Guards Division, meeting the 1st Battalion of their Regiment, then returning from the front line a few weeks later and playing the guardsmen back to their billets.

In May 1917 the Band, resplendent in full dress, formed part of the massed bands of the Brigade of Guards which gave concerts at the Trocadero and the Tuileries Gardens, Paris. Later the massed bands visited Italy, performing in Rome and Milan; during the tour, each musician was presented with a silver cigarette case by Queen Elenor. In May 1918, at the request of the American Embassy, the Band played at the Memorial Service in Paris, and in July 1919 it took part in the great Victory March in Paris, where it had the honour of playing the Colours of the British Army through the Arc de Triomphe.

Bandmaster Harris was commissioned as Lieutenant on 1 March 1919, and went on to become Senior Director of Music, Brigade of Guards, eventually retiring in the rank of major at the end of 1937. At his final appearance at the Albert Hall for the Festival of Remembrance, he was able to tell the audience that he would be sitting with them the following year as an old comrade having completed

BAND OF THE

WELSH GUARDS

50 years service. His legacy is a fine series of recordings, eighteen of which, dating from 1929-34, have recently been reissued on compact disc.

Major Harris was succeeded by Lieutenant 'Tommy' Chandler who was to stay with the Welsh for eleven years, retiring in the rank of major and as Senior Director of Music of the Brigade. In the spring of 1945 the Band made a short tour of Europe playing at the Paris Opera House and the Cirque Royale in Brussels amongst other venues. The same year saw the last parade of the Guards Armoured Division, for which the Band of the Welsh joined the Band of the Scots Guards.

The next director of music was Leslie Statham, renowned as a composer both under his own name and also under the pen name of Arnold Steck. Amongst his most popular and famous marches are 'Drum Majorette', the original signature tune to the BBC's *Match of the Day*, and 'Birdcage Walk', inspired by the London road linking Wellington Barracks to Horse Guards.

In September 1948 the Band visited Canada to play at the National Exhibition in Toronto. It was estimated that the Band's 127 concerts were attended by nearly one and a half million people and during the course of the engagement the Band played 1174 programme items. The Band made a further visit to the Canadian National Exhibition following the Coronation in 1953. These trips were something of a return engagement for Major Statham, who had been featured as a solo pianist when the Kneller Hall Band had visited Canada in 1931.

Major Statham retired from the service in 1962 to concentrate on a career as a composer and arranger.

In 1965, the Band under Captain Arthur Kenney appeared at the British Week in Milan and two years later, together with the Pipes, Drums and Dancers of the Scots Guards, they visited America where they presented a Military Tattoo which included the Ceremony of the Keys, as performed nightly at the Tower of London.

In July 1969 the Band played a prominent part in the celebrations connected with the Investiture of Prince Charles as the Prince of Wales. This was one of Major Kenney's last important engagements, for he resigned his commission in October of that year in order to devote more time to his interests in the world of civilian music.

Major Desmond Walker took over but, less than five years later, he died suddenly at the age of 50, a few weeks before the Band was to embark on a three-months tour of Canada and America.

Above: Welsh Guards musicians c1920   (Eagles/Ogilby)
Right: Massed Bands of the Household Division conducted by Yehudi Menuhin at Windsor Castle, 1970
((RMSM)

Both he and the Band were at the pinnacle of success with recording contracts, frequent broadcasts and appearances at many major sporting events. He was due to appear at the Royal International Horse of the Year Show at Wembley when it was announced that he had died.

Captain Derek Taylor was quickly appointed Director of Music and he took the Band on the American tour. Accompanied by the pipes and drums of The Argyll and Sutherland Highlanders they played in 73 principal towns and cities. A review in the *Washington Star-News* commented:

The Welsh Guards have an unusually creamy, velvety sound when they play legato and a bright crisp sound when they are war-like . . .

And the pipes and drums were also greatly appreciated, the *Montreal Star* reporting that 'The pipes were magnificent, and the lone piper's "Sleep Dearie Sleep" awed with its tenderness.'

The Band visited Houston, Texas in three successive years from 1984.

Captain Peter Hannam took over the leadership of the Band in January 1986, and maintained the international connexions. In 1988 five overseas trips were undertaken: to Seattle for the retirement dinner of the chairman of the Boeing Corporation, to Sydney, Australia for the Boeings' Bi-Centenial Air Show, to Japan for an International Tattoo, to Paris as the first British contingent to take part in the Armistice Day Parade, and finally to Georgia in the United States. The Band also appeared that year for the first time at the Royal Tournament.

In March 1989 there was a return to Macon, Georgia for the Cherry Blossom Festival, followed by a trip to Belize to see the Battalion. The following year the men visited Houston, Texas yet again; included in the itinerary was a concert with the Houston Symphony Orchestra. Further overseas performances included the Longchamps Races in Paris in 1990 and 1991, and the International Trade Fair in Vigo, Spain.

It was at home, however, that perhaps the greatest challenge was to be faced. The ambulance workers dispute of 1989 saw the musicians called upon to provide emergency medical cover; amongst their achievements was the delivery of a baby by Bandsman Julian Kirk, an event celebrated by *The Sun* in typical fashion: 'Soldier Julian is 999 Midwife!'

In 1990 Peter Hannam became the first director of music in the Welsh Guards to be promoted to Lieutenant-Colonel. He also holds the distinction of having been awarded the BEM as a corporal in the Band of The Gloucestershire Regiment whilst on active service in Cyprus 1964-65, adding the MBE to his honours in 1992. At the time of his retirement in 1993, he was the last remaining national serviceman still serving in army music.

Major Cliff Ross was with the Band for less than two years before being chosen to become the Principal Director of Music (Army) and moving to the newly constituted Headquarters Army Music, based at Kneller Hall. He was replaced by Major Stuart Watts, previously Director of Music of the Grenadier Guards.

Regimental Music

The quick march is an arrangement by Jacob Adam Kappey of the old Welsh song 'The Rising of the Lark'. The song dates back to the 18th century and is believed to have been composed by David Owen, an harpist from Caernarvon who, returning from a feast in the early hours of the morning, heard a lark herald the dawning of a new day.

Welsh Guards marching through the devastated town centre of Coleraine, Northern Ireland, 1992, Director of Music Lt-Col Peter Hannam   (Welsh Guards)

The slow march is 'Men of Harlech'. This song, which first appeared in print in Edward Jones' 1794 collection *Musical and Poetical Relics of the Welsh Bards*, is said to commemorate the heroic defence of Harlech Castle when it was besieged by the Earl of Pembroke during the Wars of the Roses. Another patriotic Welsh song, 'Men of Glamorgan', is also used as a slow march.

BANDMASTERS AND DIRECTORS OF MUSIC OF THE WELSH GUARDS

1915-1937 **HARRIS**, Andrew MVO LRAM psm. Born 1873 died 1953. Enl 1 Ox LI 19/8/87; WO (BM) 2 S Lanc R 24/4/1900; WO (BM) RA (Gib) 23/3/10; WO1 (BM) WG 1/10/15; Lt (DoM) 1/3/19; retd 31/12/37 rank of Maj.

1938-1948 **CHANDLER**, Thomas Samuel MVO LRAM ARCM psm. Born 1888 died 1963. Enl 1 R Ir Fus 6/3/05; WO1 (BM) 2 King's Own R 13/2/18; WO1 (BM) RTC 4/9/35; Lt (DoM) W Gds 1/1/38; retd 5/3/48 rank of Maj.

1948-1962 **STATHAM**, Frank Leslie MBE LRAM ARCM psm. Born 1905 died 1974. Enl 2 RS 30/1/24; WO1 (BM) 2 Manch R 24/7/35; WO1 (BM) RMC 27/7/45; Lt (DoM) 11/8/47; Lt (DoM) WG 6/3/48; retd 10/6/62 rank of Maj.

1962-1969 **KENNEY**, Horatio Arthur LRAM ARCM psm. Born 1919 died 1994. Enl 2 SLI 15/6/34; trans 1 KOYLI 4/45; WO1 (BM) 1 Ox & Bucks LI 22/9/49; WO1 (BM) 1 GJ 6/9/58; Lt (DoM) RA (Plym) 6/4/60; Lt (DoM) RTR (Alamein) 23/4/61; Capt (DoM) WG 22/5/62; retd 19/10/69 rank of Maj.

1969-1974 **WALKER**, Desmond Kiernan ARCM psm. Born 1924 died 1974. For full details see Royal Leicestershire Regiment.

1974-1986 **TAYLOR**, Derek Noel MBE LTCL ARCM psm. Born 1929. Enl 1 R Ir Fus ?/12/44; WO1 (BM) 16/5L 30/9/55; WO1 (BM) RMSM 5/5/68; Capt (DoM) RMA (Sand) 25/4/69; Capt (DoM) WG 8/74; retd 19/2/86 rank of Maj.

1986-1993 **HANNAM**, Peter MBE BEM psm. Born 1938. For full details see RRF.

1993-1994 **ROSS**, Clifford James ARCM psm. Born 1942. Enl 1 BW 8/4/58; WO1 (BM) Kings Own Border 19/3/73; Capt (DoM) PoW Div (badged RRW) 2/3/81; Capt (DoM) REME 18/11/85; Maj Snr DoM BAOR 3/2/91; Maj (DoM) WG 22/2/93; Lt-Col Principal DoM Army 4/7/94.

1994 **WATTS**, Stuart Alastair LRAM psm. Born 1945. For full details see 3rd Royal Anglians.

Bandmaster (Training Officer)

1994 **GREENER**, Paul Michael. Born 1959. Enl 4/7DG 9/9/75; WO1 (BM) 13/18H 23/7/90; WO1 (BM) LD 2/12 '92; WO1 (BM) WG 22/8/94.

THE SCOTTISH DIVISION

THE LOWLAND BRIGADE

	1881		1959
1st Foot	The Royal Scots		
21st Foot	The Royal Scots Fusiliers	)	Royal Highland Fusiliers
71st Foot	) Highland Light	)	
74th Foot	) Infantry	)	
25th Foot	King's Own Scottish Borderers		
26th Foot	) Cameronians		
90th Foot	) (Scottish Rifles)		

The Cameronians (Scottish Rifles) were disbanded in 1968. In 1994 the remaining three regimental bands were disbanded and replaced by The Lowland Band. The first Director of Music appointed was Captain Graham Jones and the first Bandmaster was WO1 Tony Clarke.

THE HIGHLAND BRIGADE

	1881	1961	1994
42nd Foot	) The Black Watch		
73rd Foot	) (Royal Highland) Regiment)		
79th Foot	The Queen's Own Cameron Highlanders	) Queen's) Own) High-)	) The High- landers)
72nd Foot	) The Seaforth	) landers)	
78th Foot	) Highlanders	)	
75th Foot	) The Gordon		)
92nd Foot	) Highlanders		)
91st Foot	) The Argyll and		
93rd Foot	) Sutherland) Highlanders		

In 1994 the regimental bands were disbanded and replaced by The Highland Band. The first Director of Music appointed was Captain David Thompson and the first Bandmaster was WO1 Jimmy Ridgeway.

BANDS OF THE

ROYAL SCOTS

(The Royal Regiment)

THE ROYAL SCOTS
(The Royal Regiment)

1633-78	In French service as Le Régiment d'Hébron and Le Régiment Douglas except for two brief periods at home between 1661 and 1667
1678	Earl of Dumbarton's Regiment of Foot
1684	The Royal Regiment of Foot
1751	1st, or Royal Regiment of Foot
1812	1st Regiment of Foot, or Royal Scots
1821	1st, or The Royal Regiment of Foot
1871	1st, or The Royal Scots Regiment
1881 (May)	The Lothian Regiment (Royal Scots)
1881 (July)	The Royal Scots (The Lothian Regiment)
1920	The Royal Scots (The Royal Regiment)

Raised by Royal Warrant in 1633, the Royal Scots is the oldest surviving regiment in the British Army. Under the command of Sir John Hepburn, the Regiment moved to France to fight in the service of Louis XIII during the Thirty Years War, thus continuing a tradition of Scottish involvement in French military affairs that dated back to the early 15th century.

Contemporary reports from the 1630s mention a pipe band of some 36 musicians – just one of whom survived the war unwounded – and refer too to 'The Scottish March', believed to be the march now known as 'Dumbarton's Drums' (see Regimental Music below).

Having officially become part of the Scottish establishment in 1661, the Regiment returned to Britain in 1678. By the following year it was reported to consist of 21 companies, each of which had two drummers; there was also a Drum Major and a Pipe Major, this latter suggesting the presence of pipers, perhaps drummers doubling up.

The first reference we have to a military band comes with General Dilke's inspection of the 1st Battalion in 1763, when it was noted, 'This regiment hath fifers and a band of music.' The following decade an inspection report mentions '8 music', though this was evidently a fast-growing ensemble, for by 1800 there is a complaint that the Band is 'too large'.

Dance Band of 2nd Battalion, The Royal Scots, Egypt 1928, Bandmaster A Macdonald   (Eagles/Ogilby)

This was to become a common theme in the early years of the 19th century. There was a concerted attempt to hold down the size of regimental bands in the infantry – the struggle to limit the cavalry bands had effectively been lost by now – and the strength of the musical establishment was in a constant state of flux. In 1815 the 1st Battalion could produce 22 musicians on parade; by 1822 this was down to one sergeant and 14 privates. The 2nd Battalion Band, similarly restricted to 15 members in the early 1820s, was by 1826 expanding again to include a sergeant, eight corporals and ten privates. And disapproval was also registered of the 4th Battalion in 1813, though the usefulness of having additional soldiers was also recognized:

Musicians: Playing very correct marching time; rather exceed the limited numbers but all are fit and trained for the ranks. Only clothed as musicians.

Perhaps the only battalion that did not incur the displeasure of inspectors was the 3rd, whose reports in 1813 and 1815 state simply 'There is no band of music.'

Despite these struggles with authority, and despite the cost of maintaining musicians (accounts show that the 2nd Battalion spent £400 simply on clothing its bandsmen in 1802/3), the role of the band in the social life of the battalion was highly valued. The atmosphere of the golden age of empire, and the band's contribution to it, is captured in an 1844 account by Colonel Bell of the 2nd Battalion:

I had my men on St George's Island and I believe everyone had a fishing rod. We caught lots of sea-fish and speared lobsters by torchlight; serenaded the Fleet in Karlow with our band and choir by moonlight, and had some nice picnic parties by daylight.

Sketches from the 1860s show the 1st Battalion wearing white tunics with blue facings, wings of blue cloth, laced white and piped red, white waist-belt and band pouch with a brass St Andrew's cross.

Above: Extract from one of Jimmy Howe's compositions, as published in prisoner of war newspaper, 1941
(Howe)
Right: 1st Battalion, The Royal Scots, Paris 1946, Bandmaster J O'Reilly (RMSM)

White pill-box hats with blue bands and lancer piping to the crown, a blue figure and a white button in the centre and a white St Andrew's cross in front were worn, though a photograph taken in Malta in 1878 shows this headwear replaced by a Glengarry, adorned with a badge similar to that worn today.

The 2nd Battalion Band in 1882 were wearing the usual uniform with a red embroidered bandsman's badge on the right arm, a white music pouch on the right-hand side of the waist-belt and a large shoulder plaid and silver brooch. The plaid and brooch, however, were abandoned soon after.

The first bandmasters to be mentioned are Mr Paolo Castaldini of the 1st Battalion and Mr Moynaugh of the 2nd; it is not known whether they were enlisted men or civilians, though the latter is more likely. What is certain is that Mr Castaldini was anything but popular with his own men. In 1847 a number of bandsmen were court martialled for an assault upon him; it appears that he was tied up in a sack and severely beaten.

Mr Moynaugh was succeeded by one of his own bandsmen, Samuel Griffiths, who had been on a student's course at Kneller Hall prior to his appointment. Mr Griffith's abilities were such that, after 16 years with The Royal Scots, he moved on to the Royal Military College (Sandhurst) and thence to Kneller Hall, where he served as Director of Music in the rank of 2nd Lieutenant.

Renowned as a composer – particularly memorable are an overture *Hermolin* and a motet 'God be Merciful unto Us' – Samuel Griffiths was also an important theorist. His work *The Military Band* is believed to be the first treatise on military band arranging, and his *Hints on the Management of Army Bands* was also influential.

During the Great War, whilst the bandmasters and boys remained at the depot to form the basis of new bands, most of the men went on active service. This was, of course, common to most of the musicians in the army, and amongst those fighting was Alexander MacDonald, who was awarded a Distinguished Conduct Medal in the ranks of the East Lancashire Regiment. Immediately following the war he took over the 2nd Battalion Band, re-building it and establishing it again as a popular attraction, especially in the seaside resorts of southern England.

The 1st Battalion, meanwhile, appointed Sam Rhodes as Bandmaster in 1926. One of the great

1st Battalion, The Royal Scots, France 1949, Bandmaster J O'Reilly   (RMSM)

military musicians of the century, Mr Rhodes was eventually to become Director of Music of the Scots Guards and Senior Director in the Army.

In 1933 the Regiment celebrated its tercentenary, and in recognition of its continued service, King George V gave the pipers the privilege of wearing the Royal Stewart tartan.

With the outbreak of the Second World War, bandsmen again joined the troops to fight, with tragic consequences for both battalions. The 1st was part of the British Expeditionary Force, but was not destined to escape from Dunkirk. Following a series of rear-guard actions that took a heavy toll, the survivors were overrun at la Bassée Canal by the SS Totenkopf Division. Amongst those taken prisoner were the band sergeant and Lance-Corporal Jimmy Howe of the Band. Jimmy recalls:

After our capture we were marched three hundred miles through Belgium and Holland to the German border. Then for three days and nights we travelled in cattle trucks into Poland, to Lamsdorf Stalag VIIIB near Breslau. There were about twenty-five thousand prisoners when we arrived. There were so many of us that the Germans left us to our own devices in some ways, under supervision of course.

It quickly became a question of survival of the fittest. For every prisoner the main thing in such circumstances was to occupy the mind. Given this situation, it is amazing what can be achieved from nothing.

By February 1941 musical instruments had been obtained from various sources, some from the Red Cross, others bartered from the German guards and from other prisoners – Jimmy, for example, acquired a piano accordian from a Polish prisoner of war in exchange for his watch. With such improvised instrumentation, the Stalag VIII Band was born. LCpl Howe's major contribution was composing and arranging; one of his songs, 'When I Come Home Sweetheart' appeared in the Stalag newspaper and, some 40 years later, was to form the trio tune in his march 'Stalag'. By this time, having held appointments with the Argyll & Sutherland Highlanders and the Scots Guards, Jimmy Howe had emerged as one of the most successful military musicians in the country.

Even worse was in store for the 2nd Battalion. Stationed in Hong Kong when the Japanese attacked, they put up a desperate but doomed defence of the colony that ended with surrender on Christmas Day 1941. There were just four officers and 98 other ranks left of the Battalion, one of the casualties being the Bandmaster, Mr Jordan, killed in action on 10 December. Those who remained were taken prisoner, the majority dying when the Japanese ship they were on was sunk.

The bands were re-formed, but for the 2nd Battalion it was a short-lived revival; in 1948 the Battalion went the way of the 3rd and 4th in the previous century and was disbanded.

During the '50s further action was seen by the bandsmen, then stationed in Cyprus. Tasks such as searching for EOKA arms were a regular part of life. Though this was perhaps the most tense posting, it was far from the only overseas service by the Band; it also played throughout Europe and as far afield as Japan, Canada, East Africa and Israel.

In 1983 the Regiment celebrated its 350th anniversary with a parade at Holyrood Park and an inspection by the Queen.

The last photograph of the Band, taken in 1994, shows it to be just 15 strong. On 15 March of that year, under the Options for Change programme, it was amalgamated with the bands of The Royal Highland Fusiliers and The King's Own Scottish Borderers to form The Lowland Band. The new Director of Music was Captain Graham Jones, and the Bandmaster was WO1 Tony Clarke.

Regimental Music

The regimental quick march is 'Dumbarton's Drums', the origins of which are obscure. Lord George Douglas, the 1st Earl of Dumbarton, was the colonel of the Regiment from 1678, and the march is named in his honour, but there are many who believe it pre-dates this and may derive from the early years spent in French service.

It is also possible that this is the same piece known from the time of the Thirty Years War as variously 'The Scottish March', 'The Scotch March' and 'The Scots March'. References to the piece and to its association with the regiment are plentiful and include a comment by Samuel Pepys whilst in Rochester in June 1667 that 'here in the streets I did hear the Scotch March beat by the drums before the soldiers, which is very odde.'

When a member of the Royal Family is present for a parade, 'The Daughter of the Regiment' is also played. This is in commemoration of the birth of the future Queen Victoria at a time when her father was Colonel of the Regiment, and was played thus for the first time at Aldershot in 1889 when the 2nd Battalion marched past the Queen. It comes from Donizetti's opera *La Fille du Régiment*.

The regimental slow march is 'The Garb of Old Gaul'. (For further details see the Scots Guards.)

BANDMASTERS OF THE 1ST BATTALION THE ROYAL SCOTS

184?-1851 **CASTALDINI**, Paolo. Civ BM (possibly Sgt) 1 Ft 184?; retd 1851.

1851-1856 **MAANEN** Van J C. Born 1827 died 1899. Sgt (BM) 52 Ft 1845; Sgt (BM) 1 Ft 1851; Sgt (BM) Bengal Artillery 1856; Sgt (BM) Scots Fus Gds 1869; BM Royal Irish Constabulary 1875; died in service.

1856-1883 Bandmaster(s) not known.

1883-1900 **McGILL**, Alexander Thompson. Born 1845 died 1907. Enl 92 Ft 8/11/60; WO (BM) 1 RS 1/2/83; retd 8/6/1900.

1900-1921 **ELLIS**, Arthur William. Born 1869 died 1948. Enl 1 King's 14/8/83; WO (BM) 1 RS 9/6/1900; retd 16/9/21.

1921-1926 **MARSHALL**, Oswald Edgar. Born 1888 died 19??. Enl 2 Midd'x R 7/8/02; WO1 (BM) 21 L 23/12/19; WO1 (BM) 1 RS 30/11/21; retd 11/6/26; BM 9 HLI 1928-39.

1926-1935 **RHODES**, Sam MVO MBE Mus Bac ARCM psm. Born 1900 died 1977. Enl 2 Seaforth 24/6/15; WO1 (BM) 1 RS 12/6/26; WO1 (BM) RA (Mtd) 20/11/35; Lt (DoM) SG 12/12/38; Lt-Col Snr DoM Bde Gds 1949; retd 26/8/59.

1935-1942 **MacPHERSON**, Hugh Charles. Born 1898 died 19??. Enl 7 H 9/9/24; WO1 (BM) 1 RS 15/12/35; WO1 (BM) 2 S Stafford R 27/3/42; retd 1948.

1942-1948 **ADAMS**, Charles Alfred MBE ARCM. Born 1913 died 1954. Enl 2 E York R 27/9/27; WO1 (BM) 1 RS 27/3/42; seconded to Recce Corps 1943; WO1 (BM) RA (Wool) 1/2/1946; WO1 (BM) 1 N Stafford R 25/11/48; died 12/54 whilst still serving.

1948-1951 **O'REILLY**, Joseph Clement ARCM. Born 1911. For full details see 2 RS.

1951-1958 **SMITH**, Cornelius Edwin. Born 1916. Enl 2 North'n R 2/1/34; WO1 (BM) 1 RS 8/1/51; retd 8/1/58; BM London Fire Brigade 1973-19??.

1958-1964 **SUTTILL**, Dennis George. Born 1930. Enl REME 20/2/46; WO1 (BM) 1 RS 9/1/58; WO1 (BM) Aden Protectorate Levies 17/11/64; WO1 (BM) RAC Jnr Ldrs 4/66; retd 21/7/69.

1964-1967 **MEEK**, Albert Percy LGSM FRSA. Born 1929. Enl RTR 2/2/50; WO1 (BM) 1 RS 17/11/64; retd 6/2/67.

1967-1971 **MANNIFIELD**, Douglas LGSM ARCM. Born 1933. Enl 1 York & Lanc R 19/11/47; WO1 (BM) 1 RS 7/2/67; retd 17/9/71.

1971-1977 **BRIGGS-WATSON**, Bryan Edgar Peter LTCL ARCM FVCM (Hons). Born 1933. Enl 1 HLI 3/9/47; transf 1 RHF 20/1/59; WO1 (BM) 1 RS 18/9/71; retd 1/9/77; DoM Royal Mounted Band Oman 1977.

1977-1984 **REEVES**, Colin John LTCL. Born 1944. Enl RA 25/7/59 – served RA (Mtd) & RA (Wool); WO1 (BM) 1 RS 14/7/77; WO1 (BM) Scot Div Sch Mus 13/7/84; Capt (DoM) Scot Div 16/9/85; Capt Snr DoM BAOR 13/1/87; Capt (DoM) RA (Alan) 7/12/87; Capt (DoM) LG 23/10/89; Maj (DoM) 1/10/91.

1984-1992 **HODGETTS**, Anthony John. Born 1954. Enl 1 Staffords 25/8/71; WO1 (BM) RS 16/7/84; WO1 Company Commander RMSM 8/6/92; retd 9/12/94.

1992-1994 **WILLIAMS**, Geoffrey ARCM BBCM. Born 1961. Enl 1 Kings 13/9/77; WO1 (BM) 1 RS 6/4/92; retd 31/10/94.

Drum Major and Bandsmen of 2nd Battalion, The Royal Scots. Aldershot c1890   (Eagles/Ogilby)

BANDMASTERS OF THE 2ND BATTALION THE ROYAL SCOTS

18??-1874 **MOYNAUGH**, F. Civ BM (possibly Sgt) 2/1 Ft 18??; retd 1874.

1874-1890 **GRIFFITHS**, Samuel C. Born 1847 died 1896. Enl 2/1 Ft 17/2/62; Sgt (BM) 2/1 Ft 31/3/74; WO (BM) 1/7/81; WO (BM) RMC (Sand) 3/5/90; Lt (DoM) RMSM 24/12/90; died whilst serving 24/3/96.

1890-1897 **CAWLEY**, Edward. Born 1857 died 1929. Enl 74 Ft 21/10/71; WO (BM) 2 RS 3/5/90; retd 31/8/97.

1897-1913 **REILLY**, William Robert. Born 1870 died 1946. Enl 1 York & Lanc R 17/12/85; WO (BM) 2 RS 1/9/97; retd 4/9/13; BM 5 R W Kent R (TA) 1929-39.

1913-1919 **GRACE**, Joseph Edward LRAM. Born 1882 died 1919. Enl 1 KSLI 18/6/96; WO (BM) 2 RS 5/9/13; retd 28/2/19.

1919-1934 **MacDONALD**, Alexander White DCM. Born 1887 died 19??. Enl 1 E Lan R 8/12/02; WO1 (BM) 2 RS 1/11/19; retd 17/11/34.

1934-1941 **JORDAN**, Herbert B ARCM. Born 1906 died 1941. Enl 1 Devon R 28/8/24; WO1 (BM) 2 RS 18/11/34; killed in action 10/12/41.

1941-1948 **O'REILLY**, Joseph Clement ARCM. Born 1911. Enl 1 R Sussex R 21/10/25; WO1 (BM) 2 RS 19/12/41; WO1 (BM) 1 RS 25/11/48; retd 7/1/51.

THE ROYAL SCOTS FUSILIERS

1678	Earl of Mar's Regiment of Foot
1686	The Scots Fusiliers Regiment of Foot
1712	The Royal North British Fusiliers
1751	21st (Royal North British Fusiliers)
1877	21st (Royal Scots Fusiliers)
1959	amalgamated to form The Royal Highland Fusiliers (Princess Margaret's Own Glasgow and Ayrshire Regiment)

That The Royal Scots Fusiliers had some music present from its earliest days is clear from the regimental rolls for 1682, showing a provision for two drummers for each of the ten companies, together with three pipers. The records from 1715 allow for drummers' pay at 1/- per day.

When the Band came into existence is less certain. A report dated 26 October 1798 talks of a 'Band consisting of 5 Sergeants, 10 Corporals, 5 Drums and 3 Privates', but some kind of musical combination must have existed prior to this, since we know of a set of instruments being presented in 1789. These instruments, however, were not destined for long service – at the end of the Peninsular War, they were lost when the *Mackerel*, bringing Captain Grant and some of the Regiment home to Perth, was sunk.

In 1832 white double-breasted tunics with regimental facings were ordered for the Band (as distinct from the scarlet tunics of the troops), and around the same time the old regimental pattern lace – white with a blue stripe – was replaced by plain worsted.

The 2nd Battalion was created in 1858 and soon afterwards the first bandmaster in the Regiment of whom we have any records was appointed; Sergeant G McQuade transferred from the Band of the 90th Foot in November 1860. His replacement in 1863 was Samuel Traise, the first appointment from Kneller Hall.

A couple of years later Kneller Hall also provided the 1st Battalion with a bandmaster: James, or possibly Thomas, Brophy. (There is some confusion about his name – handwritten reports give the initial T, whilst the printed copy of the 3rd Dragoons' regimental march 'The 3DGs' gives it as J.)

Though Sgt Brophy was undoubtedly a successful musician, the brevity of his tenure set an unfortunate pattern – the first four known band-

BAND OF THE

ROYAL HIGHLAND FUSILIERS

(Princess Margaret's Own Glasgow and Ayrshire Regiment)

Left: Drummers, 2nd Battalion The Royal Scots Fusiliers, Aldershot c1903

(Eagles/Ogilby)

Right: 1st Battalion, The Royal Scots Fusiliers, Shorncliffe 1958, Bandmaster W Allen (Eagles/Ogilby)

masters of the Battalion between them served for just 13 years, a sequence that culminated in the dismissal of Bandmaster Strudwick in 1880. His final confidential report was a terse 'Unsatisfactory'. It was left to his successor Sergeant James Reardon to provide some stability to the Band, remaining in the post for nearly 18 years.

Nor was this the only problem the Regiment needed to resolve. The pipes that had been a feature of the establishment since the outset seem to have disappeared some time around the middle of the century, and in 1870 ten men had to be equipped and trained to restore the tradition.

The 2nd Battalion meanwhile had its own difficulties establishing musical continuity. In 1879 the whole battalion, including the Band, was rushed to South Africa to assist in prosecuting the Zulu War. The bandsmen served as medical orderlies and as fighting troops. The Zulu uprising was swiftly suppressed, but two further years of service in the Transvaal were then required before a move to

India was authorized.

In December 1881 the 2nd relieved the 1st Battalion at Secunderabad. For a while it enjoyed a more settled period, but by the end of the decade it was back in South Africa for the Boer War.

Worse was yet to come, of course, and both Bands laid down their instruments in 1914 to fight in the Great War. The 2nd Battalion was to suffer particularly terrible losses in the slaughter at Ypres – casualties accounted for all but two lieutenants and thirty other ranks, with many bandsmen amongst those lost.

In 1917, however, both bands were re-formed and returned to their battalions in a musical capacity.

With the retirement of William Gidney, who had taken the 1st Battalion Band through the trauma of the war years, William Withers was appointed Bandmaster in 1923. He remained with the Regiment until the eve of the Second World War, the last few months being spent in the 2nd Battalion, having swapped appointments with Henry Roberts. An

extremely talented musician, Bill Withers was well known in military circles as a march composer, though his tendency to sell off his works to less able writers meant that his name was less familiar to the general public.

In later years, Mr Withers was employed as senior instrument-storeman at Kneller Hall, but he made his reputation in the glory days between the wars, playing summer seasons in seaside resorts and parks. Typical of the programmes of the time is one given at the Leas Cliff Bandstand in Folkstone in 1931:

March	Rienzi	Wagner
Overture	Poet and Peasant	Suppé
Highland Dances		
Selection	La Bohème	Puccini
Combined Bagpipes		
and Band		arr Withers
	Interval	
Highland Dancing		
Piccolo Solo	Cassiopeia	Barsotti

Selection	Stand up and Sing	Porter
Fantasia	The Thistle	Myddleton
March of the 21st		
21st Regiment	The British Grenadiers	
	God Bless The Prince of	
	Wales	
	God Save The King	

During the Second World War, the able-bodied joined the ranks, leaving the bandmasters, the infirm and the boys behind at the depot to form the nuclei of new bands.

In 1947 the 2nd Battalion was disbanded and Bandmaster Holyoak transferred to the 1st. Twelve years later the Regiment was amalgamated with the Highland Light Infantry.

Regimental Music

'The British Grenadiers' became the official quick-step of all Fusilier regiments in 1882, though it had been in use by The Royal Scots Fusiliers since 1858, played alongside 'Highland Laddie' (for further details see the Grenadier Guards and the Scots Guards). The slow march was 'The Garb of Old Gaul' (for further details see the Scots Guards).

Other quicksteps associated with the Regiment include 'The Sheriff's March' – an adaptation of the tune 'The Rock and Wee Pickle Tow' – and 'March of the 21st Regiment'. This latter, originally a slow march, was inherited from the old Ayrshire Militia, which in 1881 became the 4th Battalion.

It is believed that prior to 1800 the Regiment used a tune entitled 'The Scots Fusiliers'. Written in triple time, it was played as both a slow march and a quickstep. Rediscovered in the British Museum by Alexander W Inglis early this century, it was finally published by him in 1918 in *The Lowland Scots Regiments*.

1st Battalion, The Highland Light Infantry, Coronation 1937, Bandmaster H Jarman (RMSM)

THE HIGHLAND LIGHT INFANTRY
(City of Glasgow Regiment)

1777	1st Bn 73rd (Highland) Foot	1787	74th (Highland) Foot (also The Assaye Regiment, 1803)
1786	71st (Highland) Foot		
1808	71st (Glasgow Highland) Foot	1816	74th Foot
1809	71st (Glasgow Highland Light Infantry) Regiment	1845	74th (Highlanders) Foot
1810	71st (Highland) Light Infantry		

1881	The Highland Light Infantry (City of Glasgow Regiment)
1959	amalgamated to form The Royal Highland Fusiliers (Princess Margaret's Own Glasgow and Ayrshire Regiment)

The name of The Highland Light Infantry is somewhat misleading since the Regiment was actually based in Glasgow, and did not march at light infantry speed. Indeed, for much of the Regiment's existence, the men did not even wear kilts – the 71st abandoning them in 1809 and the 74th in 1847. When the two were amalgamated in 1881, the decision whether to re-adopt the kilt was passed over to the Regiment and, mainly due to pressure from the new 2nd Battalion, was resolved in favour of trews; it was not until the disbandment of the 2nd Battalion after the Second World War that the kilt was re-introduced.

References to music in the early days are sketchy, though the future Duke of Wellington, writing from Chittendore in South India in May 1804 does mention the pipers of the 74th, saying that they played delightfully. Since the Regiment had by then been in India for 17 years, any taste of home was presumably welcome also to the troops.

Before the keeping of official records, there are mentions of a bandmaster in each regiment. The 51st spent the period between 1838 and 1852 in Montreal, and it is suggested that throughout this time Joseph Maffré – a well-known choral and orchestral teacher from the town – served as Bandmaster.

In the 1850s the 74th were at the Cape of Good Hope, and Sergeant James McKay in his *Reminiscences of the Last Kaffir War* tells us that 'the Bandmaster, a native of Germany, was held in great esteem by both Officers and men'. The past tense is explained by the capture of Bandmaster Hartong during the conflict; he was subsequently tortured to death.

No further details are known of Mr Hartong, and it is equally unclear whether he was immediately replaced, since the next known incumbent was Herr Kohl, another German, who did not take up the post of Bandmaster of the 74th until 1858. He was to remain with the Band for twelve years, suggesting that he was held in some regard, and his influence was felt elsewhere; the first two Kneller Hall-appointed bandmasters of the 71st – Donald McInnes and John Simpson – had served in the 74th as sergeants, and it is reasonable to suppose that they had learnt their trade from Herr Kohl.

The relationship in Scottish regiments between the military band and the pipe band is notoriously sensitive. When the 71st was in India in the early 1860s, Sir Hugh Rose inadvertently stepped into this minefield by allowing the pipers to play the regiment off parade, a task normally performed by the military band. The resultant dispute spilled over into the Regiment's return to Scotland; when the men had been played into Edinburgh Castle by the Band to the strains of 'When Johnny Comes Marching Home Again', the pipes attempted to have the last word, striking up their own air in response. It was not until 1870 that orders were issued specifying which combination should play on which occasion.

It took Queen Victoria herself to resolve another dispute, this time concerning the question of whether the pipes should march in front of or behind the band. In 1871 the Queen decreed that 'the Regiment should on all occasions march past to the Pipes . . . When marching past the Pipes will fall in before the Band.'

In this context it is worth noting that the 71st pipe and bugle band did not have drums until 1908, which must have made marching to the pipes extremely difficult.

The two regiments were amalgamated in the great restructuring of the infantry in 1881. Photographs taken the previous decade show the 71st just 19. The Bandmaster of the 71st, Donald McInnes, shown wearing civilian clothes, despite his military rank.

The three quarters of a century that The Highland Light Infantry existed produced one major musical figure from each battalion. The 1st was dominated in the inter-war years by Henry Jarman, who remained with the Battalion for twelve years before going on to become the first Bandmaster of the Royal Army Ordnance Corps, where he was later promoted to Director of Music, finally retiring in the rank of Major.

The 2nd Battalion saw the first important appointment of the famous John Judd, who also spent twelve years with the Regiment. He was one of the first to specialize in arrangements for combined military band and pipes and drums, starting a tradition that was to reach its peak with the chart-topping 'Amazing Grace' in 1971; there are still some who have never quite forgiven him. Judd himself went on to become Senior Director of Music in the Army.

The Second World War hit both bands heavily, with many pre-war bandsmen amongst the early casualties. In the immediate aftermath, the 2nd Battalion was disbanded and Mr Wilson, the then Bandmaster, and his men transferred to the 1st.

In 1959 the Regiment was amalgamated with The Royal Scots Fusiliers; Mr Ray Mitchell of the Highland Light Infantry became Bandmaster of the new Regiment.

Regimental Music

The regimental quick march of the 1st Battalion was 'Whistle o'er the Lave o't'. The tune was composed in 1720 by John Bruce, a Braemar violinist who later fought in the '45 rising. The original words remain unprintable, but thankfully Robbie Burns produced a more acceptable version in 1780, despite his personal opinion that Bruce was 'a stark mad Highlander'.

The 74th used 'Blue Bonnets over the Border'. The origins of the tune are lost; it was known at one point as 'General Leslie's March to Longmarston Moor', which would date it to 1644, but it may be older. The words are more modern, coming from Sir Walter Scott's novel *The Monastery*:

March, march, Ettrick and Teviotdale.
Why the De'il dinna ye march forward in order?
March, march, Eskdale and Liddesdale,
All the Blue Bonnets are bound for the Border.

A popular re-writing of the words produced a variation:

March, march, over the Border,
Some of them drunk, and some of them sober.

The slow march was 'The Garb of Old Gaul' (for further details see the Scots Guards).

The regimental double past of the 71st was 'Monymusk' for the Band and 'Bulcairns' for the pipes.

Top: Dance Band of the 2nd Battalion, The Highland Light Infantry c1938, Bandmaster J Judd (RMSM)

Left: 1st Battalion, The Royal Highland Fusiliers, Edinburgh 1959, Bandmaster R Mitchell
(Eagles/Ogilby)

THE ROYAL HIGHLAND FUSILIERS
(Princess Margaret's Own Glasgow and Ayshire Regiment)

1959   The Royal Highland Fusiliers
(Princess Margaret's Own Glasgow
and Ayrshire Regiment)

The Band of the new regiment fulfilled its regimental duties in Scotland, Cyprus and Germany, though its most notable successes were to occur further afield. A 1966 tour of America and Canada was so successful that the men were later presented with a plaque for the Best Band Tour of North America 1960-1970.

In November 1970 the Band and Pipes played at the British Trade Fair in Buenos Aires, where Bandmaster John Brush re-arranged the popular Argentinian march 'San Lorenzo' for pipes, bugles and band.

The tasks of modern military musicians, however, often have little to do with music. As medical assistants, the men of The Royal Highland Fusiliers helped with the horrific aftermath of the Lockerbie bombing, later being awarded the 1989 Wilkinson Sword of Peace. 1990 saw them employed on Operation Orderly during the ambulance workers' strike, and later in the Gulf War. In between came the relative comfort of a stay in Belize and a trip to Los Angeles for British Week.

In 1993 they were back in Belize for a three-month tour, finding time to make a visit to Mexico.

On 15 March 1994 the Band was subsumed into the new Lowland Band under the Options for Change reforms.

Regimental Music

The regimental quick march is a combination of 'Whistle o'er the Lave o't' and 'British Grenadiers', arranged by Bandmaster John Brush.

The slow march is 'The Garb of Old Gaul' (for details see Royal Scots). The march of the 21st Regiment (arranged by Bandmaster Brush) is also used.

The regimental hymn 'Rhu Vaternish' was adopted by the Regiment in 1960 whilst in Aden. The music is an old pipe tune, and the words were written by the regimental padre, Reverend Morrison.

BANDMASTERS OF THE 1ST BATTALION THE ROYAL SCOTS FUSILIERS

1867-1869 **BROPHY**, Thomas (James). Enl 1/6 Ft; Sgt (BM) 1/21 Fus 13/8/67; Sgt (BM) 101 Ft 18/1/69; Sgt (BM) 3DG 1/10/74; retd 16/2/80.

1869-1874 **CARBETT**, T. Enl 48 Ft; Sgt (BM) 1/21 Fus 18/1/69; retd 2/4/74.

1874-1877 **HEWSON**, George. Born 1845 died 1877. Enl 49 Ft; Sgt (BM) 21 Fus 3/4/74; died 30/6/77 whilst serving.

1877-1880 **STRUDWICK**, J G. Enl 2/20 Ft; Sgt (BM) 1/21 Fus; retd 7/3/80.

1880-1898 **REARDON**, James Thomas. Born 1846 died 1932. Enl 1/2 Fus 17/7/61; Sgt (BM) 21 Ft 8/3/80; WO (BM) 1/7/81; retd 17/5/98.

1898-1904 **RICH**, Thomas H. Born 1867 died 1950. Enl 23 Ft 20/3/83; Sgt (BM) RGA (Templemore) 1894; WO (BM) 1 R S Fus 18/5/98; retd 19/3/04; Professor RNSM 1904; WO (BM) 5 R Sussex R (TA) 1908; WO1 (BM) Royal Hibernian Military School 1916; WO1 (BM) London Irish Rifles (TA) 1923-25.

1904-1905 **FREEMAN**, Thomas Hamilton Frazer. Born 1870 died 1905. Enl 4 Worc R 30/1/84; WO (BM) 1 R S Fus 20/3/04; retd 22/12/05.

1905-1923 **GIDNEY**, William Francis. Born 1874 died 19??. Enl 2 Queen's R 23/10/89; WO (BM) 1 R S Fus 23/12/05; retd 28/7/23.

1923-1938 **WITHERS**, William Charles ARCM. Born 1897 died 1968. Enl 2 Worc R 1/11/12; WO1 (BM) 1 R S Fus 29/7/23; WO1 (BM) 2 R S Fus 19/12/38; retd 31/8/39.

1938-1946 **ROBERTS**, Henry William Valentine ARCM. Born 1902 died 1954. (For full details see 2 R S Fus).

1947-1950 **HOLYOAK**, Harry W LRAM ARCM. Born 1904 died 19??. Enl 1 Essex R 17/1/21; WO1 (BM) 2 R S Fus 1/9/39; WO1 (BM) 1 R S Fus 1947; retd 19/5/50.

1950-1954 **PAYNE**, Frederick Arthur ARCM. Born 1910. Enl 2 RWF 31/8/25; WO1 (BM) 1 E York R 15/12/45; WO1 (BM) Sierra Leone Regt 1946; WO1 (BM) 1 R S Fus 20/5/50; retd 26/1/54.

1954-1959 **ALLEN**, William MBE ARCM psm. Born 1921 died 1987. Enl 1 Loyal R 19/4/37; WO1 (BM) 1 R S Fus 27/1/54; WO1 (BM) 1 R North'd Fus 21/1/59; WO1 (BM) Home Counties Bde 25/10/63; Lt (DoM) RA (BAOR) 10/3/66; Major (DoM) RCT 3/10/69; retd 30/6/78.

BANDMASTERS OF THE 2ND BATTALION THE ROYAL SCOTS FUSILIERS

1860-1863 **McQUADE**, G. Enl 90 Ft; Sgt (BM) 2/21 Fus 23/11/60; WO1 (BM) 64 Ft 9/4/63; retd 18/4/82.

1863-1868 **TRAISE**, Samuel. Sgt (BM) 2/21 Fus 9/4/68; Sgt (BM) 1/14 Ft 6/10/68; retd 31/12/75.

1868-1869 **LAY**, E H. Born 18?? died 1869. Sgt (BM) 43 Ft 1/1/63; Sgt (BM) 2/21 Fus 1/6/68; died 25/7/69 whilst serving.

1869-1882 **DANIELS**, Frederick. Born 18?? died 1930. Enl 21 Fus 1869; Sgt (BM) 21 Fus 26/7/69; retd 24/6/82.

1882-1887 **HANCOCK**, Robert. Born 1850 died 1887. Enl 2/14 Ft 10/2/64; Sgt (BM) 2 R S Fus 25/6/82; retd 23/5/1887.

1887-1900 **BARRETT**, William. Born 1856 died 1930. Enl 1 R Sussex R 17/1/70; WO (BM) 2 R S Fus 24/3/87; retd 16/1/1900.

1900-1922 **ROBERTSON**, William. Born 1868 died 1946. Enl 2 R S Fus 3/5/82; WO (BM) 17/1/1900; retd 8/9/22; BM Marlborough School 1922-38.

1922-1933 **GRAVES**, Walter Paramour. Born 1881 died 19??. Enl 1 RS 18/1/96; WO1 (BM) 2 Dub Fus 28/6/17; WO1 (BM) 2 R S Fus 9/9/22; retd 17/1/33.

1933-1938 **ROBERTS**, Henry William Valentine ARCM. Born 1902 died 1954. Enl 2 Queen's R 15/2/16; WO1 (BM) 2 R S Fus 18/1/33; WO1 (BM) 1 R S Fus 19/12/38; retd 1946.

1938-1939 **WITHERS**, William Charles ARCM. Born 1897 died 1968. For full details see 1 R S Fus.

1939-1947 **HOLYOAK**, Harry W LRAM ARCM. Born 1904 died 19??. For full details see 1 R S Fus.

BANDMASTERS OF THE 1ST BATTALION THE HIGHLAND LIGHT INFANTRY

1838-1852 **MAFFRÉ**, Joseph. Civ BM.

1852-1872 Bandmaster(s) not known.

1872-1878 **McINNES**, Donald. Born 1834 died 18??. Enl 74 Ft; Sgt (BM) 71 Ft 31/5/72; retd 5/2/78.

1878-1882 **SIMPSON**, John. Born 18?? died 1882. Enl 74 Ft; Sgt (BM) 71 Ft 6/2/78; retd 5/12/82.

1882-1902 **ANDERSON**, John. Born 1853 died 1908. Enl 99 Ft 5/4/64; Sgt (BM) 1 HLI 6/12/82; retd 5/12/02.

1902-1908 **BARTRAM**, Horace John. Born 1872 died 1930. Enl 2 DCLI 21/8/86; WO (BM) 1 HLI 6/12/02; retd 21/4/08.

1908-1918 **STOCKEY**, Herman. Born 1869 died 19??. Enl 3 Worc R 18/4/86; WO (BM) 1 HLI 22/4/08; retd 26/8/18.

1918-1924 **GEOGHEGAN**, Maurice William. Born 1880 died 1950. Enl 3 KOSB 4/4/94; WO1 (BM) 1 HLI 27/8/18; retd 13/11/24.

1924-1938 **JARMAN**, Henry Clay LRAM ARCM. Born 1894 died 1974. Enl 1 The King's R 17/3/09; WO1 (BM) 1 HLI 14/11/24; WO1 (BM) RAOC 1/1/39; Lt (DoM) RAOC 11/8/47; retd 13/1/52 rank of Maj.

1939-1948 **CARRICK**, John Alfred. Born 1906. Enl 2 R Fus 14/7/21; WO1 (BM) 1 HLI 1/1/39; retd 1948.

1948-1951 **WILSON**, Archibald James LRAM ARCM ATCL. Born 1911. For full details see 2 HLI.

1952-1953 No bandmaster.

1953-1959 **MITCHELL**, Ronald Alexander Young ARCM psm. Born 1926. Enl 1 Camerons 1/7/41; WO1 (BM) 1 HLI 1/6/53; WO1 (BM) RHF 20/1/59; Capt (DoM) RAOC 8/6/68; retd 16/1/68; DoM Royal Australian Air Force 1968.

BANDMASTERS OF THE
2ND BATTALION
THE HIGHLAND LIGHT INFANTRY

1858-1870 **KOHL**, Herr. Civ BM 74 Ft 1858-70.

1870-1881 **BUCHANAN**, J. Civ BM 74 Ft 1870; retd 25/4/81

1881-1889 **MOWBRAY**, Samuel. Born 1848 died 1889. Enl 18H 16/5/63; WO (BM) 2 HLI 18/3/81; retd 5/3/89.

1889-1898 **McKINNON**, John. Born 1860 died 1929. For full details see The Argyll & Sutherland Highlanders.

1898-1903 **EVANS**, Robert George, psm. Born 1868 died 1946. Enl RA 23/3/85; transf Coldm Gds 1889; WO (BM) 2 HLI 1/3/98; WO (BM) RA (Plym) 1/4/03; Lt (DoM) Coldm Gds 25/3/20; retd rank of Capt 22/11/30.

1903-1912 **BICKS**, Charles Robert. Born 1871 died 1941. Enl 1 RS 3/1/85; WO (BM) 2 HLI 1/4/03; retd 31/5/12.

1912-1920 **ADAMS**, Frederick. Born 1882 died 1948. Enl 2 E Lan R 17/6/96; WO (BM) HLI 1/6/12; WO1 (BM) 10H 30/9/20; retd 17/2/26.

1920-1930 **FRIEND**, Charles Albert. Born 1890 died 19??. Enl 1 DLI 6/4/05; WO1 (BM) 13/12/20; retd 8/11/30.

1930-1942 **JUDD**, John Leonard MBE MSM BMus (Dunhelm) LRAM ARCM AmusTCL psm. Born 1903 died 1980. Enl 2 R Innis Fus Aug 1917; WO1 (BM) 2 HLI 9/11/30; WO1 (BM) R Signals 12/7/42; Lt (DoM) R Signals 11/8/47; retd 27/2/62 rank of Lt-Col.

1942-1948 **WILSON**, Archibald James LRAM ARCM ATCL. Born 1911. Enl 1 RS 3/2/33; WO1 (BM) 2 HLI 12/7/42: WO1 (BM) 1 HLI 1948; retd 31/12/51.

Above: Bandmaster C Bicks, 2 HLI (RMSM)

BANDMASTERS OF THE
ROYAL HIGHLAND FUSILIERS

1959-1962 **MITCHELL**, Ronald Alexander Young ARCM psm. Born 1926. For full details see 1 HLI.

1962-1969 **COOKE**, Gordon Thomas F LRAM ARCM. Born 1929 died 1995. Enl 1 DLI 25/2/47; WO1 (BM) RHF 23/2/62; retd 12/68.

1969-1972 **BRUSH**, John Alfred psm. Born 1934. Enl 3 Para 3/8/51; transf RMA (Sand) 16/1/59; WO1 (BM) York & Lanc R 7/7/66; WO1 (BM) RHF 19/3/69; WO1 (BM) PoW Div 14/9/72; Capt (DoM) Royal Brunei Malay Regiment 7/3/75; retd 17/7/79.

1972-1979 **SIMPSON**, William John FVCM LTCL ATSC. Born 1936. Enl 11H 2/12/52; WO1 (BM) RHF 14/9/72; retd 19/2/79.

1979-1989 **TYRER**, James Brian. Born 1950. Enl Kings 21/9/65; WO1 (BM) RHF 19/2/79; transf to long service list regimental duty 3/7/89.

1989-1993 **GREER**, Daniel Buttar. Born 1958. Enl KOSB 2/4/58; WO1 (BM) RHF 3/7/89; retd 31/10/94.

1993-1994 **JONES**, Graham Owen ARCM psm. Born 1957. Enl RA (Wool) 10/5/72; WO1 (BM) 16/5L 5/5/85; WO1 (BM) RHF 30/6/93 Capt (DoM) Lowland Band 1/4/94.

BANDS OF THE

KING'S OWN SCOTTISH BORDERERS

THE KING'S OWN SCOTTISH BORDERERS

1689	The Edinburgh Regiment of Foot
1751	25th (Edinburgh) Foot
1782	25th (Sussex) Foot
1805	25th (The King's Own Borderers) Foot
1881 (May)	The York Regiment (King's Own Borderers)
1881 (July)	The King's Own Borderers
1887	The King's Own Scottish Borderers

Though the 25th Foot can be assumed to have had drummers at an earlier date, the first reference to a band comes with a passing comment in an inspection report dated 13 May 1768. The following decade an inspection in June 1777 notes:

The Drum-Major plays on the cymbal. 15 Music. The Musicians now wear hats with red feathers, instead of caps, which they had last year.

The musicians' headwear is a perennial concern of these inspections. The report from 1768 had mentioned drummers wearing 'fur hats with plain fronts', whilst in 1803 complaint is made that the drummers are 'incorrectly dressed, as having queues with their bearskin caps instead of plaits'. Evidently the Regiment allowed its musicians some leeway when it came to sartorial expression.

A further exemption from normal practice was authorized from Horse Guards in 1816; though the size of infantry bands had been set at one man per company plus a Master of the Band in 1803, the 25th Foot was allowed two extra men to carry the Turkish cymbals presented to the Regiment by General Sir James Leith.

The first bandmaster we know of with the Regiment is Ernst Klussman, in charge of the 1st Battalion Band during the 1820s and early '30s. Though we know little of him save for his name and the fact that he transferred to the 9th Lancers in 1835, it seems a fair assumption that, following the fashion of the times, he was a German musician.

The immediate succession is unclear, but Sergeant F H Torrington took over at some point in the middle of the century, and on his retirement was followed by a Kneller Hall appointee. Sergeant McEwan had served with the Band prior to his Kneller Hall training.

Pipers of 1st Battalion, The King's Own Scottish Borderers, Shoreham 1940   (Eagles/Ogilby)

By this stage too the 2nd Battalion had come under the centralizing influence of Kneller Hall, its first official bandmaster being Sergeant William Davies, appointed in 1869.

In 1858 authorization was finally received for the Regiment to have pipes, at which stage it was discovered that they had actually been present all along (a painting of the Regiment in Minorca shows a piper as early as 1770), though no-one could remember who had sanctioned them. The Adjutant-General's Department took up the issue with the Duke of Cambridge, the Commander-in-Chief, and a ruling was eventually given that pipers were to be allowed but that:

These men are to be on the footing of bandsmen and not of drummers, as regards their being borne on the strength of the Regiment, and also the public is to be put to no expense for their clothing as pipers.

There were three official pipers – one with the Colonel's Company and one each with the flank companies, the Grenadiers and the Light – but it is likely that, in common with other Scottish regiments, there were also men from the ranks who could play the pipes. Certainly by the 1880s both battalions had sizeable pipe and drum bands in addition to the military bands.

The pipers adopted the Royal Stewart tartan, though again official approval was not given until well after the fact in 1920. (The piper in the 1770 painting is wearing what appears to be a Government No. 1 tartan, more commonly known as the Black Watch.)

By 1880 the 1st Battalion Band had begun to earn itself a reputation for its string orchestra. Stationed in India, the strings were in constant demand for dances and other engagements and when the 2nd Battalion relieved the 1st in 1890, it appears that many musicians chose to remain.

During the Boer War the bandsmen of the 1st Battalion served both as stretcher bearers and as fighting troops, but the Band was re-formed in the aftermath. Meanwhile, the string band seems to have gone from strength to strength, and was to be one of the great successes of the 1911 Coronation

Durbar in India. 2nd Lieutenant Hutchenson tells the story of that day:

'The King's Own String Band' was playing softly from a tent immediately behind the throne. Suddenly there was a cry of 'Fire!' . . [At] this moment a drummer from the band stepped through the aperture behind the throne and without the least concern leaned forward confidentially towards His Majesty and broke the tense silence, announcing 'Some mucker's done this on purpose', in the broadest Scots accent. The King Emperor roared with laughter, so infectious that it immediately communicated itself to everyone present.

Drummer Dalton was later awarded the Durbar Decoration in recognition of his presence of mind under fire.

With the coming of war, the call to military duty again took precedence over music, and most musicians served in the ranks. At the outbreak the 1st Band had been 50 strong; some 21 men and boys remained behind, and were attached to the 3rd Battalion. A Divisional Band, under Band Sergeant T McDonald MBE, was also active in Egypt in 1916.

The pipers, meanwhile, fulfilled what has long been accepted as their battlefield role, that of inspiring the troops. Amidst the horrors of the trenches, Piper Daniel Laidlaw, a reservist with the 7th Battalion, won enduring fame as the Piper of Loos, playing fearlessly along the parapet. Though wounded, he continued to play 'The Standard on the Braes o' Mar' and the regimental march 'Blue Bonnets'. During the same battle, Robert MacKenzie, a former pipe-major of the 2nd Battalion, returned to service at the age of 59 as Pipe-Major of the 6th Battalion. He too played the men over the top, and was fatally wounded.

In September 1924 Walter FitzEarle was appointed Bandmaster of the 2nd Battalion; he was to remain with the Regiment for 25 years, transferring to the 1st in 1938. Most of his time with the 2nd Band was spent abroad in Egypt and India, where he built it back to its pre-war strength, though the string band had sadly disappeared forever.

When war was again declared, the Band of the 1st Battalion – then engaged in a series of concerts on the South Parade Pier in Southend – packed away its instruments once more and reverted to

Far Left: War-time dance band of The King's Own Scottish Borderers, Hawick 1943

(Packer)

Left: The King's Own Scottish Borderers, Edinburgh 1961, Bandmaster D Bayton

(Eagles/Ogilby)

Below: The King's Own Scottish Borderers, Tunbridge Wells 1984, Bandmaster P Butler

(Colin Dean)

its war-time establishment of one sergeant and 20 stretcher-bearers. Mr FitzEarle and the boys returned to the depot and the remaining bandsmen were issued with rifles and sent to join the British Expeditionary Force in France.

Band Sergeant 'Skip' Skinner, who had enlisted in 1924, commanded a platoon in the first conflict in North-West Europe, and was awarded the Regiment's first Military Medal of the hostilities, later being promoted to the rank of Captain. Completing a unique succession, the first band sergeant after the war, Charles Packer, was also the recipient of a Military Medal, the citation concluding that 'No praise is too high for the magnificent work that he has done.'

Writing in *Fanfare* magazine in 1989, Mr Packer recalled the cost to the Band of the conflict:

> *At Dunkirk, we had one of our bandsmen killed, two went missing and one was taken prisoner, but in the D-Day landings and the days that followed, we lost five former members of the band, amongst them Sergeant Major Wally McLeish.*

Between the two North-East Europe campaigns,

a nine-man dance band was formed, featuring Mr Packer. It survived for a short while after the conclusion of hostilities, and even spent five months in Norway, having been selected by the War Office to accompany a composite Foot Guards regiment assisting the return of King Haakon VII.

Back home the depot band gradually re-built during the war, and was soon performing at recruiting functions and morale-boosting events. It was to form the basis of the post-war band. The 2nd Battalion, however, was disbanded in 1948 and its band disappeared.

Memories of the war were re-kindled in 1969, when the Band returned to the island of Walcheren for the 25th anniversary of the great battle to open the port of Antwerp, in which the 4th and 5th Battalions had fought so famously.

1989 was the tercentenary of the Regiment and the Band played a great many engagements in celebration, including 21 beatings of retreat throughout the country, from Stanraer to London.

On 15 March 1994, under Options for Change, the Band of The King's Own Scottish Borderers disappeared into the amalgamated Lowland Band.

Regimental Music

The quick march is 'Blue Bonnets' (for further details see Royal Scots Fusiliers), adopted for obvious reasons by a Border regiment, and the slow march is 'The Garb of Old Gaul' (for further details see the Scots Guards). The pipes and drums have their own slow march 'The Borderers'.

BANDMASTERS OF THE 1st BATTALION THE KING'S OWN SCOTTISH BORDERERS

182?-1835 **KLUSSMANN**, Ernst. Civ BM (possibly a Sgt) 1/25 Ft 182?; transf 9 L 1835; retd 1841.

1835-18?? Bandmaster(s) not known.

18??-1875 **TORRINGTON**, F H. Sgt (BM) 1/25 Ft 18??; retd 30/9/75.

1875-1881 **McEWAN**, W H. Enl 1/25 Ft ?; Sgt (BM) 1/25 Ft 1/10/75; retd 16/3/81.

1881-1886 **JAMES**, Alfred. Born 1847 died 1923. Enl 4 H 16/10/62; Sgt (BM) 1 KOSB 17/3/81; WO (BM) 1/7/81; retd 20/4/86.

1886-1900 **RAFTER**, William. Born 1857 died 1943. Enl 2 King's Own R 7/8/71; WO (BM) 1 KOSB 21/4/86; retd 28/2/1900.

1900-1922 **WILSON** Alfred James. Born 1868 died 1946. Enl 2 Midd'x R 9/6/83; WO (BM) 1 KOSB 1/3/1900; retd 24/4/22.

1922-1938 **JARVIS**, Thomas Kingston MBE MSM. Born 1885 died 1982. Enl 1 W York R 24/1/99; WO1 (BM) 1 KOSB 25/4/22; retd 14/2/38; BM London Fire Brigade 1938-1951.

1938-1950 **FITZEARLE**, Walter Henry ARCM. Born 1895 died 19??. For full details see 2nd Battalion.

1950-1960 **STOCKHAM**, Leonard Eric LRAM ARCM. Born 1915. Enl The Bays 16/12/29; WO1 (BM) 1 KOSB 14/1/50; WO1 (BM) Lowland Bde 10/8/60; retd 19/10/63.

1960-1963 **BAYTON**, Dennis Arthur. Born 1928. For full details see Royal Lincolnshire Regiment.

1963-1969 **DANIEL**, Geoffrey Russell. Born 1929. Enl 9 L 18/7/45; WO1 (BM) KOSB 22/1/63; att Lowland Depot 29/3/69; retd 24/9/69.

1969-1971 **MACKAY**, Douglas Hunter LGSM ARCM psm. Born 1931. Enl RS 4/12/46; WO1 (BM) The Royals 19/1/66; WO1 (BM) KOSB 29/3/69; WO1 (BM) RMSM 16/8/71; Capt (DoM) RAC Jnr Ldrs Regt 4/9/74; Capt (DoM) RA (Alan) 6/3/79; retd 26/7/82 rank of Maj.

1971-1975 **LAVERTY**, George Malcolm (Changed surname to **HENRY** whilst Bandmaster). Born 1938. Enl R U Rifles (later 2 R Irish) 31/5/65; WO1 (BM) KOSB 17/8/71; retd 16/11/75.

1975-1978 **WALL**, David Frederick LTCL BBCM psm. Born 1945. Enl KSLI 10/6/60; WO1 (BM) KOSB 17/11/75; WO1 (BM) Scottish Div Dep 1978; Capt (DoM) HQ Queen's Div 13/8/84; Capt (DoM) AJSM (Bov) 20/1/86; Capt (DoM) R Signals 18/5/87; Maj (DoM) 13/8/92.

1978-1987 **BUTLER**, Peter George BBCM psm. Born 1945. Enl 3 LI 2/9/66; WO1 (BM) KOSB 26/11/78; Capt (DoM) (badged KOSB) Jordanian Armed Forces 20/4/87; retd 6/9/89.

1987-1991 **CHAPMAN**, John Ernest BA ARCM Cert Ed. Born 1956. Enl 2 Para 12/8/71; WO1 (BM) KOSB 7/1/87; commissioned RAEC 31/7/92; retd rank of Capt 10/94.

1991-1994 **PERRY**, Martin Alfred. Born 1956. Enl QOH 13/9/71; WO1 (BM) D and D 1/9/89; WO1 (BM) KOSB 8/7/91; WO1 (BM) R Signals 17/4/94.

BANDMASTERS OF THE 2nd BATTALION THE KING'S OWN SCOTTISH BORDERERS

1869-1876 **DAVIES**, William. Enl 1/11 Ft 18??; Sgt (BM) 2/25 Ft 16/9/69; retd 30/6/76.

1876-1892 **DOUGLASS**, James. Born 1840 died 1913. For full details see The Buffs.

1892-1902 **COOPER**, William Frederick. Born 1866 died 1937. Enl 71 Ft 5/1/81; WO (BM) 2 KOSB 1/12/92; WO (BM) 5 R Gar R 8/6/02; WO (BM) 2 R North'd Fus 1/3/06; retd 3/1/16; BM Halifax Police 1916-1928; BM Royal Jersey Militia 1929-1936.

1902-1909 **DUNN**, John Joseph. Born 1867 died 1938. Enl 1 The Cameronians 23/7/81; WO (BM) 2 KOSB 8/6/02; retd 19/1/09.

1909-1912 **CARLETON**, William. Born 1881 died 1952. Enl 1 RS 21/7/95; WO (BM) 2 KOSB 20/1/09; retd 23/6/12.

1912-1923 **WILSON**, Thomas. Born 1880 died 1953. Enl 1 Lincoln R 5/9/94; WO (BM) 2 KOSB 10/7/12; retd 31/12/23.

1924-1924 **MARSHALL**, Reginald. Born 1891 died 1924. Enl The Bays 31/8/05; WO1 (BM) 2 KOSB 1/1/24; died whilst serving 16/9/24.

1924-1937 **FITZEARLE**, Walter Henry ARCM. Born 1895 died 19??. Enl 1 Camerons 1/9/10; WO1 (BM) 2 KOSB 17/9/24; WO1 (BM) 1 KOSB 15/2/38; retd 13/1/50.

1937-1948 **KENDALL**, Walter M. LRAM ARCM. Born 1906. Enl 2 Seaforth 14/8/25; WO1 (BM) 2 KOSB 2/11/37; retd 1948.

THE CAMERONIANS
(Scottish Rifles)

1689	The Earl of Angus's Regiment	1794	90th Perthshire Volunteers
1751	26th Foot (The Cameronians)	1815	90th Perthshire Light Infantry
1786	26th Cameronian Regiment		

1881	The Cameronians (Scottish Rifles)
1968	disbanded

It is not known when the Band of the 26th Foot first started to take shape, though it seems certain that it was not during the first century of the Regiment's history, for an inspection report of 1785 states confidently 'No Band'.

There were, however, pipers as early as 1713, records showing that they were distinguished from other ranks by the wearing of a single heron's feather in the front of their bonnets. With the formal establishment of pipe-majors and pipers for Highland regiments after the Crimean War, the Lowlanders also claimed the same privilege; it is recorded that the central plank of the Cameronians' case was the evidence of an unnamed bandmaster who recalled in 1862 that there had been pipers in the Regiment when he had joined some 30 years earlier.

Though the identity of this bandmaster has been lost with the passage of time, his presence in the Regiment in the 1830s is the first reference we have to a band in The Cameronians; it can be assumed that the band had come into existence some time earlier.

The first bandmaster for whom full records survive was Josef Sommer. Trained at Kneller Hall, he had served with the 17th Foot prior to his appointment to the 26th in 1874. His confidential report of 1889 was signed by Major S H Lomax and was fulsome in its praise: 'I cannot speak too highly of him, either as a Bandmaster or as to his personal character.' He left in 1890 to take up a position with the Hyderabad Contingent and subsequently to become Director of Music of the Royal Engineers.

A photograph taken of the 90th Foot in Nowshera in 1866 shows 33 bandsmen together with 26 buglers, despite an official establishment for bat-

BANDS OF THE

CAMERONIANS
(Scottish Rifles)

90th Foot (Perthshire Light Infantry) c1877   (Eagles/Ogilby)

talion bands at the time of just 22 musicians and 16 buglers.

Amongst those in the photograph is Sergeant Bullard, who had joined the 90th sometime in the 1860s and was for a period the acting Bandmaster in the rank of sergeant. Later on, having attended a course at Kneller Hall, he was appointed to the 24th (2nd Warwickshire) Foot, and killed in action in 1879 at the Battle of Isandhlwana. Whether he was replaced immediately is unknown, but in 1882 the first recorded bandmaster was appointed, with the move of William Fitzgerald from the 28th Foot.

With the amalgamations of 1881, Scottish dress was introduced for the Lowland regiments, and both the Battalions of The Cameronians chose to adopt the Douglas tartan of their first Colonel, the Earl of Angus. Being Scottish Rifles, they also retained the Scottish helmet and doublet, but in a dark rifle green with black buttons.

During the Boer War, most of the men from the 2nd Battalion Band were employed as stretcher bearers or riflemen. The 1st meanwhile were stationed in the Punjab. Front-line service was also seen in the Great War.

In June 1929 Lawrence Dunn was appointed Bandmaster of the 1st Cameronians; he was to remain with the Regiment for two decades, some of that time spent with the 2nd Battalion.

Stationed in India in the late '30s, the bandsmen of the 1st Battalion saw a full range of military life: 'Stretcher bearing, khud climbing, digging, wiring and weeding are calls of the day,' recorded the Band Notes on the regimental magazine *The Covenanter* in 1936, whilst at a battalion rifle meeting that year, the Band beat all other platoons, with the pipes coming in second. Musical duties were not forgotten, however, and weekly retreats and concerts were also given.

During the same period, the bugle section was also flourishing and had sufficient strength of numbers to perform in its own right.

The 2nd Cameronians spent much of the interwar era at home. 1939 saw the Band engaged in ceremonial duties at the Tower of London, and Brigadier Barclay records in his *History of The Cameronians, Vol III* the retirement that year of Bandmaster Leslie Seymour who had been with the Battalion since before the Great War:

The Cameronians, Singapore 1950, Bandmaster C Pike   (Pike)

He departed in April and all ranks gave him a rousing send off. Subsequently, Mr Seymour took up a musical appointment in the Channel Islands and only just succeeded in getting away when the Germans occupied the islands.

Mr Seymour's new position was with the Royal Guernsey Militia, though it was of course only a brief appointment.

He was replaced by Mr Dunn of the 1st Battalion, who had the task of re-building the Band after the War. The range of a concert programme given in Queen's Park, Glasgow with the 2nd Argyll & Sutherland Highlanders in July 1945 suggests that the process was already well under way:

Coronation March	Le Prophète	Meyerbeer
Overture	Light Cavalry	Suppé
Suite	Three Bavarian Dances	Elgar
First New Sullivan Selection		arr Godfrey
Tone Poem	Finlandia	Sibelius
Potpourri	The Thistle	arr Myddleton
Post Horn Trio	Vivacity	Barsotti
Selection	White Horse Inn	Benatszky
Overture	Solonelle 1812	Tchaikovsky

Regimental Marches	Within a Mile o' Edinboro' Town
	Highland Laddie
	God Save The Queen

With the disbandment of the 2nd Battalion, Laurie Dunn returned to the 1st, taking the Band on a posting to Gibraltar in October 1946. A variety of engagements included being the pit orchestra for a production of *The Gondoliers*, playing chamber music at the Calpe Institute and providing music for the Feast of Corpus Christi, a Catholic procession a long way removed from the Cameronians' Presbyterian history.

Mr Dunn remained with the Cameronians until his commission in 1949 to become the first Director of Music of the Royal Engineers (Aldershot). The Band was then in Trieste, and the promotion of Mr Dunn was accompanied by the departure of Band Sergeant North and several of the more experienced musicians. The new Bandmaster, Clifford Pike, was therefore obliged to rebuild. The fact that he was successful is evidenced by the Kneller Hall inspection some five years later, when the Band was classified as 'Outstanding', the highest grade possible.

Under Cliff Pike's leadership, an old custom was revived of giving a concert in the Sergeants' Mess immediately after church, to which officers and families were also invited. And the traditional involvement of musicians in regimental sport was also upheld, as Captain Pike later remembered:

The Band were indeed very popular and this was further enhanced by the Battalion winning the BAOR Basketball Cup, in which the team consisted almost entirely of Band members. The Battalion was also finalists in the BAOR Hockey Cup and here the team was represented by six or seven bandsmen.

Amongst more official engagements undertaken during their posting in Germany, the combined Band, pipes and drums played at the Liberation Celebrations at Brunssum, Holland in July 1955.

The late '50s saw a 14-piece dance orchestra created from the ranks of the military band. It proved highly popular, though it faced some intense competition from a rival dance band formed by the pipes and drums.

In the same period both military and pipe bands made prestigious overseas visits, the Band to the Nairobi Festival of Remembrance in November 1957, and the pipes to Amman to beat retreat with the Band of the Jordan Arab Army.

Even more memorable was 1961, a year in which the Band not only played a successful tour of the UK, including seasons in the Glasgow Parks and the Edinburgh Tattoo, but also accepted an invitation to visit Germany. There it combined with the 3rd Musickorps of the Bundeswehr to play a concert at the Musikhalle, Hamburg attended by veterans of the Afrika Korps to commemorate the 70th anniversary of the birth of Erwin Rommel. The Cameronians' contribution featured pieces by Wagner, Leutner and Lehar.

The reforms of 1968 saw the disappearance of The Cameronians and its Band. This fiercely independent regiment, whose antecedents went back to 1650 and the National Covenant that bound the Presbyterian cause to the restoration of the Monarchy, chose to disband rather than face amalgamation.

Regimental Music

The quick march was 'Within a Mile o' Edinburgh Town' written by James Hook in 1780. A hugely

The Cameronians playing National Anthem, Scarborough 1953, Bandmaster C Pike   (Pike)

prolific composer, Hook wrote well over 2000 songs, the best known of which is 'The Lass of Richmond Hill'. Shortly after the regiment was raised, it was stationed at Edinburgh, returning there in 1861 to the Castle. It is thought that these links helped influence the choice of tune as regimental march.

The slow march was 'The Garb of Old Gaul'. (For further details see Scots Guards.)

The quick march used by the pipes of the 1st Battalion was 'Kenmuir's On an' Awa'' (also known as 'Kenmure's Up and Awa''). It was written in celebration of William Gordon, 6th Viscout Kenmure, one of only two peers executed for their part in the Fifteen uprising; the adoption of the tune is curious, since The Cameronians fought on the side of the government troops who defeated Kenmure at Preston.

The pipes of the 2nd used 'The Gathering of the Grahams', an adaptation of 'The Atholl Highlander' re-named after Sir Thomas Graham who raised the Perthshire Light Infantry.

Bandmaster L Dunn   (RMSM)

BANDMASTERS OF THE 1st BATTALION, THE CAMERONIANS (Scottish Rifles)

1874-1890 **SOMMER**, Josef MVO. Born 1843 died 19??. Enl 65 Ft or 84 Ft 5/4/64; Sgt (BM) 17 Ft 8/12/66; Sgt (BM) 26 Ft 31/7/74; Sgt (BM) Hyderabad Contingent 30/1/90; Lt (BM) RE 1/3/91; retd 8/1/05.

1890-1912 **BIRMINGHAM**, John. Born 1857 died 1912. Enl 88 Ft 11/5/72; WO (BM) 1 Cameronians 30/1/90; believed to have died 10/11/12 whilst still serving.

1912-1929 **DOWELL**, Horace Edwin LRAM psm. Born 1878 (possibly 1879) died 1945. Enl 2 N Stafford R 7/7/94; trans to RA (Port); WO (BM) 1 Cameronians 11/11/12; Lt (DoM) SG 21/6/29; retd 11/12/38 rank of Capt; DoM unofficial Band RAPC 1940.

1929-1939 **DUNN**, Lawrence Norman MBE ARCM. Born 1902. Enl 1 Seaforth 27/1/16; WO1 (BM) 1 Cameronians 21/6/29; WO1 (BM) 2 Cameronians 7/4/39; WO1 (BM) 1 Cameronians 5/12/46; Lt (DoM) RE (Ald) 22/11/49; retd 31/12/58 rank of Maj; DoM Bermuda Militia 1/59 – 13/3/75.

1939-1946 **PENNELL**, Sydney William ARCM. Born 1908 died 1951. Enl 1 S Lan R 21/2/24; WO1 (BM) 1 Cameronians 8/4/39; WO1 (BM) 2 Ox & Bucks LI 5/12/46; WO1 (BM) 1 Para 1/11/47; retd 9/3/51.

1946-1949 **DUNN**, Lawrence Norman MBE ARCM. For full details see above.

1949-1956 **PIKE**, Clifford LRAM ARCM. Born 1919. Enl RE 24/4/34; WO1 (BM) 1 Cameronians 22/11/49; WO1 (BM) Lowland Bde 16/6/56; Lt (DoM) RTR (Rhine) 17/7/60; Lt (DoM) R Signals 28/2/62; retd rank of Capt 12/4/69.

1956-1962 **QUINN**, Robert MBE LRSM psm. Born 1921 died 1990. Enl 1 A&SH 8/9/36; WO1 (BM) 2 Inniskilling Fus 5/9/52; WO1 (BM) 1 Cameronians 16/6/56; Lt (DoM) RA (BAOR) 29/9/62; Capt (DoM) RA (Wool) 10/3/66; retd 15/12/76 rank of Maj.

1962-1968 **CHARLTON**, Thomas. Born 1928. Enl 1 Somerset LI 15/10/43; WO1 (BM) 1 Cameronians 29/2/62; retd 14/5/68.

BANDMASTERS OF THE 2nd BATTALION, THE CAMERONIANS (Scottish Rifles)

187?-1877 **BULLARD**, Henry. Born 1845 died 1879. Enl 90 Ft 186?; Sgt (acting BM) 90 Ft 187?; Sgt (BM) 24 Ft 13/5/78; killed in action 22/1/79.

1877-1882 Bandmaster(s) not known.

1882-1895 **FITZGERALD**, William Thomas Godfrey. Born 1850 died 1895. Enl 28 Ft 15/1/65; WO (BM) 2 Cameronians 13/6/82; retd 9/3/95.

1895-1912 **LAVEROCK**, Albert Robert Victor. Born 1865 died 1936. Enl 24 Ft 12/5/79; WO (BM) 2 Cameronians 10/3/95; retd 30/11/12; BM 3rd Monmouthshire Regt (TA) 1933-1936.

1912-1939 **SEYMOUR**, Rupert Leslie. Born 1887 died 1947. Enl 1 Loyal R 13/1/02; WO (BM) 2 Cameronians 1/12/12; retd 7/4/39; BM Royal Guernsey Militia 1939-1940.

1939-1946 **DUNN**, Lawrence Norman MBE ARCM. Born 1902. For full details see 1st Battalion above.

BANDS OF THE

BLACK WATCH

(Royal Highland Regiment)

THE BLACK WATCH

1725	Independent Companies – The Black Watch	1758-62	2nd Bn 42nd (The Royal Highland) Foot
1739	The Highland Regiment of Foot	1779-86	2nd Bn 42nd (The Royal Highland) Foot
1751	The 42nd Foot		
1758	42nd (The Royal Highland) Foot	1786	73rd Highland Regiment of Foot
1861	42nd (The Royal Highland) Foot (The Black Watch)	1809	73rd Foot
		1862	73rd (Perthshire) Foot

1881	The Black Watch (Royal Highlanders)
1934	The Black Watch (Royal Highland Regiment)

The 42nd Foot is the oldest Highland regiment in the British Army, dating back to the 1720s. In 1758 it added a second battalion to its strength, which subsequently became a separate regiment, the 73rd Foot, before the two were finally re-united in 1881 to form The Black Watch.

The title of the Regiment – 'Am Freiceadan Dhu' in Gaelic – is believed to be in reference to the dark tartan, which was specially designed to have no association with any particular clan, and to the regimental duty of keeping a watch over the Highlands at a time when the threat of the Jacobites was still very real.

Inspection reports from as early as 1768 refer to pipers in the 42nd, and in 1773 mention is made of '2 pipers and a very good Band of Music'. Two years later this band is shown as '10 Music', and by 1790 it had more than doubled to 21 musicians. The 73rd meanwhile was slower in acquiring a Band, and did not even have pipes prior to the 1881 amalgamation.

In his *Retrospect of a Military Life*, QMS James Anton of the 42nd writes of the fashion in the British Army for holding balls during the Napoleonic era, and his comments give some indication of the position of bandsmen within the hierarchy:

> *Our Corporals followed the example set by the Sergeants, the musicians that by the Corporals, the drummers that of the musicians, and last, though not least, the officers' servants had a ball.*

Less information survives of the early bandmasters. There are passing mentions of two German musicians in the 1850s and '60s, but little more. In 1851 the 42nd moved to Halifax, Nova Scotia, following postings in Malta and Bermuda, and the following year, we are told, the Bandmaster, Mr Goldbergh, was dismissed as being unsatisfactory. There is then a gap in the available evidence until early 1863, when Private A W McIntosh recorded in his diary (now in The Black Watch Regimental Museum) that:

A Band Master had been engaged for the Band and joined us here, he is a German named I I Bader, he has a wife and two children who came along with him.

The same source also gives us an insight into the music played by the Band in the mid-19th century; Pte McIntosh mentions at various points 'The Girl I Left Behind Me', 'Hurrah for the Highlands', 'Here's a Health Bonnie Scotland to Thee', 'Blue Bonnets Over the Border' and 'Auld Lang Syne'.

The secondary medical role of bandsmen was becoming established by this time, and the musicians of the 42nd served in the Crimea, having been taught the basics of medical care en route from Turkey. These skills, however, were of little use a few years later in 1861, when the Regiment was stationed at Agra, Bengal in the midst of a cholera epidemic. A policy known as 'cholera dodging' was introduced, moving camp every day in an attempt to stay ahead of the infection; the Band's task was to play the men out onto the road with a selection of up-beat strathspeys, reels and hornpipes to help maintain morale. The ravages of the disease were not entirely avoided, and amongst those who died was Pipe-Major Irvine.

The first official bandmasters were James Wilson of the 42nd, who had risen through the ranks and attended a course at Kneller Hall before being appointed in 1868, and Walter Buck of the 73rd, who joined from the 14th Foot the following year.

Mr Wilson was succeeded by William Scott, who remained at his post for a quarter of a century before being in turn replaced by Edward Murray. It was during the latter's incumbency that a hugely successful tour of Canada was undertaken in 1904. Two weeks at the Canadian National Exhibition in Toronto were followed by a 50-concert tour that covered some 6000 miles. The President of the National Exhibition later wrote that:

Conductor Murray won golden opinions from the public for the modest and unassuming, yet artistic manner in which he conducted the concerts . . .

the popularity of the Band increased every day, reaching its climax at the extra concert given by them at the close of the Exhibition.

Around the same time the 2nd Battalion acquired the services of Percival O'Donnell as bandmaster. Mr O'Donnell was one of three brothers who were all destined to become directors of music in the Royal Marines (see 'Musical Families' in *Volume One*).

Despite a peaceful existence, the musicians were still serving soldiers, a fact that the Standing Orders of the 1st Black Watch, published in 1906, reiterated: 'As bandsmen are liable to serve in the ranks on any emergency, they are to make themselves thoroughly efficient.' It was a timely reminder; in 1914 the Bands returned to the battlefield for the first time since the Crimean War. As on that occasion, the men acted in the capacity of medical orderlies and stretcher-bearers.

Bass drummer of the Pipes and Drums, 1st Battalion The Black Watch, Edinburgh Castle c1912
(Eagles/Ogilby)

1st Battalion The Black Watch, 1924, Bandmaster H Rowe   (RMSM)

In 1915, when most Scottish battalions were bringing back their pipers, the 1st Battalion, The Black Watch went a stage further and revived its military band, though the members continued on active service. A photograph taken in Flanders that year shows the Regimental Medical Officer and his RAMC sergeant sitting in the midst of the Band.

The 2nd Battalion had appointed Harold Austing as Bandmaster in 1915, and under his leadership, its Band too was soon rebuilt. Mr Austing evidently possessed some technical imagination; at a time when the Boehm system had yet to replace the old simple system clarinet, he patented a device for the instrument that facilitated more flexible fingering.

It appears too that he was a man of uncompromising musical tastes, as hinted at by a correspondent in the regimental journal, *The Red Hackle*, in 1922: 'I hear favourable comments everywhere, but it is possible that if the Band played more numbers familiar to their audiences the comments and bookings would have been even better.'

Nonetheless, the effort seems to have been worthwhile. By the late '20s, when the Band instituted Sunday evening concerts during the winter months and announced that it would welcome requests for anything in the library, the same magazine could report: 'The pieces asked for have shewn

a surprisingly high level of musical appreciation: Beethoven's "Leonora" overture, the 5th Symphony, Schubert's "Unfinished Symphony", Wagner's "Flying Dutchman" overture and "Lohengrin".'

These concerts became a regular feature of battalion life, particularly as the Depression began to eat into the civilian bookings that could normally be expected. 1932 is recorded in the Band Notes of *The Red Hackle* as 'our poorest year to date', though by 1934 the engagements seemed to be picking up again; the season that year included twelve days at the *Daily Mail* Brighter Homes Exhibition. The 1st Battalion, meanwhile, was stationed in India, where the Band made a number of broadcasts on the Calcutta Broadcasting Station.

Again in 1939 instruments were put aside and the bandsmen joined the ranks. For the 1st Battalion, it was to be a disastrous war; as part of the 51st Highland Division, it was trapped at St Valéry long after the Dunkirk evacuations and was forced to surrender. Under the leadership of Lionel Maiden, however, and with many of the bandsmen repatriated in 1943, the Band was re-formed. By October 1944 it was back in France on tour, later playing though the Low Countries and into Germany.

The 2nd Battalion was disbanded in 1949 and the Band, which had won great acclaim in the '30s

The Black Watch, Sydney 1949, Bandmaster L Hicks (RMSM)

as far afield as Finland and Italy, was amalgamated with that of the 1st under the baton of Laurie Hicks. There was a revival of the Battalion for four years in the mid-'50s that saw the re-emergence of the Band under Bandmaster Babbs, but it was a short-lived episode.

In 1951 the Band toured Australia and New Zealand, the 39 musicians augmented by six pipers. The opening programme is typical of the concerts of the times:

Grand March Slav	Tchaikovsky
Excerpts from La Traviata	Verdi
The Pipers of The Black Watch	
Waltz: Gold and Silver	Lehar
An Exhibition of Highland Dancing	
Melodies from The Dancing Years	Novello

Interval

Overture: Mirella	Gounod
Xylophone Solo: On The Track	Simpson
Song (to be selected)	
Morceau: A Walking Tune	Grundman
Ballet Music: Prince Igor	Borodin
Regimental marches: The Garb of Auld Gaul	
Blue Bonnets over the Border	

The demonstrations of Highland dancing were

courtesy of sixteen bandsmen, amongst them Brian Smith, who would later become better known as Director of Music of the RMA Sandhurst.

The tour was so successful that it cost the Regiment its Bandmaster. Returning to England just long enough to resign, Bandmaster Hicks left to become Director of Music of the Royal Australian Air Force.

In 1959 Duncan Beat, son of a former Bandmaster of the Argyll and Sutherland Highlanders, was appointed Bandmaster. He was to end his career as Director of Music at Kneller Hall in the rank of Lieutenant-Colonel, but even this lofty height was to be surpassed by his successor in The Black Watch. Sam Holmes left the British Army in 1974 to take up a post as Director of Music of the South African Police, where he was eventually to be promoted to Brigadier; this is believed to be the most senior rank attained by a former British bandmaster.

His replacement was Norman Rogerson, who was to stay with the Regiment for just over a decade. During that time, the Band released a total of 24 albums, claimed to be a record for a British Army band under a single bandmaster. The most successful was the top twenty hit *Scotch on the Rocks*, the title track of which reached the top ten singles in 1975; the chart success brought in its wake appear-

Highland Dancers, Hilton Hotel, Panama City, June 1951, LCpl Brian Smith on right   (Brian Smith)

ances on *Top of the Pops* and a top of the bill appearance at the London Palladium.

Demonstrating that the British were prepared to let bygones be bygones, the Band combined with that of the Royal Marine Commando Forces for a tour of the US to celebrate the Bicentennial Independence Celebrations in 1976. Seventy musicians of The Black Watch, including pipes and drums, under Bandmaster Rogerson and 60 Marines under Captain W Shillito played 63 concerts in 47 cities. The Band returned three years later for a further tour.

In early 1994, under Options for Change, the Band of The Black Watch came to the end of its distinguished existence and was amalgamated into The Highland Band.

Regimental Music

In the early days of the Independent Companies, it is believed that a march known as 'The Highland Watch's Farewell' was used. The piece is perhaps better known as 'For the Sake of Some Bray', the title of the Burns poem for which it became the setting.

The quick marches of the 42nd – and later of the combined Regiment – were 'Blue Bonnets over the Border', adopted at the beginning of the 19th century, and 'Highland Laddie', adopted around 1850. (For further details of the former, see The Highland Light Infantry, and of the latter, see the Scots Guards.)

The slow march is 'The Garb of Old Gaul' (see the Scots Guards), which The Black Watch claim as their own; it is believed that in the late 18th century the piece was also known as 'The Highland March' and 'The 42nd Regimental March'.

Prior to the 1881 amalgamation, the 73rd Foot used 'My Love is Like a Red, Red Rose' as a march past.

BANDMASTERS OF THE 1st BATTALION, THE BLACK WATCH

184?-1852 **GOLDBERGH**. Believed to be German.

1852-1863 Bandmaster(s) not known.

1863-186? **BADER**, I I. Believed to be German.

1868-1877 **WILSON**, James. Enl 42 Ft 186?; Sgt (BM) 42 Ft 10/3/68; retd 31/10/77.

1877-1903 **SCOTT**, William John. Born 1850 died 1911. Enl 1/28 Ft 21/8/63; Sgt (BM) 42 Ft 1/11/77; retd 30/6/03.

1903-1919 **MURRAY**, Edward Thomas. Born 1868 died 1943. Enl 1 Leins R 31/10/82; WO (BM) 1 BW 1/7/03; retd 31/10/19.

1919-1927 **ROWE**, Henry Arnold. Born 1891 died 19??. Enl R Fus 25/9/06; WO1 (BM) 1 BW 1/11/19; retd 16/5/27.

1927-1933 **TURNER**, Thomas William. Born 1886 died 19??. Enl 1 Leicester R 27/9/01; WO1 (BM) 1st West Indian Regt 20/6/23; WO1 (BM) 1 BW 17/5/27; retd 10/3/33.

1933-1945 **MAIDEN**, Lionel John LRAM ARCM. Born 1900 died 19??. Enl 2 KRRC 25/1/16; WO1 (BM) 1 BW 11/3/33; retd 1/7/45.

1945-1949 **BARNETT**, Louis Jack ARCM. Born 1914. Enl 1 Manch R 19/9/29; WO1 (BM) 1 BW 2/7/45; WO1 (BM) 1 Midd'x R 9/4/49; retd 25/4/50.

1949-1951 **HICKS**, Laurence Henry OBE LRAM ARCM. Born 1912. For full details see 2nd Battalion.

1951-1959 **BAKER**, John Arthur LRAM ARCM. Born 1910 died 1959. Enl 2 The Buffs 9/1/25; WO1 (BM) 1 BW 3/9/51; died 8/2/59 whilst serving.

1959-1965 **BEAT**, Duncan Ritchie LVO ARCM psm. Born 1931. Enl RA (Wool) 8/1/47; WO1 (BM) BW 9/2/59; WO1 (BM) Highland Bde 2/4/65; Capt (DoM) RAOC 14/6/68; Capt (DoM) SG 28/8/74; Lieut-Col (DoM) RMSM 1/12/82; retd 28/2/88; DoM Metropolitan Police 1988.

1965-1973 **HOLMES**, Samuel Patrick ARCM AmusTCL ALCM. Born 1932. Enl 3 DG 17/12/50; WO1 (BM) BW 2/4/65; WO1 (BM) Scottish Div 2/2/73; retd 8/12/74; DoM South Africa Police retiring in rank of Brigadier.

1973-1984 **ROGERSON**, Norman Mollart MBE ARCM A(Mus)LCM FVCM(Hons) LTCL. Born 1941. Enl 13/18H 3/9/57; WO1 (BM) BW 2/2/73; retd 6/1/84.

1984-1985 **MAYCOCK**, Raymond Edward William LRAM ARCM LmusTCL LGSM psm. Born 1944. Enl 1 RRF 21/4/61; WO1 (BM) 4/7DG 9/12/74; WO1 (BM) RA (Wool) 1979; WO1 (BM) BW 6/1/84; Capt (DoM) Para 16/8/85; Capt (Dep Ch Inst) RMSM 27/1/86; Maj (loc) AJSM (Bov) 4/5/87; Capt (DoM) RCT 3/9/90; Maj (DOM) 16/8/93; Senior Instructor RMSM 7/94.

1985-1992 **CARLTON**, Trevor. Born 1951. Enl LI 10/8/66; WO1 (BM) BW 15/8/85; retd 1992.

1992-1994 **PEAPLE**, Ian Roger. Born 1957. For full details see Queens (Alb).

BANDMASTERS OF THE 2nd BATTALION, THE BLACK WATCH

1869-1894 **BUCK**, Walter Gresson. Born 1839 died 1902. Enl 1/14 Ft 6/1/53; Sgt (BM) 73 Ft 1/1/69; retd 5/1/94.

1894-1905 **JONES**, Robert. Born 1860 died 1949. Enl 91 Ft 22/6/75; WO (BM) 2 BW 6/1/94; retd 7/10/05.

1905-1915 **O'DONNELL**, Percival Sylvester George MVO B Mus LRAM ARCM psm. Born 1882 died 1945. Enl 2 S Wales Bord 26/2/97; WO (BM) 2 BW 8/10/05; WO1 (BM) RA (Gib) 1/10/15; WO (BM) RM (Plym) 27/6/16; Lt

Bandmaster H Austing (RMSM)

(DoM) 1921; Capt (DoM) RM (Chat) 11/6/28; retd 23/10/37 rank of Maj.

1915-1933 **AUSTING**, Harold Edgar. Born 1885 died 1951. Enl SC 11/7/05; WO1 (BM) 2 BW 12/11/15; retd 11/11/33.

1933-1938 **LEWIS**, Frederick George ARCM. Enl 21 L 20/9/10; WO1 (BM 2 Suffolk R 12/1/2/21; WO1 (BM) 2 BW 12/11/33; retd 14/3/38; BM 66 RA (TA) 1938-39.

1938-1949 **HICKS**, Laurence Henry OBE LRAM ARCM. Born 1912. Enl 1 Cameronians 17/12/26; WO1 (BM) 2 BW 15/3/38; WO1 (BM) 1 BW 9/4/49: retd 2/9/51; DoM Royal Australian Air Force 2/6/52; retd 23/6/68.

1949-1952 Battalion disbanded.

1952-1956 **BABBS**, Walter LRAM ARCM. Born 1917. Enl 16/5L 8/2/33; WO1 (BM) 2 BW 2/9/52; WO1 (BM) 1 Camerons 2/12/57; WO1 (BM) 1 QO Hldrs 7/2/61; WO1 (BM) British Military Mission, Libya 15/4/63; WO1 (BM) attached RMSM '64; retd 1/3/65.

BANDS OF THE

QUEEN'S OWN HIGHLANDERS

(Seaforth and Camerons)

SEAFORTH HIGHLANDERS
(Ross-Shire Buffs, The Duke of Albany's)

1778 78th Highland Regiment (Seaforth's Highlanders)	1793 78th (Highland) Regiment, or The Ross-shire Buffs
1786 72nd (Highland) Regiment	
1823 72nd, or The Duke of Albany's Own Highlanders	

1881   Seaforth Highlanders (Ross-shire Buffs, The Duke of Albany's)

1961   amalgamated to form the Queen's Own Highlanders (Seaforth and Camerons)

The regiment that was to become the 1st Battalion, Seaforth Highlanders was originally raised as the 78th but was subsequently re-numbered the 72nd. A new 78th was raised in 1793 and, in the 1881 programme of infantry amalgamations, this became the 2nd Battalion.

A regimental roll from May 1778, the first year of the senior regiment's existence, lists an establishment of 22 pipes and drums, a total which included the first Pipe-Major, Roderick McKenzie. When the military band was formed is not known, though an article in a 19th century edition of the regimental magazine *Cabar Feidh* (Stag's Head, named after the cap badge) states:

A Brass Band, or 'Band of Musik' was added some years after the regiment was raised, and which at first, as in other corps, had several foreigners (Germans or Swiss) in it.

Certainly the Band was fully functioning by 1824, for there is a report that in that year the Regiment had keyed bugles and was considering the purchase of a 'Royal Patent Basso – Hibernicon' and a 'Hibernicon – Tenor Horn'.

Around this time too was appointed the first bandmaster of whom we know. Mr Ricks, believed to have been of German origin, took up the post some time in the 1820s, and was succeeded in 1854 by his son Seaton Ricks. He in turn was replaced in November 1865 by John Murdock, who had joined the Band at the age of thirteen nearly twenty years earlier and had completed a short course at Kneller

Bandmaster H Maxwell, 1st Battalion The Seaforth Highlanders, Aldershot 1894 (Eagles/Ogilby)

Hall; the next incumbent, Charles Frederick Murdock, is thought to have been his brother.

The first Kneller Hall-approved bandmaster of the 78th came in September 1868 with the arrival from The Essex Regiment of Mr McEleney.

The 72nd were posted to Dublin during the late 1860s, and the military band was in great demand playing at public functions.

More pressing demands were made on the 78th the following decade. Stationed in India, the Regiment was ordered to Kohat on the outbreak of war with Afghanistan in 1878 and the Band was reduced to the regulation strength of 24, with the remainder of the bandsmen taking their places in the ranks. The march to Kohat took a month, and the men were accompanied by the military band and the pipe band playing whenever it was possible so to do. During the ensuing campaign, the bandsmen worked both as musicians and as medical orderlies.

Further military action was seen in the Egyptian war of 1882, before the Regiment returned home to Parkhurst on the Isle of Wight. There the Band played at the funeral of HRH The Duke of Albany.

Later that decade the Band of the 2nd Battalion played at the Edinburgh Exhibition of 1886, where the composition was recorded as: 1 flute/piccolo, 2 oboes, 2 Eb clarinets, 2 bass clarinets, 2 bassoons, 4 horns, 4 cornets, 2 trumpets, 3 trombones, 2 baritones, 1 euphonium, 4 basses and 2 drummers.

In common with most infantry regiments, the Seaforths had a fife and drum band for some years, though it appears to have been disbanded some time after 1885.

It was in the latter part of the 19th century that a regimental custom was established of not playing when going to or coming from church parade on Sundays. Tradition has it that the practice originated at the Inverness depot, where the local authorities did not encourage bands playing in the streets on the Sabbath. When this was brought to the attention of Queen Victoria, she expressed her wish that it be continued.

The Band of the 2nd Battalion built up a good reputation as a concert band in the years leading up to the Great War. A typical programme was at the Alexandra Palace in 1913:

March	The Rifle Regiment	Sousa
Overture	William Tell	Rossini
Valse	Sourire d'Eté	Waldteufel
Cornet solo	Because	Thompson
Selection	Gipsy Love	Lehar
Fantasia	A Highland Scene	Moore
Selection	Lohengrin	Wagner
Morceau	The Wedding Glide	Hirsch
	Hungarian Fantasy	Tobani

At the outset of the Great War most of the bandsmen were immediately employed either as stretcher bearers or in the ranks as soldiers. Mention should be made of drummer Walter Ritchie of the 1st Bat-

Above: 2nd Battalion The Seaforth Highlanders, India 1922, Bandmaster M Webber   (Eagles/Ogilby)
Below: The Seaforth Highlanders, Proclamation of Coronation, Edinburgh 1952, Bandmaster A Brundsen
(Eagles/Ogilby)

talion, who, on the first morning of the 1916 Battle of the Somme, stood on the parapet of the trench under heavy gunfire, sounding the regimental call and the charge; he was awarded the Victoria Cross.

Musicians in the Army, of course, have always occupied a curious position in the wider military world, and nowhere is the ambivalent attitude of the regular soldier to the bandsman better expressed than in the June 1929 issue of *Cabar Feidh*:

In our time one could pick out a bandsman any-where. Nice oily hair . . . clean shaven, despite King's Regulations, an Oxford drawl, and an unwholesome appetite for wads and chocolate – so we pictured a bandsman . . . . It was an easier job following in Beethoven's footsteps, than picking feet in the Company.

But there is another side to the medal. Who made up the regimental football team – The Bands-men. Cricket, hockey and swimming – The Band. Winners of individual running and sporting events – The Band. Battalion and company shots – The Band. And, finally, bandsmen in our parti-cular battalion gained more DCMs in proportion to their strength than any of the other companies during the War. There were no flies on them when it came to doing a job of work under fire. So when all is said and done, though they may be easy and greasy in peace time, they take a lot of beating when the real thing comes along.

One such band member to win the DCM was Band Sergeant W H Platt.

The bands and the pipes and drums also contri-buted to the war effort in less direct ways. A visit to America was reported by a US newspaper:

The Brass Band left N'Yark stone cold, but when the Pipes began to skirl in front of the Town Hall 1000 New Yorkers enrolled in one evening and set the war spirit simmering.

Stationed in India, the Band of the 2nd Battalion played for the visit to Delhi of HRH The Duke of Connaught in February 1921, and then the follow-ing decade for the visit of HRH The Prince of Wales. A decade later both Battalions were in Palestine and the Bands combined for a retreat in Haifa in honour of HRH The Princess Royal. The royal connexion continued in May 1935, when the Band of the 1st was chosen to play for the King's Jubilee celebrations in Cyprus.

In the early 1930s the Band of the 1st, conducted by George Hespe, enjoyed great popularity with civilian audiences, but later it was the 2nd, under

Sgt Harper, Seaforth Highlanders, Egypt 1955
(Eagles/Ogilby)

Arthur Brunsden, which became the favourite.

With the restructuring of the Army after the Second World War, the 2nd Battalion was disbanded in 1948 and Bandmaster Brunsden transferred to the 1st. On 7 October 1953 he was piped out of Fort George on his retirement after 38 years' service. He had been promoted to sergeant in September 1921 and was now reputed to be the oldest serving WO1 in the British Army. Whilst serving in Malaya in 1950, he had been mentioned in dispatches, and he was awarded the MBE in 1952.

In summer 1953 the pipes and drums toured Sweden and Denmark.

Whilst in the Canal Zone the following year, the military band massed with the Middle East Air Force Band, under the baton of Wing Commander Sims, for the El Alamein commemorations.

After serving in Egypt, the Regiment moved to Gibraltar in 1956 and then on to Germany in 1958.

Regimental Music

The quick march was 'Blue Bonnets over the Border' (see The Highland Light Infantry). The slow march was 'The Garb of Old Gaul' (see Scots Guards). In 1881 'Highland Laddie' became the official quickstep of all Highland regiments (see Scots Guards). Also popular with the regiment is 'Scotland the Brave', sometimes known to the Regi-ment as 'Scotland for Ever!'.

THE QUEEN'S OWN CAMERON HIGHLANDERS

1793   79th Foot (Cameronian Volunteers)
1804   79th foot (Cameron Highlanders)
1806   79th Foot or Cameron Highlanders
1873   79th Regiment, The Queen's Own
         Cameron Highlanders
1897   2nd Battalion formed
1961   amalgamated to form the Queen's Own
         Highlanders (Seaforth and Camerons)

The date of birth of the Camerons' band is unknown; in early inspection reports, musicians are conspicuous by their absence – a report from April 1799 states 'No Band of Music', whilst one from 1801 mentions only drummers.

Presumably there were also pipes; certainly there were by the time of Waterloo, for the actions of Piper Kenneth MacKay in playing outside the square on the battlefield so impressed George III that he presented the man with a set of silver-mounted pipes. Also remembered from the long wars with Napoleon is Drummer Charles Bogle, a black musician who was killed at the 1812 Siege of Burgos.

There is also an account of the 79th at Waterloo, however, that tells us the Regiment marched to the battle to the sound not of pipers but of a military band playing 'Loudon's Bonnie Woods and Braes', so we must assume that such a formation existed by this stage. Further evidence of a band comes in an extant document from the early 19th century, 'Orders for the Assistance and Guidance of the Non-Commissioned Officers of the 1st Battalion 79th Regiment':

When the Regiment is marching to the Music, he [the Master of the Band] is never to play tunes but such as are particularly adapted for that purpose and in which the greatest accuracy of time can be maintained. At other times such as route marching he may play any good tunes.

The first bandmaster in regimental records is Adam Schott, who is believed to have joined the 79th on its return from Canada in 1836 and who stayed until 1844, when he moved to the Grenadier Guards.

An issue of the regimental magazine, the *79th News*, from the end of the century, talks of Herr Schott's replacement being another German, Ernest Fromm, who had been recruited from the Prussian Army. Herr Fromm, according to this article, remained with the regiment until its return from India in 1871. There is mention elsewhere, however, of a different succession: Sgt McLaren (1844-59), Sgt White (1866-69) and Sgt Frome (1869-72). It is possible that these three were Band Sergeants – as opposed to being Bandmaster Sergeants – and that they were thus responsible for parades and other military functions, whilst Herr Fromm handled the musical training of the Band. This interpretation is supported by the facts that all three came from within the 79th and that the first bandmaster appointed by Kneller Hall, James McDonald, took charge in 1872.

The Regiment had by this stage already made a contribution to the emergence of Kneller Hall, with one of the pupils on the first ever course being Lance-Corporal R Sweeney of the 79th, later to be appointed Bandmaster of the 2nd Buffs.

An 1868 photograph taken in Mussoorie in North India shows Herr Fromm in civilian clothes whilst the bandsmen are resplendent in kilts. The strength at the time was: 2 flutes/piccolos, 1 Eb clarinet, 8 Bb clarinets, 4 bassoons, 2 horns, 4 cornets, 2 trumpets, 1 baritone, 2 tenor trombones, 2 bass trombones, 1 euphonium and 2 basses.

This complement of 31 musicians was over-strength, but this was a situation tolerated by commanding officers at the time, so long as the surplus bandsmen returned to the ranks for inspections and when military duty called. In this latter role, Bandsman David Hogg was killed in the battle at Kosheh Fort in December 1885.

The second half of the 19th century saw the establishment of a remarkable dynasty within the regiment. Terence Sweeney, a soldier in the 79th, produced five sons who all went on to serve in the Band; the first to enlist was Robert, later Bandmaster of The Buffs, in 1843, followed by William (who went on to become a bandmaster in America), Donald Spence, John and James. Donald Spence Sweeney retired in 1875 as Band Sergeant, a position later occupied by his son, Daniel. Another son, Richard, was also a bandsman, though he was to die at Aisne during the Great War.

The quality of musicianship in the later years of the century was evidenced by this report from a Scottish newspaper in 1892:

The Queen has been pleased, on the recommendation of the Secretary for Scotland, to approve the appointment of Mr Robert White, late Band Ser-

geant of the 79th Highlanders, to be Her Majesty's trumpeter for Scotland.

This is assumed to be the Sgt White referred to above, who had retired from the Regiment in 1869.

The amalgamations of 1881 paired off the infantry regiments, but because there was an odd number of regiments in the Army, the Camerons remained unaffected, becoming instead the only foot regiment to have just one battalion. This anomalous position gave rise to fears that the Camerons would be subsumed into the Scots Guards, but the personal intervention of Queen Victoria – who had earlier bestowed the title 'Queen's Own' upon the Regiment – ensured its survival, and in 1897 it raised a second battalion to bring itself into line with the rest of the Army.

The following year a bandmaster was appointed from Kneller Hall, Henry Fisher, who was evidently a success for he stayed with the 2nd Battalion until 1921. During his time with the Band he formed an orchestra, and there are several accounts of a string quartet playing at various functions.

The '90s were good years too for the 1st Battalion. It spent some years stationed in Malta, a favourite with the troops because of its warm but not unreasonable climate and the quality of the accommodation it offered. There were other bands also on the island, providing the opportunity for massed band events. One such was a Grand Military Tattoo held on 28 September 1893, when the band and pipes of the Camerons combined with the bands of the 2nd Royal Irish Rifles, 1st Royal West Surreys and 1st North Staffords, and with the Royal Artillery trumpeters. The programme demonstrates the popularity of Wagner:

> Retreat sounded by massed bugles, fifes and drums
> 'Invocation to Battle' (Wagner)
> 1st Post sounded by massed bugles
> Overture – 'Rienzi' (Wagner)
> 1st Post sounded by massed trumpets
> 'Cavalieria Rusticana' (Mascagni)
> 2nd Post sounded by massed trumpets
> 'Princess May Gavotte'
> Selection – 'Lohengrin' (Wagner)
> Finale – 'Grand Military Tattoo'

Regimental variety concerts, with contributions from a variety of performers, were also popular. A concert in the Garrison Recreation Rooms in December 1895 featured Suppé's overture, 'Pique Dame',

1st Battalion The Queen's Own Cameron Highlanders, c1890, Bandmaster R Wakelin   (Eagles/Ogilby)

Bandmaster W Abbot, The Queen's Own Cameron Highlanders, c1907 (RMSM)

Mr Abbott conducted as though inspired with the spirit of the music, and the band responded with confidence from the 'Priests War March' of Mendelssohn's Athalie, with which the concert opened, to Handel's 'Hallelujah Chorus', with which it concluded. Lance-Corporal Michie played 'The Lost Chord'. In Tours' 'Hymn to the Angels', the harmonious melody was beautifully rendered, the euphonium being especially fine. A selection from Rossini's 'Stabat Mater' and another from Beethoven's works displayed the resources of the band at their best.

Other favourite composers included Tchaikovsky, Sullivan and Verdi.

The Great War saw both the military band and the pipes disbanded, though both were to re-form – the pipes in 1916 and the band the following year.

In 1931 the Band of the 2nd Battalion under Bandmaster Griggs was chosen by the War Office to play at the British Trade Exhibition in Buenos Aires, an exhibition opened by the Prince of Wales. Concerts were also given in San Paulo, Santos, Monte Video, Rio di Janeiro and Lisbon.

Mr Griggs was a prolific arranger – signing his pieces 'Arranged C.W.G.' – and most of the Band's programmes featured his works. He specialized in Scottish fantasias, which he called Grand Cameron Finales, and which included such titles as: 'The Castle Ruins', 'The Kilt and the Sporran', 'Chief of the Clan', 'The Cameron Country', 'Loch Ness' and 'The Dirk and the Thistle'.

At the outbreak of the Second World War, the bandsmen joined the ranks, with the two bandmasters returning to the depot at Inverness with the boys.

Part of the task of the military band, of course, is to embody the living history and tradition of the regiment, and a key element in this has long been the regimental drums, with the battle honours emblazoned upon them. When, therefore, the 4th Battalion was forced to surrender at St-Valéry with the 51st (Highland) Division in 1940, the drums were thrown into a pond to avoid capture. In 1987 two of the five drums were finally returned to the Regiment.

Regimental Music

The quick march was 'The March of the Cameron Men', both words and music written by Mary Maxwell Campbell (1812-1886). The slow march was 'The Garb of Old Gaul' (see Scots Guards). In 1881 'Hielan' Laddie' was adopted as the quick

alongside a humorous trio of two oboes and a bassoon and a display of sword dancing by the pipers.

The 2nd Battalion also served on a Mediterranean island, in this case Gibraltar, where the local newspaper reported in 1900 that Bandmaster Fisher had premiered his new march, 'Buena Vista', at a concert in Barrack Square, Buena Vista. Mr Fisher was noted in his day as a fine military composer; one of his successors, Wally Babbs, was impressed many years later by 'a splendid march incorporating the Scottish Lament "The Flowers of the Forest"'.

By 1908 the 1st Battalion was back in Britain, stationed in Tidworth, from where trips were undertaken to play at various south coast resorts. A report from the *Sussex Daily News* shows the depth and quality of the repertoire in those times:

march of all Scottish regiments (see Scots Guards).

The quick step used by the pipes was 'Pibroch O' Donuil Dhu', an old highland marching tune composed in honour of the Cameron Chief, Donuil Dhu (Black Donald).

As with the Seaforths, 'Scotland the Brave' was also much used.

QUEEN'S OWN HIGHLANDERS
(Seaforth and Camerons)

1961	The Queen's Own Highlanders (Seaforth and Camerons)
1994	amalgamated with The Gordon Highlanders to form The Highlanders

When the Seaforths and Camerons were amalgamated in 1961, the Bands came together under the leadership of Wally Babbs, formerly Bandmaster of the Camerons. Two years later he left to take up a post with the British Military Mission in Libya, and was replaced by Barry Langton.

1989 was a particularly busy and successful year for the Band, with trips to Italy, Holland, France and Poland. The latter was to participate in the commemorations of the fiftieth anniversay of the outbreak of the Second World War, and included a visit to the site of Auschwitz concentration camp, where Pipe Sergeant John MacDonald played a lament for the dead. With the Band on the tour were 150 ex-prisoners of war.

During the Second Gulf War the men were employed in their secondary role as medical orderlies. They did, however, take their instruments with them and possibly the high-point was a trip to Riyadh to play for the 215th anniversary of the US Marine Corps.

Regimental Music

The quick march was a compilation of 'Scotland the Brave' and 'The March of the Cameron Men', arranged by Bandmaster Henderson of the Seaforths. The slow march was 'The Garb of Old Gaul' (see Scots Guards).

BANDMASTERS OF
1st BATTALION, THE SEAFORTH HIGHLANDERS
(Ross-shire Buffs, The Duke of Albany's)

1845-1857 **RICKS**. Civ BM.

1854-1865 **RICKS**, Seaton. Sgt (BM) 72 Ft 18??; Sgt (BM) 19 Ft 24/11/65; retd 28/5/72.

1865-1871 **MURDOCK**, John James Brocklebank. Born 1832 died 1904. Enl 72 Ft 26/3/46; Sgt (BM) 72 Ft 24/11/65; Sgt (BM) 15 Ft 1/3/81; retd 31/3/85.

1871-1875 **MURDOCK**, Charles Frederick. Enl 72 Ft ?; Sgt (BM) 72 Ft 1/3/85; retd 30/9/75.

1875-1895 **MAXWELL**, Henry Albert. Born 1845 died 1920. Enl 76 Ft 14/1/60; Sgt (BM) 72 Ft 1/10/75; retd 10/6/95.

1895-1896 **WILLE**, William. Born 1862 died 1943. Enl The Royals 10/12/77; WO (BM) 1 Seaforth 11/6/95; WO (BM) 7 DG 24/6/96; retd 31/3/03.

1896-1912 **MARSH**, George. Born 1868 died 1947. Enl SG 12/2/83; WO (BM) 1 Seaforth 24/6/96; retd 12/2/12.

1912-1928 **GRAYSON**, George William Edward, LRAM ARCM psm. Born 1881 died 19??. Enl 1 RWF 25/6/97; WO (BM) 1 Seaforth 13/2/12; Lt (DoM) RM (Plym) 11/6/28; retd 31/10/30.

1928-1933 **HESPE**, George William, LRAM ARCM. Born 1920 died 19??. Enl 1 Queen's R 31/12/18; WO1 (BM) 1 Seaforth 12/6/28; retd 1/9/33; BM Sheffield Police 33-43.

1933-1939 **BAKER**, Edward, ARCM. Enl 1 R North'd Fus 31/7/18; WO1 (BM) 1 Seaforth 2/9/33; retd 30/7/39.

1939-1947 **KEELING**, Donald, LRAM ARCM. Born 1912 died 19??. Enl 1 Queen's R 20/12/28; WO1 (BM) 1 Seaforth 31/7/39; WO1 (BM) 2 Para 1/11/47; WO1 (BM) Pakistan School of Music 5/3/52; WO1 (BM) 48th Highlanders of Canada 4/54.

1947-1953 **BRUNSDEN**, Arthur, MBE ARCM. Born 1900 died 19??. Enl 2 R Fus 26/11/15; WO1 (BM) 2 Seaforth 6/12/32; WO1 (BM) 1 Seaforth 1/11/47; retd 28/10/53.

1953-1961 **HENDERSON**, Albert George. Born 1923. Enl R W Kent R 4/7/38; WO1 (BM) 1 Seaforth 29/10/53; WO1 (BM) Highland Bde 7/2/61; retd 1/4/65.

BANDMASTERS OF
2nd BATTALION, THE SEAFORTH HIGHLANDERS
(Ross-shire Buffs, The Duke of Albany's)

1868-1875 **McELENEY**, A. Enl 1 Essex ?; Sgt (BM) 1 Essex 10/1/67; Sgt (BM) 1 Essex 1/9/68; retd 9/75; BM Duke of York's Royal Military School 1/9/80-10/2/88.

1875-1887 **BUNCH**, James Alexander. Born 1841 died 1924. Enl 1BW 26/3/56; Sgt (BM) 2 Seaforth 21/7/75; retd 12/7/87.

1887-1897 **McCHESNEY**, Francis. Born 1854 died 19??. Enl 16/7/67; WO (BM) 2 Seaforth 13/7/87; retd 16/2/97.

1897-1902 **BIRKHEAD**, Christopher. Born 1857 died 1938. For full details see The Buffs.

1902-1912 **FOWLES**, James. Born 1871 died 1930. Enl 1 Conn Rang 12/4/86; WO (BM) 2 Seaforth 17/11/02; retd 16/11/12.

1912-1923 **WILTSHIRE**, Thomas Bevan Frederick. Born 1884 died 1923. Enl 1 R Ir Fus 29/7/99; WO (BM) 2 Seaforth 17/11/12; retd 18/12/23.

1923-1932 **WEBBER** Stanley Thomas, ARCM. Born 1899 died 19??. Enl 1 Queen's R 14/7/14; WO1 (BM) 2 Seaforth 19/12/23; retd 5/12/32.

1932-1947 **BRUNSDEN**, Arthur, MBE ARCM. Born 1900. Enl 2 R Fus 26/11/15; WO1 (BM) 2 Seaforth 6/12/32; WO1 (BM) 1 Seaforth 1/11/47; retd 28/10/53.

BANDMASTERS OF
1st BATTALION THE QUEEN'S OWN
CAMERON HIGHLANDERS

1837-1844 **SCHOTT**, Adam J. Civ BM 79 Ft 183?; Sgt (BM) (or possibly Civ BM) Gren Gds 1844; retd 1/7/56.

1844-1859 **McLAREN**, James. Enl 79 Ft 18??; Sgt (BM) 79 Ft 1844; retd 1859.

1859-1866 Bandmaster(s) not known

1866-1869 **WHITE**, Robert. Enl 79 Ft 18??; Sgt (BM) 79 Ft 1866; retd 1869.

1869-1872 **FROME**, James. Enl 79 Ft 18??; Sgt (BM) 79 Ft 1869; retd 12/9/72.

1872-1885 **McDONALD**, James. Born 1840 died 1902. Enl 2 RS Fus 27/7/58; Sgt (BM) 79 Ft 13/9/72; retd 31/10/85.

1885-1903 **WAKELIN**, Richard Bailey Baxter. Born 1858 died 1922. Enl 1 Camerons 21/3/23; WO (BM) 1 Camerons 1/11/85; retd 10/7/03.

1903-1907 **SAUNDERS**, Charles Obediah. Born 1868 died 19??. Enl KDG 31/1/82; WO (BM) 1 Camerons 11/7/03; retd 25/9/07.

1907-1920 **ABBOTT**, William Henry. Born 1874 died 1956. Enl 2 RS Fus 11/9/88; WO (BM) 1 Camerons 26/9/07; WO1 (BM) 2 Leins R 1/4/20; WO1 (BM) 1 R Norfolk R 30/6/22; retd 29/7/23.

1920-1932 **JONES**, David William LRAM ARCM psm. Born 1884. Enl 1 North'n R 1/8/99; WO1 (BM) 1 Camerons 25/10/20; Lt (DoM) RE 15/11/32; Capt 15/11/38; retd 31/1/44.

1932-1943 **POPE**, Douglas Alexander, OBE FRCM psm. Born 1903 died 1984. Enl 2 R Sussex R 8/1/18; WO1 (BM) 1 Camerons 15/11/32; WO1 (BM) RMC 8/9/43; WO1 (BM)

RASC 1/2/44; Lt (DoM) Coldm Gds 5/9/44; Lt-Col Snr DoM Bde Gds 1960: retd 20/11/63; DoM (Retd Off) JMW 1963-6/8/70; Professor of Instrumentation RMSM 1966-78.

1943-1955 **START**, Douglas Vernon, ARCM. Born 1912 died 19??. Enl 2 North'n R 23/9/27; Wo1 (BM) 1 Camerons 8/9/43; retd 5/3/55; DoM Royal Canadian Black Watch 1955-60.

1955-1957 **BUCK**, Clarence Henry. Born 1917. Enl 1 Para 7/2/50; Wo1 (BM) 1 Camerons 6/3/55; retd 1/12/57.

1957-1961 **BABBS**, Walter. Born 1917. For full details see Black Watch.

BANDMASTERS OF
2nd BATTALION THE QUEEN'S OWN
CAMERON HIGHLANDERS

1898-1921 **FISHER**, Henry. Born 1871 died 1931. Enl 1 Seaforth 16/2/66; WO (BM) 2 Camerons 1/10/98; retd 28/6/21.

1921-1922 **WINTERS**, Robert. Born 1886 died 1950. Enl 1 Gordons 3/10/01; WO1 (BM) 2 Camerons 29/6/21; retd 12/10/22.

1922-1938 **GRIGGS**, Charles William, MBE. Born 1889 died 1950. Enl Royal Garrison Artillery 11/11/03; WO1 (BM) 2 R Innis Fus 26/9/18; WO1 (BM) 2 Camerons 13/10/22; retd 10/11/38.

1938-1947 **WEBSTER**, Victor Ernest, MBE ARCM. Born 1908. Enl 1 Suffolk R 26/6/24; WO1 (BM) 2 Camerons 11/11/38; WO1 (BM) 6th King's African Rifles 15/12/47; retd '52; BM Tanganyika Police '52; BM Zambia '64; retd '73.

BANDMASTERS OF
THE QUEEN'S OWN HIGHLANDERS
(Seaforth and Camerons)

1961-1963 **BABBS**, Walter, LRAM ARCM. Born 1917. (For full details see 2 BW).

1963-1970 **LANGTON**, Barry Victor. Born 1930. Enl 1 RHF 6/11/47; WO1 (BM) QO Hldrs 15/4/63; retd ?/7/70.

1970-1977 **MALLAS**, Peter, ARCM. Born 1938. Enl RA (Wool) 4/9/59; WO1 (BM) 4 Queen's 15/1/69; QO Hldrs 1/7/70; WO1 (BM) Depot LI 15/6/77; retd '80; Maj (DoM) Sultan of Oman Land Force.

1977-1982 **COMPSON**, Gary Michael. Born 1945. Enl WFR 14/4/61; WO1 (BM) QO Hldrs 15/6/77; retd 18/5/82.

1982-1987 **JARVIS**, Guy Westron Coombe, LTCL ARCM. Born 1952. Enl LG 4/4/68; WO1 (BM) QO Hldrs 19/5/82; Lt (regt duty) 24/4/87; Capt 24/4/93.

1987-1994 **WHITTINGHAM**, Terence W, LTCL. Born 1956. Enl RE(Ald) 8/8/72; WO1 (BM) QO Hldrs 7/12/87; WO1 (BM) Gren Gds 30/3/94.

GORDON HIGHLANDERS

1758	75th Foot	1794	100th (Gordon Highlanders) Foot
1763	disbanded	1798	92nd (Highland) Regiment
1764	75th (Invalid) Foot	1861	92nd (Gordon Highlanders) Foot
1765	disbanded		
1778	75th (Prince of Wales's) Foot		
1783	disbanded		
1787	75th (Highland) Regiment		
1809	75th Foot		
1862	75th (Stirlingshire) Foot		

1881	The Gordon Highlanders
1994	amalgamated with The Queen's Own Highlanders to form The Highlanders

At the 1813 Battle of Vittoria, it is said, the pipes of the 92nd screamed high above the noise of the artillery bombardment and the fire of the musketry; as ever, the bagpipes were expected to terrify the enemy as much as to inspire the troops.

By this stage the military band was already in existence – a record from 1810 refers to the purchase of 'clarionetts, a bassoon, a bass drum head, a tamborrin and reeds' – and it can be assumed that the bandsmen also served in the Napoleonic wars, for shortly after Waterloo a Court of Enquiry was established to investigate, amongst other business, why some of the bandsmen lost their instruments during the battle.

Following the defeat of Napoleon, the 92nd returned home for a brief period, before being posted to Ireland and then Jamaica. In 1827 it came back to Scotland, with the Band still engaged on regimental duties, as described by Lieutenant-Colonel Gardyne in his history of the Gordons:

Soon after the death of the 4th Duke of Gordon, his remains arrived in Edinburgh . . . . On 12 July 1827 the remains were removed from Holyrood on their journey to Gordon Castle, being escorted by two companies of the 92nd with their band playing the Dead March in 'Saul'.

The early days of the Band of the 75th are undocumented, though the regiment was censured in 1834 for having more NCOs than was permitted in the band. The first bandmaster of whom we have

BANDS OF THE

GORDON HIGHLANDERS

any records was William Collender, appointed in January 1869. Later that year Charles Farrell took up a similar position in the 92nd.

Perhaps the most important of Sergeant Collender's engagements was playing for the visit of the Prince of Wales to Lahore in 1876. The Band and pipes also played in the Imperial Assemblage in Delhi to commemorate the proclamation of Queen Victoria as Empress of India.

The amalgamation in 1881 was not universally popular in the Army, and a stone at Floriana Barracks in Malta commemorates the event from a 75th perspective:

Here lies the poor old 75th,
But under God's protection
They'll rise again in kilt and hose,
A glorious resurrection.
For by the transformation power
Of Parliamentary laws,
We go to bed the 75th,
And rise the Ninety-twas.

The 92nd was no happier about the merger, even though the name The Gordon Highlanders was to survive. At midnight on 30 June 1881, as the old regiment ceased to exist, a torchlight funeral was staged, with a coffin containing a flag inscribed '92' being carried to its grave by officers wearing full highland dress. An oration was given by Lieutenant-Colonel George Luck of the 15th Hussars, the pipers played a lament, and the Band gave their rendition of the 'Dead March'.

Despite this initial sense of distrust, the new regiment proved successful. In the fighting on the North-West Frontier at the end of the century, Piper Findlater of the 1st Gordons was awarded a Victoria Cross for his courage in continuing to play the men into the assault on the Dargai Heights, despite being wounded in both legs. During the first battle of Ypres in the Great War, Drummer William Kenny won the same honour 'for conspicuous bravery'; as a stretcher-bearer, he rescued wounded men under fire on five occasions.

The bandsmen of both battalions also served as stretcher-bearers in the Boer War.

In the inter-war years, both Bands spent time overseas. The Band of the 1st Battalion served in Malta, Turkey, Egypt, India and Palestine and – though it returned to Britain with the Battalion in January 1935 – it was soon off again on a trip to Brussels.

The following year, together with the pipes and drums, it sailed to South Africa, playing for six

Above: Bandsman, The Gordon Highlanders, Kneller Hall c1891 (Eagles/Ogilby)
Right: Bandmaster W Windram, 2nd Battalion The Gordon Highlanders, c1896 (Eagles/Ogilby)

weeks at the Empire Exhibition in Johannesburg and then going on tour. Thirty-nine concerts, together with ceremonies at twelve war memorials, were played in four weeks. Whilst there, an unofficial mascot was adopted in the form of a dog, whom the bandsmen named 'Champ'. It was claimed that Champ could recognize the drum roll for the National Anthem, and would stand to attention.

The 2nd Battalion Band was also active, playing at the 1932 British Exhibition in Copenhagen, and moving to Gibraltar in 1934. To commemorate the visit, the Danish composer Hermann Pecking wrote the march '92nd in Copenhagen', later shortened to 'Copenhagen'.

A typical programme of the era was given by the 1st in July 1936 at Pittencrieff Park, Dunfermline:

Extracts from	Orpheus in the Underworld	Offenbach
Cornet Duet	The Humming Birds	Sutton
Overture	Tannhauser	Wagner
Trombone Solo	The Dragon Fly	Scholes
Humoresque	Wedded Whimsies	Alford

The Bydand Dance Orchestra
in tunes from their repertoire

A Display of Piping and Highland Dancing

Rhapsody	Slavonic No. 1	Friedmann
Xylophone Solo	On The Track	Simpson
Vocal Solo	Misty Islands of the Highlands	Carr
	Suite for Pipes and Band	Campbell
Regimental March	Cock of the North	
	God Save The King	

The Second World War saw disaster overtake both Battalions: the 1st was captured with the 51st (Highland) Division at St Valéry, whilst the 2nd was in the garrison of Singapore and was taken prisoner by the Japanese in 1942; Bandmaster Reg Ashton was amongst those killed in the construction of the notorious Siam-Burma railway.

In anticipation of the disbandment of the 2nd Battalion in 1948, Bandmaster Bill Lemon was not replaced when he left to join the Royal Tank Regiment in September 1947.

The late '40s saw the Band active in Germany, France, Belgium and Denmark, as well as Scotland, where the Regiment received the Freedom of Aberdeen on 20 August 1949.

In 1951 it embarked on the *Empire Halladale* for Port Said, before moving on to Malaya. Massed band performances were given with the Seaforths and the Cameronians, but there were also military duties to be undertaken; 'Band Notes' from the regimental journal of the period read:

At the moment of writing, the whole Band excluding the scribe are out on a forty-eight hour operation chasing the elusive Yong Hoi, the area bandit commander.

Recent years have seen the Band, pipes and drums take on a highly successful tour of Japan in 1986. There was a slight hitch when Japanese customs

'He has an ear for music and likes the bagpipes,' commented Bandmaster Campbell, in what some would regard as a contradiction in terms. So attached did the men become to Champ that permission was given for him to accompany them home.

In 1937 a visit to France saw the men attend the opening of the British Pavilion at the Paris Exhibition.

2nd Battalion The Gordon Highlanders, India 1907, Bandmaster E Blake   (Eagles/Ogilby)

showed some reluctance to allow two claymores, sixteen dirks and seventeen Sgean dubhs into the country, but the remainder of the tour went ahead as planned. It culminated in a concert at the British Embassy in Tokyo where the guests included the Prince and Princess of Wales and the Crown Prince and Princess of Japan.

In November 1990 the bandsmen were again on an overseas tour, though this time it was to the Gulf, where they served as medical assistants with 32 Field Hospital RAMC.

The last major tour abroad came in October 1993 when a visit to Italy ended in Lucia, home of Puccini, where a concert was attended by 2500 enthusiastic fans.

In 1994, as the Regiment was amalgamated, the Band of The Gordon Highlanders disappeared into the new Highland Band.

Regimental Music

Originally 'Highland Laddie' was used as the regimental quick march, but in 1932 it was replaced by 'Cock of the North', a piece that had long been associated with the regiment. (It was this march that Piper Findlater played at the Dargai Heights.) The composer is unknown, though some believe him to have been William Marshall, a composer who also had the job of being butler to the Duke of Gordon; his employer's sobriquet was 'Cock of the North'.

The tune is thought to date from around 1816, when it first appeared as a violin tune. A later publication in a collection of bagpipe music by Donald MacDonald around 1822 gives it the title 'Gairm n'an Coileach' – 'The Cock's Crow'. One set of words associated with it runs:

> *Come gather, come gather, ye lads of the heather,*
> *An' down thro' the glen in the piper's wake;*
> *Baith gentles and commons, gie heed tae the*
> *   summons,*
> *An' haste tae the muster make.*
> *MacPherson's comin', Cameron's comin',*
> *Campbell, MacNeill, an' the men o' the island;*
> *An' a' tae enlist in the Gordons, the best,*
> *An' the brawest o' lads in the Highlands.*

The slow march was 'Garb of Old Gaul' (see Scots Guards).

Another piece associated with the Regiment was 'The Plains of Waterloo', a seven-verse ballad written by Sergeant Grant, who served in the battle with the 92nd Regiment.

BANDMASTERS OF THE 1st BATTALION THE GORDON HIGHLANDERS

1869-1894 **COLLENDER**, William. Born 1845 died 1931. Enl 2/19 Ft 12/9/59; Sgt (BM) 75 Ft 1/1/69; retd 21/11/94.

1894-1900 **RUNCIMAN**, John B. Born 1866 died 1931. Enl 74 Ft 21/6/78; WO (BM) 22/10/94; retd 10/1/1900.

1900-1918 **PALLANT**, Ernest Robert. Born 1863 died 1923. Enl 2 Border R 21/2/85; WO (BM) 1 Gordons 11/1/1900; retd 3/12/18.

1918-1938 **CAMPBELL**, William Norris LRAM ARCM. Born 1887 died 1975. Enl SG 21/10/01; WO1 (BM) 1 Gordons 4/12/18; retd 20/9/38.

1938-1955 **WILLIAMS**, William MBE ARCM psm. Born 1909 died 1990. Enl 2 E Lanc R 31/10/27; WO1 (BM) 1 Gordons 21/9/38; WO1 (BM) High Bde 20/7/55; Lt (DoM) RA (Mtd) 17/3/58; retd 18/1/66 rank of Maj.

1955-1963 **FORD**, Roy Douglas. Born 1924. Enl 1 York & Lanc R 3/8/39; WO1 (BM) Gordons 20/7/55; WO1 (BM) Lowland Bde 10/10/63; retd 28/1/65.

1963-1969 **HARPER**, Colin Alastair MBE ARCM AmusLCM. Born 1932. Enl 1 Seaforth 14/5/46; WO1 (BM) Gordons 18/10/63; WO1 (BM) R Anglian Depot 29/7/69 ; WO1 (BM) Queen's Div 1/5/70; retd 3/72; DoM Royal Australian Air Force.

1969-1976 **RENTON**, Frank Anthony ARCM psm. Born 1939. Enl RHG 19/1/59; WO1 (BM) Gordons 29/7/69; WO1 (BM) King's Div Depot (badged DWR) 6/8/76; Capt (DoM) Para Bde 8/5/78; Capt (DoM) RA (Mtd) 10/11/82; Capt (DoM) RA (Alan) 26/7/84; Capt (DoM) RA (Wool) 30/1/85; Lt-Col (DoM) RMSM 7/1/88; retd 22/9/92.

1976-1980 **BATHAM**, Trevor ARCM. Born 1942. Enl 16/5L 20/10/58; WO1 (BM) 1 Gordons 19/7/76; retd 30/4/80.

1980-1984 **DARKE**, Richard Colin ARCM. Born 1949. Enl RTR (Rhine) 1/1/66; WO1 (BM) Gordons 30/4/80; WO1 (BM) 3RTR 16/3/84; retd 1/1/89.

1984-1991 **KNOX**, David. Born 1956. Enl RS ; WO1 (BM) Gordons 16/3/84; regt commission 15/5/91; Capt 16/5/93.

1991-1994 **COOPER**, Timothy John. Born 1961. Enl Glosters 18/10/78; WO1 (BM) Gordons 20/5/91; WO1 (BM) LG 1994.

BANDMASTERS OF THE 2nd BATTALION THE GORDON HIGHLANDERS

1869-1879 **FARRELL**, Charles. Enl 92 Ft; Sgt (BM) 92 Ft 20/10/69; retd 6/6/79.

1879-1891 **KING**, Joseph. Born 1850 died 1912. Enl 1 The Buffs 6/6/64; Sgt (BM) 92 Ft 7/6/79; retd 1/1/91.

1891-1898 **WINDRAM**, William Charles. Born 1860 died 1935. Enl 3 H 27/11/75; WO (BM) 2 Gordons 2/1/91; WO (BM) HMS *Excellent* 11/8/98; Commissioned Bandmaster 1905; retd 1911.

1898-1910 **BLAKE**, Edward. Born 1863 died 1935. Enl 1 RS 9/10/87; WO (BM) 2 Gordons 11/8/98; retd 13/11/10.

1910-1928 **BARTLETT**, William Henry. Born 1879 died 19??. Enl 3 Rifle Bde 12/12/94; WO (BM) 2 Gordons 14/11/10; retd 11/12/28; BM City of London Police 1933-1941.

1928-1934 **McPHERSON**, Albert Henry ARCM. Born 1898 died 19??. Enl R North'd Fus 14/12/14; WO1 (BM) 12/12/28; retd 31/12/34; BM HAC (TA) 1935-1939.

1935-1943 **ASHTON**, Reginald George ARCM. Born 1904 died 1943. Enl 4H 31/5/20; WO1 (BM) 2 Gordons 1/1/35; died whilst serving 2/9/43.

1945-1947 **LEMON**, William George ARCM psm. Born 1914. Enl 2 Bedfs & Herts 4/4/29; WO1 (BM) 2 Gordons 15/12/45; WO1 (BM) RTR (C Band) 1/10/47; Lt (DoM) RTR (Alamein) 9/1/50; Maj (DoM) 23/4/61; retd 22/5/64.

'The Big Band' of The Gordon Highlanders   (Gordons)

BANDS OF THE

ARGYLL AND SUTHERLAND HIGHLANDERS

(Princess Louise's)

THE ARGYLL AND SUTHERLAND HIGHLANDERS
(Princess Louise's)

1794	98th (Argyllshire Highlanders) Foot	1799	93rd Highlanders
1796	renumbered 91st Argyllshire Highlanders) Foot	1861	93rd (Sutherland Highlanders) Foot
1809	91st Foot		
1821	91st (Argyllshire) Foot		
1864	91st (Argyllshire) Highlanders		
1872	91st (Princess Louise's) Argyll-shire Highlanders		

1881 (May)	The Princess Louise's (Sutherland and Argyllshire) Highlanders
1881 (July)	The Princess Louise's (Argyll and Sutherland) Highlanders
1920	The Argyll and Sutherland Highlanders (Princess Louise's)

The regiment that was later renumbered the 91st had pipes from the outset, but it seems likely that the military band took a few years to establish. In a letter dated 13 January 1801, the first Colonel of the Regiment, Duncan Campbell, expresses his regret that other duties have prevented him from 'looking out for a man as master' of the incipient band:

I shall however write to our friend Wortley to speak to the man who made the First Regiment's Band, to be looking out for a proper person and also choosing Instruments and Materials for Clothing.

It is assumed that the post was filled shortly afterwards and that a Band was created.

The 93rd would certainly have had a band from its earliest days, for General Wemyss of Wemyss, who raised the regiment in 1799, had a reputation for furnishing his units with brass instruments. His accounts from 1800 show that he paid Broderick and Williamson £6.0.2d for musical instruments, and Kolak £12.4.7d for French horns. His purchases appear to have been satisfactory, for while an 1809 inspection in Capetown reported that the band were merely 'tolerable', it adds 'instruments good'. A year later the musicians were said to be 'improving'.

2nd Battalion The Argyll & Sutherland Highlanders, c1925, Bandmaster F Ricketts second from left
(Eagles/Ogilby)

General Wemyss' legacy survives in the form of a Jingling Johnny inherited by the 93rd from one of his previous regiments, the 3rd Sutherland Fencibles; still in the possession of the Regiment, this instrument is engraved with the initials W.W.

The first bandmasters of the two regiments are known by little more than their names. Sergeant James McKenzie was responsible for the Band of the 93rd between 1835 and 1839, whilst a brief entry in the Commanding Officer's Rough Book of the 91st in 1860 mentions a Mr Davies, who had offered to conduct a weekly band practice whilst the regiment was in Kamptee in India. With Mr Davies' successor, however, we enter better documented territory, for Sergeant Peter Kelly had attended a course at Kneller Hall prior to taking over in 1862.

In 1871 the Band, pipes and drums of the 91st played at the wedding of Princess Louise, the Duchess of Argyll and fourth daughter of Queen Victoria, leading the procession with a rendition of 'Bonnie Mary of Argyll'. The following year the regiment incorporated the Duchess's name into its title.

During the winter of 1873 the 91st Band, pipes and drums played weekly at the Assembly Music Room in Edinburgh, collecting a total of £42 from the admission charges. The money was used to erect a drinking fountain on the Edinburgh Castle Esplanade.

The same year the 93rd was posted to Aldershot, the Band arriving in such small numbers that it was dubbed 'The Twelve Apostles', a nickname that was to survive for some time.

Soon after the 1881 amalgamation, the 1st Argylls departed for the outposts of the Empire, the pipes and drums finding themselves in great demand for local weddings in Ceylon. Whilst in Johannesburg in 1902-3, the Band and pipes played a regular afternoon concert in the public gardens each week, again proving highly popular.

The 2nd Battalion also spent time abroad, with a

1st Battalion The Argyll & Sutherland Highlanders, Holyrood Palace, Edinburgh 1934, Bandmaster A O'Connor   (Eagles/Ogilby)

posting to India at the turn of the century. The staple musical diet of the Army abroad at the time consisted of regimental concert parties, and the new Bandmaster, Mr Walsh, soon established himself as a regular item on the programme, singing songs accompanied by his wife. The orchestra at these events was organized by Band Sergeant Hall.

A different role was adopted in 1908 when the Regiment sent a detachment of officers and men, including the Band, pipes and drums to London for guard duties, whilst the Foot Guards were on manoeuvres.

The most famous bandmaster to serve with the regiment was undoubtedly F J Ricketts, who – under the name Kenneth J Alford – composed many of the finest British marches. (See Musical Families – *Volume One*). Appointed Bandmaster of the 2nd Battalion in 1908, he joined the Band at Tempe in the Orange River Colony.

During the Great War, Bandmaster Ricketts and the bandboys joined the 3rd Battalion in Edinburgh, whilst the remainder of the musicians became stretcher bearers and medical orderlies.

The '20s were perhaps the highpoint of the 2nd Battalion Band. Under Mr Ricketts' baton, it became a popular fixture in the London parks and elsewhere. For the following programme at Alexandra Palace in December 1923, the Band and pipes combined with the Band of the 1st Sherwood Foresters and the drums and fifes of the Scots Guards, with contributions by Miss Jennie Bleasdale (soprano) and Mr Gwynne Davies (tenor):

March Heroique	Szabadi	Massenet
Song	Jewel Song (Faust)	Gounod
Tone Poem	Finlandia	Sibelius
Song	The Minstrel	Martin
Naval Patrol	Britain's First Line	Williams
Duet from 1st Act	La Bohème	Puccini
Grand Overture Solemnele	1812	Tchaikovsky

Interval

Humoresque	A Musical Switch	Alford
Song	The Market	Carew
Scottish Suite for Pipes and Band	(a) Highland Marches (b) A Lament (c) A Folk Song	
Song	O Sole Mio	Capua
Finale	Rheingold	Wagner
Descriptive Fantasia	For Service Overseas God Save The King	Ricketts

In 1925 the Band of the 2nd undertook a six-month tour to New Zealand, where it was the resident band for the New Zealand and South Seas Exhibition. Whilst there, Mr Ricketts wrote 'Dunedin' and 'Old Panama'.

Such was his popularity with the public that when in 1927 Bandmaster Ricketts handed the baton over to Charles Beat – having been appointed Director of Music at the Royal Marines depot in Deal – 15,000 people turned up to wish him well.

Following a period in India, the 2nd Battalion moved to Singapore in 1936. It was still there when the island surrendered to the Japanese in 1942; apart from the human casualties, all the instruments and equipment were lost. The Bandsmen of the 1st Battalion meanwhile were training for service in the Western Desert.

The post-war years have been uncertain ones for the Band. The 2nd Battalion was disbanded in 1947, and the two Bands came together under Bandmaster O'Connor of the 1st. In 1970 a proposal that the entire Regiment disappear saw the Band disbanded in anticipation, though it was to return in January 1972 when the Regiment was reprieved. In 1994, however, the death knell was finally sounded, and the Band was subsumed into the new Highland Band.

Despite these troubles, the Band continued to function and to act as ambassadors of British military music throughout the world. Amongst the most memorable performances was a 1960 visit to the British Trade Fair in Moscow, when the men were introduced to Nikita Kruschev, whilst the most spectacular must surely have been at the Hollywood Bowl in 1962: a wildly enthusiastic audience of 40,000 saw the Band play in a reproduction of Stirling Castle.

The Band kept up these international commitments to the very end, visiting the men of the Regiment in the Falklands in 1986, touring Australia the following year, and spending three months in the USA and Canada at the end of 1989.

In February 1990 Bandmaster Kevin Lamb was appointed Deputy Chief Instructor at Kneller Hall,

becoming the only Argyll ever to wear the uniform as a commissioned Director of Music.

His replacement was Bandmaster Peter Hunt, under whose leadership in 1993 the men joined the International Military Pilgrimage to Lourdes, playing at various church services en route, whilst the dance band performed each evening.

Bandmaster K Lamb, The Argyll & Sutherland Highlanders (Lamb)

Regimental Music

For many years the quick march of the 1st Battalion was 'The Campbells Are Coming', a song of the Campbell clan which was first published in 1745 as a country dance entitled 'Hob and Nob'. The 2nd Battalion used 'Highland Laddie' (for further details see Scots Guards).

When Bandmaster Ricketts was appointed to the 2nd Battalion in 1908, he arrived without any particular reputation as a composer (he had actually come last in the march competition at Kneller Hall). Nonetheless he was immediately asked by his new Commanding Officer to write a march for the Battalion, and he responded with 'The Thin Red Line', which was to become one of his most famous pieces. In 1960 it was officially adopted as the regimental quick march (Army Order 6/60).

The slow march is 'Garb of Old Gaul' (for further details see Scots Guards).

A regimental tradition is that 'Rule Britannia' should be played on Mess Nights, in commemoration of the sinking of the troopship *Birkenhead* on 28 February 1852 when 60 men of the Regiment lost their lives. An alternative account of the custom dates it to the period between 1858 and 1876, when Colonel Bertie Gordon commanded the 91st Highlanders; Colonel Gordon had earlier been involved in another shipwreck, when the *Abercrombie Robinson* was sunk.

BANDMASTERS OF
THE 1st BATTALION THE ARGYLL AND SUTHERLAND HIGHLANDERS

185?-1862 **DAVIES**. Civ BM or instructor. No other details available.

1862-1886 **KELLY**, Peter. Born 1831 died 1886. Enl 91 Ft 20/6/45; Sgt (BM) 91 Ft 1/9/62; died whilst serving 22/6/86.

1886-1889 **MacKINNON**, John. Born 1860 died 1929. Enl 74 Ft 17/2//74; WO (BM) 1 A&S 23/6/86; WO (BM) 2 HLI (74 Ft) 6/3/89; retd 1/3/98.

1889-1902 **HILL**, Michael. Born 1855 died 1902. Enl 89 Ft 28/1/70; WO (BM) 1 A&S 6/3/89; retd 28/2/98.

1902-1909 **McCLURG**, John. Born 1864 died 1946. Enl 1 BW 29/10/84; WO (BM) 1 A&S 8/1/02; retd 31/10/09.

1909-1914 **MacDONALD**, Edmund Maxwell. Born 1876 died 19??. Enl 2 KOYLI 14/9/91; WO (BM) 1 A&S 1/11/09; retd 30/12/14.

1914-1932 **GARRETT**, John. Born 1881 died 19??. Enl 1 Conn Rang 4/3/96; WO (BM) 31/12/14; Retd 30/12/32.

1932-1949 **O'CONNOR**, Alexander George ARCM. Born 1902 died 19??. Enl 1 Ir Fus 7/11/17; WO1 (BM) 1 A&S 31/12/32; retd 22/6/49; BM Cyprus Police 1949-195?.

1st Battalion, The Argyll & Sutherland Highlanders, 1970, Bandmaster R Tomlinson (RMSM)

1949-1958 **HOWE**, James Hakin MBE LRAM ARCM psm. Born 1917. Enl 1 RS 12/4/33; WO1 (BM) 1 A&SH 27/5/49; WO1 (BM) Highland Bde 17/3/58; Lt (DoM) SG 27/8/59; Snr DoM Household Division 1970; retd 10/11/74 rank of Maj.

1958-1963 **POPE**, Maurice Andrew ARCM. Born 1924. Enl KDG 3/7/39; WO1 (BM) A&S 17/3/58; WO1 (BM) RA (Wool) 13/12/63; retd 14/7/69.

1963-1969 **PEARSON**, James Henry ARCM. Born 1932. Enl RE (Chat) 17/10/48; WO1 (BM) A&S 13/12/63; retd 3/2/69.

1969-1970 **TOMLINSON**, Roger Grenfell BA FTCL LGSM ARCM psm. Born 1939. Enl R Signals 25/2/57; WO1 (BM) A&SH 4/2/69; WO1 (BM) 16/5L 28/12/70; WO1 (BM) PoW Div (badged RWF) 17/2/75; Capt (DoM) RAC Jnr Ldrs (badged 16/5L) 21/2/79; Capt (DoM) RTR (Cam) 20/4/82; Capt DoM RAC 1/4/84; Capt (DoM) RHG/D 18/6/86; Lt-Col Principal DoM (Army) 24/8/92; retd 1993.

1970-1972 Band disbanded whilst regiment at company strength.

1972-1974 **CHAMBERLAIN**, Lemuel. Born 1939. Enl Para 16/6/58; WO1 (BM) A&SH 15/1/72; retd 14/4/74.

1974-1984 **CLARK**, S R. Born 1944. Enl 1 RRF 31/8/59; WO1 (BM) A&SH 16/4/74; retd 10/1/84.

1984-1990 **LAMB**, Kevin BA DipEd FVCM BBCM psm. Born 1953. Enl RA (Mtd) 2/9/73; WO1 (BM) A&SH 10/1/84; Capt Deputy Chief Instr RMSM 19/2/90; Capt Trg & Dev RMSM 1991; Capt (DoM) REME 17/12/93.

1990-1994 **HUNT**, Peter John. Born 1958. Enl RH 10/10/75; WO1 (BM) A&SH 16/1/90; WO1 (BM) RA (Wool) 1994.

BANDMASTERS OF
THE 2nd BATTALION THE ARGYLL AND SUTHERLAND HIGHLANDERS

1835-1839 **McKENZIE**, Sgt James. Born 1818 died 18??. Enl 93 Ft 13/5/35; Sgt 93 Ft ?/7/35; retd 31/10/39.

1839-1884 Bandmaster(s) not known

1884-1894 **GRANT**, James. Born 1854 died 1901. Enl 92 Ft 13/10/68; WO (BM) 2 A&S 1/10/84; retd 2/12/94.

1895-1903 **DAVIES**, William. Born 1866 died 1912. Enl 43 Ft 21/10/80; WO (BM) 2 A&S 30/1/95; retd 14/4/03.

1903-1908 **WALSH**, John. Born 1872 died 19??. Enl 92 Ft 4/6/77; WO (BM) 2 A&S 14/4/03; retd 3/6/08.

1908-1928 **RICKETTS**, Frederick Joseph psm. Born 1880 died 1945. Enl 2 R Ir R 5/9/95; WO (BM) 2 A&S 4/6/08; Lt (DoM) RM (Deal) 13/1/28; Lt (DoM) RM (Plym) 1/11/30; retd in rank of Major 31/5/44.

1928-1947 **BEAT**, Charles Smart ARCM. Born 1894 died 1974. Enl Camerons 18/9/12; WO1 (BM) 2 A&S 13/1/28; retd 1948; Professor Royal Marines School of Music 1948-1974.

THE QUEEN'S REGIMENT

	1881		*1959-61*	*1966*
2nd Foot	Queen's Royal Regt	)))	Queen's Royal Surrey Regt	1st Bn Queen's Regt
31st Foot)	East Surrey	)		
70th Foot)	Regt	)		
3rd Foot	The Buffs	))	Queen's Own Buffs	2nd Bn Queen's Regt
50th Foot)	Royal West	)		
97th Foot)	Kent Regt	)		
35th Foot)	Royal			3rd Bn Queen's Regt
	) Sussex			
107th Foot)	Regt			
57th Foot)				4th Bn Queen's Regt
	) Middlesex Regt			
77th Foot)				

The 4th Battalion, The Queen's Regiment, was disbanded in 1970.

In 1984 the three surviving battalion bands were replaced by the Albuhera Band and the Quebec Band.

In 1992 The Queen's Regiment was amalgamated with The Royal Hampshire Regiment to form The Princess of Wales' Royal Regiment (Queen's and Royal Hampshire).

BANDS OF THE

1ST BATTALION

THE QUEEN'S REGIMENT

THE QUEEN'S ROYAL REGIMENT
(West Surrey)

1661	The Tangier Regiment
1684	The Queen's Regiment
1686	The Queen Dowager's Regiment
1703	The Queen's Royal Regiment
1715	The Princess of Wales's Own Regiment of Foot
1881 (May)	The Royal West Surrey Regiment (The Queen's)
1881 (July)	The Queen's (Royal West Surrey Regiment)
1921	The Queen's Royal Regiment (West Surrey)
1959	amalgamated with The East Surrey Regiment to form The Queen's Royal Surrey Regiment

When Catherine of Braganza, daughter of the King of Portugal, married Charles II in 1661, part of her dowry was the territory of Tangier. The regiment that was later to become the Queen's Royal Regiment (West Surrey) was raised to garrison the new colony; as the 2nd of Foot, it was the senior English infantry regiment.

An inspection report from 12 September 1781 notes the presence of a 'Good Band', but thereafter there is a gap in the records. During the first half of the 19th century, the Band was presumably under the direct command of the officers, and at some point a 2nd Battalion Band was created, but it is not until March 1863 that written records resume.

That month saw the appointment from Kneller Hall of John Gready as Bandmaster of the 1st Battalion of what was then known as The Princess of Wales's Own Regiment of Foot, and of Charles Barthmann to the 2nd. Both were to depart in unhappy circumstances.

Though Mr Barthmann's musical ability was not in doubt, his conduct appears to have left something to be desired; under that heading, reports from his Commanding Officer note: 'Irregular' in 1865, falling to 'Intemperate, discharged' in 1868. Despite this dismissal, Mr Barthmann's drinking does not seem to have unduly impeded his career; he reappears in the Kneller Hall ledgers in 1874 as Bandmaster of the 2nd Battalion, 61st Foot, and

No. 138. Vol. 6.]   FOR THE WEEK ENDING SATURDAY, NOVEMBER 10, 1894.   [Price One Penny.

BANDSMEN, GOLD COAST CONSTABULARY, CAMERON HIGHLANDERS, AND 93RD HIGHLANDERS.

(From a photograph by Gregory & Co., 51, Strand, W.C.)

*Top from left to right: Bandsman, Coldstream
Guards with slide trumpet 1830*   (RMSM);
Musician, 7th Foot with oboe c1790   (RMSM);
Cymbalist, Grenadier Guards c1850   (RMSM);
Bass drummer, Grenadier Guards c1829   (RMSM)

Far left: Fifer, 25th Foot c1770   (RMSM)
*Left: Bandsman, 93rd Foot with
ophicleide 1850*   (RMSM)
*Right: Drum Major and drummer,
9th Foot*   (Turner)

Top: Massed Drums of the Guards returning to barracks after the Queen's Birthday Parade 1992   (Colin Dean)
Above: 18th century Band of the Coldstream Guards 1991   (Colin Dean)

Opposite page: Scots Guards Orchestra, Director of Music Major David Price   (SG)
Right: Welsh Guards with Egyptian Band, Egypt 1995, Director of Music Major S Watts   (WG)

Opposite page:
Coldstream Guards,
Windsor Castle
        (Coldm Gds)
Below:
Coldstream Guards,
London 1993
        (Robin Ridewood)

Right: Fanfare
trumpeters, Welsh
Guards, Cardiff 1989
        (Colin Dean)
Below: Irish Guards,
Edinburgh, Director
of Music Lt-Col M Lane
        (IG)

THE BAND OF
HER MAJESTY'S
IRISH GUARDS

Above left: Major (now Lt-Col) D Price, Scots Guards
(Price)

Above: Major Stuart Watts, Welsh Guards (WG)
Left: Lt-Col P Hannam, Welsh Guards (Hannam)

Opposite page
Top left: Major Phil Hills, Grenadier Guards (Hills)
Top right: Major David Marshall, Coldstream Guards
(Marshall)
Below left: Major David Marshall with Oscar Peterson
(Marshall)
Below right: Major Mick Henderson, Irish Guards
(Colin Dean)

*Right: Trumpeter, The Argyll
& Sutherland Highlanders*
                    (A&SH)
*Below: The Queen's Own
Highlanders, Bandmaster
T Whittingham, c1990*
                    (QOHldrs)

*Opposite page:
Top left: Side-drummer,
The Argyll & Sutherland
Highlanders*   (A&SH)
*Top right: Bandmaster
Norman Rogerson,
The Black Watch*   (Rogerson)
*Bottom left: Trumpeters,
The Black Watch*
            (Wolfgang Luedecke)
*Bottom right: The Gordon
Highlanders, East Berlin c1992,
Bandmaster T Cooper*
            (Gordons)

Top: The Royal Scots, Bandmaster A Hodgetts, Berlin c1989 (RS)
Below: The King's Own Scottish Borderers, Bandmaster J Chapman (RMSM)

*Right: The Argyll &
Sutherland Highlanders,
Sydney Opera House,
1987, Bandmaster
K Lamb* (A&SH)

*Below: Edinburgh Tattoo
1993. Bandmasters:
Peter Hunt, A&SH;
Tim Cooper, Gordons;
Ian Peaple, BW; Graham
Jones, RHF; Captain
David Thompson, BW
(Director of Music
Infantry North);
Bandmasters:
Geoff Williams, RS;
Martin Perry, KOSB;
Terry Whittingham,
QO Hlds*

Above: The Quebec Band and Corps of Drums, The Queen's Regiment
(RMSM)

Right: Trumpeters, 3rd Battalion, The Royal Regiment of Fusiliers
(Wolfgang Luedecke)

Opposite page
Above: Stars of the TV Show 'Black Adder' with members of the Band of the 3rd Battalion, The Royal Anglian Regiment, Bandmaster T Parkinson
(Parkinson)

Below: The Duke of Kent's Band, The St George's Band and the Corps of Drums of the 1st Battalion The Royal Regiment of Fusiliers. The Drum Major's mace, drums and head-dress are decorated for St George's Day (RMSM)

Top left: Captain Bob Meldrum, Director of Music, Minden Band, The Queen's Division
(Meldrum)

Top right: Bandmaster (now Captain) Peter Clarke, Duke of Kent's Band, RRF (Clarke)

Left: The Highland Band of the Scottish Division receiving their new cap badges 1994
(Highland Band)

2nd Battalion The Queen's Royal Regiment, Dover 1930, Bandmaster R Barsotti (RMSM)

made a success of his new band, remaining with it until his retirement some fifteen years later.

Mr Gready was also dismissed from the Regiment, receiving a final report in 1879 that stated: 'Conduct – good; Musical ability – very good; General usefulness – useless; Remarks – discharged.' Like Mr Barthmann, he had previously been a sergeant in the Band, though he did serve as Bandmaster for nearly sixteen years before being discharged, which suggests that he coped adequately with his change of role. A better clue to the nature of his dismissal possibly comes from the fact that his successor, William Gidney, was returned to Kneller Hall after just fifteen months, with a comment that he was 'unsatisfactory'. Perhaps we can assume that the officers were becoming dissatisfied with the system of appointments from Kneller Hall.

The most distinguished bandmaster to serve with the regiment was John Mackenzie Rogan, who was appointed to the 2nd Battalion in 1882. Then stationed in Peshawar, India, the Band of the 2nd had more than 35 musicians, but included in that number were seventeen experienced players due to retire the following year. The new bandmaster therefore faced the task of recruiting what was effectively a new band. Some prospective musicians were found in a home for Army orphans founded

by Sir John Lawrence near Sabathu, and some from within the ranks, as Mr Rogan recounted in his memoirs *Fifty Years of Army Music*:

> I had a talk with the boys and explained to them the advantages they would gain by joining a regiment like the Queen's, in which the officers and in fact all ranks took a keen interest in the band. I was fortunate in getting the consent of six and a promise from others to join when they were old enough to enlist.
>
> Soon after this a draft of 250 men and 4 boys arrived from England and volunteers from this draft were invited to join the band. Twenty-five names were sent in, all young men of fair education and young soldiers. After a trial of a few months I decided to keep fifteen.

So successful was this exercise in recruiting that by the time Mr Rogan left The Queen's, the Band could boast a strength of nearly 60, whilst the Coldstream Guards – his next appointment – stood at just 33.

Mr Rogan was also a talented composer, responsible for many of the best known British marches. Amongst them was 'Bond of Friendship', dating from his time with The Queen's. The Battalion had been mobilized in 1885 for active service following the outbreak of the Burma War, and was sailing from Calcutta when Bandsman Murray collapsed with heat stroke. With the doctor giving him no chance of recovery, he managed to raise himself to consciousness one last time and took the Bandmaster's hand with the words: 'I'm so glad Mr Rogan you are here.' Later that night, 'Bond of Friendship' was sketched out in his memory.

The 1st Battalion spent ten years from 1895 in India, whilst the 2nd saw action in South Africa. During the Great War too, the bandsmen were called upon as medical orderlies.

But it was not only in these major national conflicts that the military role of musicians came to the fore. The religious conflicts between Muslims and Hindus in the mid-'20s saw the 2nd Battalion, including many bandsmen, despatched to Kotwali to help restore order. The musicians who remained behind were employed on guard duties.

The 1st Battalion also served abroad in the interwar years with a posting to China in 1927, followed some years later by a move to India. The Band accompanied the Battalion but, due to a restriction that prevented those under the age of nineteen from travelling, it was below full strength and suffered an imbalance in instrumentation. This was to remain a problem right through to 1933, when the situation became so serious that fifteen musicians were transferred from the 2nd Battalion to strengthen the depleted ranks.

The Band of the 2nd was at the time stationed back in the UK – making recruitment somewhat easier than it was for the 1st in the Far East – and, under the baton of Roger Barsotti, was establishing an enviable reputation. A photograph taken in November 1937 shows the Band to be 52 strong, though by this time war was looming and the bandsmen were training to take up again their secondary role.

Mr Barsotti's industry and leadership were such that, within a few months of the outbreak of war, he had built a new band at the regimental depot capable not only of playing for passing out parades and the like, but also of giving public concerts. A typical example comes from the Cliffs Bandstand, Southend-on-Sea on Whit Sunday 1942:

March Medley	American Marches	arr Barsotti
Selection	Saschinka	Schirmann
Trombone Solo	The Firefly	Moss
	soloist: LCpl G Ingle	
Selection	Classica	arr Ewing
Characteristic	The Parade of the Pirates	Bratton
	Interval	
	March of the Bowmen	
	from Robin Hood	Curzon
Selection	Palace & Hippodrome	
	Memories	arr Duthoit
Spanish Serenade	Lolita	Barsotti
Selection	Battle Dress	Debroy Somers
Regimental March	Braganza	
	God Save The King	

In November 1946 the Band of the 2nd Battalion left Britain for a tour of the Far East. Together with bands from the West Yorkshires and the Royal Northumberland Fusiliers, it played massed band performances in Singapore and Hong Kong, before proceeding to Japan, where it toured the British battalions then occupying the country.

On 9 September 1948 the 2nd Battalion trooped its colours for the last time at a parade in Berlin, and the two bands amalgamated. Though stationed in Berlin, the surviving Band returned frequently to the UK to play at military and civilian functions.

It also accompanied the Regiment to Malaya between 1954 and 1957, a gruelling and exhausting tour that few bands managed to complete, though the Queens did do so. Whilst there, the Band played for the Sultan of Johore's Diamond Jubilee Celebrations and performed in a number of towns.

Regimental Music

For over a century the 1st Battalion marched past to a version of 'God Save The King', but in 1881 the authorities insisted that the practice be ended and a new march adopted. A Portuguese tune was chosen and retitled 'Braganza', though there is no evidence that any connexion with Catherine of Braganza existed.

The 2nd Battalion, in deference to General Bruce who raised the Battalion and who had formerly served with the Highland Light Infantry, used a Scottish march, 'We'll Gang Nae Muir to Yon Toun'.

The slow march was 'Scipio' (see the Grenadier Guards).

1st Battlion The East Surrey Regiment, North Russia Campaign 1919, Bandmaster W Bradshaw

(Eagles/Ogilby)

THE EAST SURREY REGIMENT

1702	Villier's Regiment of Marines	1756	2nd Bn, 31st Foot
1711	Goring's Marines	1758	70th Foot
1714	31st Foot	1782	70th (Surrey) Foot
1782	31st (Huntingdon-shire) Foot	1812	70th (Glasgow Lowland) Regiment
		1825	70th (Surrey) Foot

1881	The East Surrey Regiment
1959	amalgamated with The Queen's Royal Regiment to form The Queen's Royal Surrey Regiment

The inspection reports of the 18th century generally tell us little more than that a band did or did not exist at a particular time, but those of the two regiments later to become the East Surreys are more intriguing. An inspection of the 70th Foot on 5 May 1777 enthuses, 'An Handsome Band of Music genteelly dressed', whilst the officers of the 31st Foot were clearly making full use of their musicians from an early stage; a report dated 29 May 1790 states, 'Band on recruiting service.'

The 31st Band was also actively involved in the Peninsular War, and an account in *Recollections of Sir George B L'Estrange, late 31st Regiment* gives some indication of the mobility of both music and musicians between the two opposing forces in that conflict:

We could distinctly hear the bands of different French regiments play, and so near that we could distinguish the air. I recollect one in particular that we afterwards discovered from two bandsmen who had deserted and come over to us, and were immediately taken into our band, to whom they taught it. It was called 'Bonaparte's March' and a very fine piece of music it was, I recollect the air of it to this day.

The first reference to a bandmaster in the 31st Foot comes in a further set of military memoirs; Lieutenant E W Bray's *Recollections of the Afghan War in 1842* records the death of 'Sergeant Reed, our Bandmaster', one of several victims of a cholera epidemic. Nothing else is known of Sgt Reed.

Further involvement by the 31st in military campaigns followed in the Crimean War and the Second Chinese War of 1860; in both conflicts, bandsmen were absorbed into the ranks.

The earliest known bandmaster of the 70th Foot is Mynheer Dittrich, presumably a continental musician, who was appointed in the late 1850s. He accompanied the Regiment to New Zealand in 1861, but appears to have stayed for only a few months. During that time, however, he formed a successful choral class at the Otahuhu Institute, and was reportedly popular with both the troops and the local population.

In 1869 Bandmaster W Vines was appointed by Kneller Hall to the 31st, with Charles Joiner coming to the 70th in 1878.

The Army reforms of 1881 brought the 31st and 70th of Foot together as the two regular battalions of

1st Battalion The East Surrey Regiment, 1941, Bandmaster C Harriott   (RMSM)

The East Surrey Regiment. The 1st Battalion moved to India the following year, where it remained until the end of the century, whilst the 2nd saw service in India, Egypt and the Sudan, before going to South Africa in 1899. Both Bands accompanied their Battalions on these postings abroad.

During the Great War the bandsmen served as stretcher-bearers, with the two Battalions meeting up briefly at Ypres.

Between the wars the Band of the 1st East Surreys spent a further twelve years abroad, in such places as North Russia, Egypt, Sudan and Hong Kong. These postings were by no means always peaceful – in 1922, for example, the bandsmen were called upon to help control riots in Cairo – but for the most part the greatest challenge came from competition in sport, the perennial preoccupation of military bands. Bandsman Wareham was a successful boxer, whilst Bandsmen Mackleworth and Hannam were part of a Hong Kong 4 × 440 yards relay team that beat the Japanese Olympic squad. (Bandsman Mackleworth was the Colony Champion over the distance.)

There was also time for music, with an orchestra being formed under the leadership of Corporal Wernham whilst stationed in Rawalpindi. And time too for less welcome military duties; the Band Notes from the February 1931 regimental journal sum up three months on the Cheklala Frontier with a sense of wearied resignation: 'Guards, engagements, guards and still more guards appear to have been our lot during the last few weeks.'

Perhaps the most memorable experience of the period was an appearance in the 1939 version of *The Four Feathers*, directed by Zoltan Korda, playing alongside the Band of the 1st Battalion, The Queen's Royal Regiment.

The 2nd Battalion Band had a quieter time of it, spending most of the '20s and '30s at home, though there were short spells in Turkey, Jersey and Gibraltar. It was in the latter that Lieutenant-Colonel (retd) Mackenzie Rogan, formerly of the Queen's and more recently Senior Director of Music of the Household Division, appeared in the audience; the bandsmen were reportedly much relieved when this respected musician praised their playing, particularly their rendition of 'Cavalleria Rusticana'.

Shortly before the outbreak of war, the 1st Battalion returned home via a posting in the Sudan and, on commencement of hostilities, Bandmaster Cyril Harriott moved to the regimental depot to build a new band.

On the other side of the world, the 2nd Battalion faced total disaster. Moved from Shanghai to Singapore, it was sent forward into Malaya to combat the Japanese invasion. There it suffered such a heavy onslaught that a composite unit, the famous British Battalion, was formed with the 1st Leicesters (see The Leicestershire Regiment). Those who survived were captured when Singapore fell; amongst them was Bandmaster Ernest Manley, who died on 15 January 1945 in Amagasaki Camp, Japan.

Back home the new Band was making good progress and was kept extremely busy. When the two battalions amalgamated in 1948, it was Bandmaster Harriott who took command of the surviving Band.

Regular performances on the bandstands of Britain dominated the remaining decade of the Band's existence, though there was a visit to Athens to celebrate the birthday of King Paul in 1949, and a two-year posting to Tripoli in 1952. It was whilst there that Mr Harriott was suddenly taken ill and died at the Tel-el-Kebir Military Hospital on 16 August 1953; he was buried the following day.

It fell to his replacement, William Snowden, to take the Band into its 1959 amalgamation with The Queen's Royal Regiment.

Regimental Music

The quick march of the 1st Battalion was 'A Southerly Wind and a Cloudy Sky', adapted from an old song for no other reason than it was good to march to.

The 2nd Battalion used 'Lass o' Gowrie', probably in memory of the 70th Foot having originally been raised in Glasgow, where it served for the first three years of its existence. (Although the Regiment became associated with Surrey in 1782, there remained a large number of Glaswegian members, which – combined with the grey facings then worn – earned it the nickname 'The Glasgow Greys'.) The tune of 'Lass o' Gowrie' was originally known as 'Loch Eroch Side'; the words are by Caroline Oliphant, the famous Jacobite writer of 'Charlie is my Darling' and 'Will Ye No Come Back Again?'

The slow march was entitled 'Lord Charles Montague's Huntingdonshire Slow March'.

THE QUEEN'S ROYAL SURREY REGIMENT

1959   The Queen's Royal Surrey Regiment
1966   re-designated 1st Battalion, The Queen's Regiment

During its brief existence, the Band of The Queen's Royal Surrey Regiment served in Bury St Edmunds, Colchester, Aden, Hong Kong and Munster. The spell in Aden was interrupted by a return to Britain to play for the Regimental Tercentenary in 1961.

One of the last engagements was a massed band performance with the Bands of The Devon and Dorsetshire Regiment and The Sherwood Foresters for the visit to Ypres of the Queen.

Regimental Music

The new Regiment adopted two quick marches from the old formations: 'Braganza' and 'Lass o' Gowrie'.

1st BATTALION, THE QUEEN'S REGIMENT

1966   1st Battalion, The Queen's Regiment
1992   The Princess of Wales' Royal Regiment (Queen's and Royal Hampshire)

The Queen's Regiment came into being on 31 December 1966 with The Queen's Royal Surrey Regiment becoming the 1st Battalion. The Band accompanied the Battalion on visits to Bahrain, Canada, Denmark, France, Northern Ireland, Berlin and West Germany.

Bandmaster Fred Short, who had taken the Band through the amalgamation, retired on compassionate grounds in 1968, and was succeeded by Tom Crichton. Mr Crichton had already enjoyed a colourful career as a bandsman in the Argyll and Sutherland Highlanders, whom he had joined in 1947 at the age of sixteen. Quite apart from his musical abilities, he was an all-round sportsman, playing hockey, basketball and rugby for his battalion, and even representing the Army in the 100 and 200 metre sprints. Despite these achievements, however, he cites as the highlight of his career meeting Nikita Kruschev when the Argylls played in Moscow in 1960.

On 4 May 1974 the bands of the regiment massed for the Presentation of Colours by Queen Margarethe II of Denmark. The following year the band accompanied the Battalion on a tour in Northern Ireland.

In 1984 the Regiment decided that rather than have three small battalion bands each of 21, it would prefer two larger bands each of 35. On 1 May 1984 therefore the Albuhera and Quebec Bands came into being, with the Band of the 1st Battalion under Bandmaster Hills forming the nucleus of the Albuhera Band.

Regimental Music

The regimental quick march was an arrangement by Major Donald Pryce of the popular song 'Soldiers of the Queen'. This was composed by Leslie Stuart at the time of Queen Victoria's Diamond Jubilee in 1897. The words of the refrain are:

It's the soldiers of the Queen my lads
Who've been my lads, who've seen my lads
In the fight for England's glory lads
Of it's world wide glory let us sing
And when we say we've always won
And when they ask us how it's done
We'll proudly point to ev'ry one
Of England's soldiers of the Queen.

The slow march was 'The Caledonian'. This was inherited from The Middlesex Regiment and has also been known as 'The Highland March' and 'The Gaelic March'. It was introduced to The Middlesex Regiment by Colonel John Campbell of Strachur when he assumed command of the 57th Foot in 1775.

BANDMASTERS OF
THE 1st BATTALION THE QUEEN'S
ROYAL REGIMENT
(West Surrey)

1863-1879 **GREADY**, John. Enl 1/2 Ft; Sgt (BM) 1/2 Ft 28/3/63; retd 16/6/79.

1879-1880 **GIDNEY**, William. Enl 1/13 Ft; Sgt (BM) 1/2 Ft 17/6/79; returned to Kneller Hall 2/9/80.

1880-1890 **GARDNER**, Samuel. Born 1850 died 1933. Enl 17L 20/11/68; Sgt (BM) 1/2 Ft 3/9/80; WO (BM) 1/7/81; retd 1/8/90.

1890-1899 **INKSTER**, Frederick James. Born 1863 died 1942. Enl 1 Lincoln R 11/7/83; WO (BM) 1 Queen's R 2/8/90; retd 28/2/99.

1899-1906 **WHELAN**, Edward. Born 1870 died 1944. Enl 1 North'n R 1/8/84; WO (BM) 1 Queen's R 1/3/99; retd 12/11/06.

1906-1915 **MATTHEWS**, John. Born 1872 died 19??. For full details see 4 R War R.

1915-1928 **BUCKLE**, John James. Born 1879 died 19??. Enl 2 R Sussex R 4/4/95; WO1 (BM) 1 Queen's R 1/1/15; retd 10/1/28; DoM Queen's Own Rifles (Canada) 1928-1947.

1928-1933 **PERRY**, Herbert ARCM. Born 1895 died 1949. Enl RA (Wool) 25/6/11; WO1 (BM) 1 Queen's R 1/3/28; retd 10/4/33; WO1 (BM) 6 W York R (TA) 1934-1936; WO1 (BM) 4 Somerset LI (TA) 1936-1939.

1933-1947 **BROOKS**, Charles Henry MBE ARCM. Born 1902 died 1985. Enl 2 Essex R 9/4/18; WO1 (BM) 1 Queen's R 11/4/33; Retd 1947; WO1 (BM) 7 R War R (TA) 1949.

1947-1956 **GAINES**, Edward. Born 1916 died 1969. For full details see 2nd Battalion.

1956-1959 **LYNES**, William Charles. Born 1928. Enl 1 Leicester R 31/3/43; WO1 (BM) 1 Queen's R 5/6/56; WO1 (BM) 1 The Buffs 14/9/59; WO1 (BM) QO Buffs 3/61; Lt (regt duty) Queens 11/5/65; retd 15/8/69 rank of Capt (QM).

BANDMASTERS OF
THE 2nd BATTALION THE QUEEN'S
ROYAL REGIMENT
(West Surrey)

1863-1870 **BARTHMANN**, Charles. Born 1834 died 18??. Enl 2/2 Ft; Sgt (BM) 2/2 Ft 3/3/63; Sgt (BM) 2 Glosters 6/5/74; retd 11/6/89.

1870-1882 **KEARNS**, Richard A. Enl 2/2 Ft; Sgt (BM) 2/2 Ft 14/5/70; retd 28/5/82.

1882-1895 **ROGAN**, John Mackenzie (also known as Mackenzie-Rogan), CVO Mus Doc Hon RAM. Born 1852 died 1932. Enl 2 Bn 11 Ft 5/2/67; WO (BM) 2 Bn R W Surr R 29/3/82; WO (BM) Coldm Gds 9/4/96; Snr BM Gds 1900; Lt 27/2/04; retd rank of Lt-Col 24/3/20.

1895-1904 **BATTISHILL**, Percy Francis, Hon RAM. Born 1866 died 1924. Enl 2 KRRC 30/10/84; WO (BM) 2 Queen's R 23/11/95; WO (BM) RA (Dover) 2/11/04; WO1 (BM) RA (Shoeburyness) 1918; retd 24/7/24.

1904-1913 **STOCK**, Albert. Born 1873 died 19??. Enl 1 Devon R 16/9/87; WO (BM) 2 Queen's R 2/11/04; retd 19/8/13.

1913-1924 **ADAMS**, William Arthur. Born 1879 died 1942. Enl 2 KOSB 1/10/94; WO (BM) 2 Queen's 20/8/13; retd 1/12/24; WO1 (BM) 6 Hampshire R (TA) 1925-1935.

THE QUEEN'S REGIMENT · 103

1924-1930 **FLECKNEY**, John Richard. Born 1897 died 19??. Enl 2 Worc R 6/9/11; WO1 (BM) 2 Queen's R 2/12/24; retd 16/8/30.

1930-1945 **BARSOTTI**, Roger ARCM. Born 1901 died 1986. Enl The Buffs 25/4/16; WO1 (BM) 2 Queen's R 17/8/30; retd 12/8/45; DoM Metropolitan Police 1946-1968.

1945-1947 **GAINES**, Edward. Born 1916 died 1969. Enl 2 The Buffs 18/4/1932; WO1 (BM) 2 Queen's R 13/8/45; WO1 (BM) 1 Queen's R 1947; WO1 (BM) Home Counties Bde 5/6/56; Retd 2/7/61.

BANDMASTERS OF
THE 1st BATTALION
THE EAST SURREY REGIMENT

184? **REED**. Sgt (BM) 31 Ft – see text for further information.

1869-1880 **VINES**, W. Enl 69 Ft; Sgt (BM) 31 Ft 24/3/69; retd 28/9/80.

1880-1890 **CHAPMAN**, William. Born 1845 died 1924. Enl 3H 25/2/59; Sgt (BM) 31 Ft 29/9/80; WO (BM) 1/7/81; WO (BM) 2 E Surr R 1890; retd 1900.

1890-1893 **TOBIN**, John. Born 1854 died 1931. For full details see 2nd Battalion.

1893-1913 **CLARK**, William. Born 1863 died 1937. Enl 106 Bombay Light Infantry 16/5/77; WO (BM) 1 E Surr R 19/11/93; retd 8/7/13.

1913-1925 **BRADSHAW**, William F. Born 1874 died 19??. Enl 2 Seaforth 4/4/05; WO (BM) 1 E Surr R 9/7/13; retd 11/6/25; WO1 (BM) 53 Bde RA (TA) 1929-1939.

1925-1938 **DOWLE**, Donald Bertram. Born 1898 died 19??. Enl 1 Cameronians 7/1/13; WO1 (BM) 1 E Surr R 12/6/25; retd 6/5/38.

1938-1953 **HARRIOT**, Cyril Francis ARCM. Born 1904 died 1953. Enl 1 Border R 21/9/26; WO1 (BM) 1 E Surr R 7/5/38; retd 16/8/53.

1953-1959 **SNOWDEN**, William ARCM. Born 1926. Enl Coldm Gds 24/11/47; WO1 (BM) 1 E Surr R 17/8/53; WO1 (BM) QR Surr 14/10/59; Lt (regt duty) Queen's 4/4/63; retd 1/10/76 in rank of Maj (QM).

BANDMASTERS OF
THE 2nd BATTALION
THE EAST SURREY REGIMENT

185?-186? **DITTRICH**, Mynheer. Sgt (BM) or Civ BM 70 Ft some time during late 1850s until possibly 1862.

186?-1878 Bandmaster(s) not known.

1878-1883 **JOINER**, Charles. Born 186? died 1883. Enl 77 Ft; Sgt (BM) 70 Ft; WO (BM) 1/7/81; died whilst serving 2/7/83.

1883-1890 **TOBIN**, John. Born 1854 died 1931. Enl 31 Ft 29/2/68; WO (BM) 2 E Surr R 1/89/83; WO (BM) 1 E Surr R 1890; retd 18/11/93.

1890-1900 **CHAPMAN**, William. Born 1845 died 1924. For full details see 1st Battalion.

1900-1912 **DURHAM**, James. Born 1871 died 19??. Enl 1 Durham LI 2/9/87; WO (BM) 2 E Surr R 25/2/1900; retd 30/11/12; WO (BM) Holkar State 1/12/12; retd 9/4/38.

1912-1932 **JENKINS**, William Henry. Born 1878 died 19??. Enl 2 S Lan R 3/5/92; WO (BM) 2 E Surr R 1/12/12; retd 9/12/32.

1932-1945 **MANLEY**, Ernest Edward ARCM. Born 1899 died 1945. Enl 1 Queen's R 23/3/14; WO1 (BM) 2 E Surr R 9/12/33; died 15/1/45 in Japanese prisoner of war camp.

BANDMASTERS OF
THE 1st BATTALION THE QUEEN'S
ROYAL SURREY REGIMENT

1959-1962 **SNOWDEN**, William ARCM. Born 1926. For full details see 1st Battalion The East Surrey Regiment.

1962-1966 **SHORT**, Fred Edwin William ARCM. Born 1931. Enl R Leic 25/10/45; WO1 (BM) QR Surr 7/12/62; WO1 (BM) 1 Queens 31/12/66; retd 29/1/68.

BANDMASTERS OF
THE 1st BATTALION
THE QUEEN'S REGIMENT

1966-1968 **SHORT**, Fred Edwin William ARCM. Born 1931. For full details see The Queen's Royal Surrey Regiment.

1968-1973 **CRICHTON**, Thomas ARCM. Born 1931. Enl A&SH 24/2/47; WO1 (BM) 1 Queens 30/1/68; retd 14/6/73; DoM Royal Guard of Oman 1977-92, retiring in rank of Colonel.

1973-1978 **MELVIN**, Andrew Wauchope Keith LTCL. Born 1938. Enl DWR 23/7/57; transf PWO 15/1/70; WO1 (BM) 1 Queens 15/6/73; retd 189/6/78.

1978-1984 **HILLS**, Phillip Elven, FLCM psm. Born 1947. Enl RA 5/6/63; trans WG 1972; WO1 (BM) 1 Queens 29/6/78; WO1 (BM) Albuhera 31/3/84; WO1 (BM) RMSM 10/9/85; Capt (DoM) Infantry (North) badged BW 2/1/87; Capt Senior DoM BAOR 15/1/88; Capt (DoM) AJSM (Bov) 2/7/88; Capt (DoM) RA (Alan) 9/10/89; Capt (DoM) Gren Gds 10/8/92; Maj (DoM) 30/9/93.

BANDS OF THE

2ND BATTALION

THE QUEEN'S REGIMENT

THE BUFFS
(The Royal East Kent Regiment)

1665	The Holland Regiment
1689	Prince George of Denmark's Regiment
1708	The Buffs
1751	3rd (or The Buffs) Foot
1782	3rd (East Kent – The Buffs) Foot
1881 (May)	The Kentish Regiment (The Buffs)
1881 (July)	The Buffs (East Kent Regiment)
1935	The Buffs (Royal East Kent Regiment)
1961	amalgamated with The Queen's Own Royal West Kent Regiment to form The Queen's Own Buffs, The Royal Kent Regiment

Though it did not come onto the official British Army establishment until 1665, The Buffs is actually the oldest of the English regiments, dating its existence back to 1572 when it was raised for overseas service and sent to support the struggle of the people of Holland against their Spanish rulers.

The Band can similarly claim a unique antiquity. The first reference comes from an advertisement in a local Sussex newspaper dated Monday 25 December 1749:

The Buffs, 3rd Regiment of Foot

At the White Hart in Lewes next Friday evening, being the 29th December, will be performed a Publick Concert of MUSICK. By the Band belonging to his Majesty's Regiment of Buffs, commanded by the Hon. Col. George Howard.

Act 1	Act 2
1 Symphony with French Horns	1 Symphony with French Horns
2 Hautboy Concerto	2 Hautboy Concerto
3 Violin Concerto	3 Solo for the Trumpet
4 Solo for French Horn	4 German Flute Concerto
5 Symphony with French Horns	5 Symphony with French Horns

Tickets to be had at the New Coffee House the White Hart and the Castle. At 1s 6d each. To begin exactly at Six O'Clock.

Bandboys, 2nd Battalion The Buffs, Brighton 1899   (Eagles/Ogilby)

The instrumentation is evidently limited – predominantly French horns with hautboy(s), flute(s) and trumpet(s), and possibly a violin – but this is the earliest mention of a recognizable band of music in the British Army, pre-dating that of the Royal Artillery by some twelve years. Nonetheless, the Gunners' boast of having the oldest permanent musical organization in Britain appears safe, for an inspection report of The Buffs in 1785 notes 'No Band', suggesting that there must have been an interruption in the band's existence.

The first bandmaster whose name has survived is Signor Giovanni Gassner, a civilian who, typically of many foreign musicians in the mid-19th century, moved between regiments on a frequent basis. He came from the 44th Foot, served briefly with the 1st Battalion of The Buffs from 1851 to 1853 and then departed for various other posts, including the Band of the 50th.

In January 1879 the 2nd Battalion was in South Africa when the Zulu War broke out. As the men marched to join the other units engaged in the suppression of the rising, the bandsmen played music and, when resistance was met, served as stretcher-bearers. Sometimes it was not clear which of the two roles was appropriate, as Brigadier-General A J Whitacre Allen noted in his diary:

The Band played the main body of the Battalion right into the advanced skirmishers of a Zulu Impi of considerable strength which was waiting for us on the slopes of the Etyoe range. The reason for this martial effort on the part of the Band was that the native contingent who were ahead had melted away on contact with the Zulus, all their Company Officers being killed, and consequently no information was sent back by them. The colours were now piled, and the Band solemnly stacked their instruments and took up their places as stretcher bearers.

The Band of the 1st Battalion was engaged in more peaceful activities, stationed in Dublin and playing for various civilian and military functions.

The Great War saw both bands put away their instruments for medical duties. Even with the cessation of hostilities, however, the dangers of military life were not over. The 1st Battalion was stationed in Fermoy when the IRA's guerilla campaign intensified in 1919-20; amongst the casualties were two members of the Band, Corporal Hall and Bandsman Gammon, killed by rebels on 26 November 1920.

The 2nd Battalion spent the immediate post-war period abroad, in Mesopotamia, India and Aden, but returned home in 1924, whilst the 1st went overseas. There was, in addition, a band at the regimental depot. A photograph from the mid-'20s

The Bandmaster of the 2nd Buffs at this time was Charles Hewitt, who had been appointed to the post in 1902 and remained right through to 1930, when he took up a position as civilian bandmaster of the Royal Army Service Corps. Under his leadership, an active dance band was formed, which rapidly became a popular attraction in its own right, whilst the military band were a regular fixture in various seaside resorts, and at the Aldershot Tattoo and Alexandra Palace. On many of these

1st Battalion The Buffs, Fermoy 1914. Last outing prior to war   (RMSM)

shows it at a strength of bandmaster and 23 instrumentalists, and it seems to have been an efficient training ground for musicians in the battalion bands: Band Sergeant Clayton of the 1st Battalion, for example, had previously been the depot bandmaster.

BSgt Clayton's name also turns up as the conductor of the last concert of the 1925/26 season in Gibraltar (Bandmaster Leach was on leave). The programme featured a number of novelty pieces, including 'Chick, Chick, Chicken', 'Variations on Three Blind Mice', a trombone quartet, and a cornet duo, 'The Two Imps', played by two bandboys. Perhaps the most interesting piece was a xylophone solo by Sergeant Roger Barsotti; as Bandmaster of The Queen's Royal Regiment, Mr Barsotti was to become well known as a march composer, and a writer of light pieces featuring xylophones, post horns and the like.

engagements, Mr Hewitt would play violin solos, his favourite being the gypsy fantasia 'Czardas', by Monti.

He was awarded the MBE in 1929, and on his departure from the Regiment was presented with a silver salver inscribed with the names of all the officers who had served during his 27-year incumbency.

His replacement was another long-serving bandmaster, Walter Foster, who stayed with the Regiment for twenty years. He maintained the reputation of the 2nd Buffs as a concert and broadcasting band, achieving a major distinction at the 1938 Empire Exhibition in Glasgow when the Buffs alternated on the bandstand with the famous Fodens Motor Works Band conducted by Harry Mortimer. The Band also played for the visit to Britain of the Crown Prince of Ethiopia in 1931, and was detailed for guard duties in London the same year.

1st Battalion The Buffs, c1920, Bandmaster C Elvin   (RMSM)

The 1st Battalion spent most of the '30s in the Far East, stationed in Burma and India, before moving to Palestine in 1938. Here music virtually ceased, with the majority of bandsmen engaged on regimental duties.

At the outbreak of war Bandmasters Salmon and Foster returned to the depot at Canterbury with the bandboys; within a short period they had built a Band good enough to begin broadcasts on the wireless. Despite the absence of a bandmaster, the musicians of the 1st Battalion, still in Palestine, managed to keep playing, and the June 1940 edition of the regimental journal noted:

As the Drums have now joined us once more, we are carrying on the weekly Retreat Beating . . . We still find time to make Tchaikovsky, Beethoven and others turn in their graves.

In 1944 Mr Salmon spent eight months at Arbor-field building up the newly formed REME Band, before returning to re-create the 1st Battalion Band.

Immediately after the war, the Massed Bands and Drums of The Buffs attended the 1946 celebrations in Denmark for the birthday of King Christan X, with Bandmasters Salmon and Foster both being awarded the decoration Knight of the Order of Dannebrog.

In 1948 the two Battalions amalgamated in Hong Kong, and Mr Foster was appointed Bandmaster. Two years later he retired and was succeeded by Trevor Sharpe, a brilliant clarinettist and a perfectionist in every way, who took the Band to new heights of musicianship. The adventurous programmes undertaken by Mr Sharpe can be seen in the following typical concert:

Fanfare	Veteri Frondescit Honore	Sharpe
March	Entry of the Gladiators	Fucik
Overture	Plymouth Hoe	Ansell

Cornet and Trombone ITMA arrange-	Softly Awakes My Heart	Saint-Saens
ments	a) British Grenadiers	arr Richardson
	b) The Irish Washerwoman	arr Richardson
Ballet music	The Dance of the Hours (from *La Giaconda*)	Ponchielli
Selection	Aida	Verdi
Entracte	Claire de Lune	Debussy
	Dance of the Comedians	Smetana
Male Voice	Selected	
	Valse des Fleurs	Tchaikovsky
Finale	Intro to Act III Lohengrin	Wagner
Regimental march	The Buffs	Handel
	God Save The King	

The association with the Danish royal family was strengthened in May 1955 when King Frederik presented new colours to the Regiment. The following day the Regiment paraded the colours through the streets of Canterbury; despite a heavy downpour of rain that split the skins of the bass drum and side drums, the event went ahead successfully – the drummers simply went through the motions as though nothing was wrong.

In 1961 The Buffs amalgamated with the Queen's Own Royal West Kent Regiment.

Regimental Music

The quick march was 'The Buffs', traditionally attributed to George Handel, who is said to have been an admirer of the Regiment. This claim has never been authenticated, but the second half of the march does resemble a theme from *Acis and Galatea*. One set of words sung to the march are:

The Buffs, the Buffs are going away,
Leaving the girls in the family way,
Leaving the Royal West Kents to,
Leaving the Royal West Kents to pay.
With a knife, fork, spoon, razor, comb and a
* lather brush,*
Knife, fork, spoon, razor, comb and a lather
* brush.*

The slow march was 'Men of Kent', believed to have been composed by James Rufus Tutton in the 1840s, and inherited by The Buffs from the old Kent Militia. James Tutton became bandmaster of the Royal Horse Guards in 1848 and was one of the founders of the Society of British Musicians.

An early march that inexplicably seems never to have been adopted was 'March of the 3rd Regt of Foot, Lord Amherst's', written by General John Reid, the celebrated composer of 'Garb of Old

Gaul'. Lord Amherst was Colonel of the Regiment between 1768 and 1779, and the march was presumably written between those dates. Neglected over the years, it was revived by Trevor Sharpe in the 1950s.

═══════════════════════════════════════

THE QUEEN'S OWN ROYAL WEST KENT REGIMENT

1756	50th Foot
1782	50th (West Kent) Foot
1827	50th (Duke of Clarence's) Foot
1831	50th (The Queen's Own) Regiment of Foot
1824	97th (The Earl of Ulster's) Regiment

1881 (May)	The Royal West Kent Regiment (The Queen's Own)
1881 (July)	The Queen's Own (Royal West Kent Regiment)
1961	amalgamated with The Buffs (Royal East Kent Regiment) to form The Queen's Royal West Kent Regiment

The 50th Foot was raised in Norwich in 1757, and appears to have had fifers from the outset, though there is no mention of a band until an inspection in June 1777: 'Drummers and Fifers wore hats, the caps not being delivered. 10 Music in all, but one was a Sergeant and 5 drums.'

By this stage the Regiment had already been active abroad, sailing for Jamaica in 1772 and subsequently fighting in the American War of Independence. It is unclear whether the Band was in existence for that campaign, but it was certainly called upon in the Napoleonic Wars, when the 50th fought in Corsica, Egypt and the Peninsula.

One memento from those days stemmed from the Battle of Vimiero in 1808. In that encounter, the 900 men of the 50th routed some 5000 French troops, and were joined in the aftermath by soldiers from the French 70th Regiment who had changed their loyalties; their long red plumes were adopted by the 50th Band as trophies.

In 1820 the Regiment was stationed again in Jamaica, and in his memoirs, *Adventures of Captain*

1st Battalion The Queen's Own Royal West Kent Regiment, Agra 1920, Bandmaster P Walmsley   (RMSM)

Patterson, an officer of the 50th pays tribute to the social value of the Band: 'Evening parade at five was the rallying-point of a grand turn-out: warlike evolutions and the military music, in strains harmonious, attracted the fair and languid belles of Kingston.'

The 97th (The Earl of Ulster's) Regiment was raised in Winchester in 1824, though it was not the first regiment to have the number; amongst the four previous incarnations was the 97th (Queen's Germans) at the turn of the century, which was believed to have had some form of band. The regiment that was to become the 2nd Battalion, The Royal West Kent Regiment also had a band from early on, with a strength in 1846 of a sergeant bandmaster and twenty privates.

The 50th served in the Crimean War, and the bandsmen evidently took their instruments with them, as is clear from an article in the *Illustrated London News* about the evacuation from Balaclava in 1856:

> *The English and Russians presented arms to each other, the Band of the 50th, and the Band belonging to the 'Algiers' then played the 'Russian Hymn', 'God Save the Queen' and 'Partant pour la Syrie' . . . . The 50th then marched off, four deep on board the 'Algiers', this being the last regiment to leave Russia.*

The Band also accompanied the Regiment to New Zealand during the Maori Wars of the 1860s.

The Bandmaster was Giovanni Gassner, previously with The Buffs. Born in 1828 of either Italian or Swiss nationality, Signor Gassner studied at the Royal Conservatoire in Naples from the age of nine. At 19 he became a 2nd Lieutenant in the 1st Regiment of Swiss Guards, coming to England after the Italian rebellion of 1848. He became the bandmaster of the 44th Regiment and in fairly quick succession served with the 3rd Foot, HMS *Bellerophon*, the 1st Royal Lanark Militia, the 5th Dragoon Guards and then finally the 50th. Here he stayed from 1856 until 1884. When he at last retired, he was presented with a cheque for five pounds by the Band to purchase an album for the photographs they had had taken for him to remember them by. (Considering that at the time, an estimated 80% of families lived off less than 30 shillings a week, this must have been an impressive album.)

Signor Gassner was the last civilian musician to serve with the Regiment, but the Standing Orders from 1891 indicate that the regularization of appointments had some benefits in asserting the bandmaster's independence:

> *No one but the Commanding Officer and the Band Committee is to interfere with the practice or public playing of the Band, and during practice, men are not to be sent for by officers commanding companies.*

The same document gives the Band establish-

Tea-room orchestra, The Buffs, Fermoy, 1920.
Two of the bandsmen were killed shortly after by the
IRA (RMSM)

ment as a sergeant, a corporal and twenty privates, with two corporals and a lance-corporal as acting bandsmen, together with as many privates as the Commanding Officer authorized.

The 2nd Battalion served with General Rundle's force during the Boer War, with the bandsmen employed as stretcher-bearers. It was subsequently stationed in Ceylon, Hong Kong, Singapore and India, whilst the 1st Battalion spent most of the period around the turn of the century at home.

In the years after the Great War, the roles were reversed, and the 1st Battalion spent nearly twenty years in India. It was not, of course, only the soldiers who went abroad on these tours, but the families as well, and the regimental journal notes the death in 1931 of Mrs Dennison, wife of the Band Sergeant.

The 2nd Battalion played at various seaside resorts and parks through the '20s and '30s, in addition to its military engagements. The Band Notes in the regimental journal suggest that the main preoccupation of the men was not always music, commenting thus on a booking at the Aldershot Tattoo:

With the arrival of the Tattoo came great financial worries, each performer having a ticket to the value of 1s to spend nightly. Some had great difficulty in spending it. Several had large suppers, some purchased cleaning gear, while others even returned their tickets, but in these exceptional cases we blame late nights and early mornings.

During the Second World War, the bandsmen served as stretcher-bearers or fighting soldiers, with the 1st Battalion in the British Expeditionary Force and the 2nd in the siege of Malta.

The war took a heavy toll on many bands, and in several cases the resultant imbalance in instrumentation made conventional military bands difficult. Bandmaster George Jackson of the 2nd Battalion (and later of the 1st, when the two were amalgamated) responded with what he called The Queen's Own Royal West Kent's Band Show, a fifteen-piece line-up consisting of five saxophones, three trumpets, two trombones and a five-man rhythm section.

Regimental Music

Prior to the 1860s, the 50th used 'Garry Owen' as a quick march, but sometime during that decade 'A Hundred Pipers' was adopted. Written in the '40s, the latter song is generally attributed to Lady Nairne, daughter of a distinguished family of Jacobites, though it is possible that she took an old Scottish folk tune, arranged it and wrote new words.

The quick march of 2nd Battalion was another Scottish tune, 'Bonnets of Blue' (not to be confused with 'Blue Bonnets Over The Border').

The slow march was 'Men of Kent'. (For full details see The Buffs.)

new combinations: the Dave Catt Quintet, playing piano-led jazz in the manner of George Shearing, and The Woodwind Quintet, specializing in chamber music. One of the highest profile engagements came at the Hong Kong premier of the Fonteyn-Nureyev film of *Romeo and Juliet*: the Band's fee for the performance included six crates of beer.

Regimental Music

The quick march was an arrangement by Bandmaster Lynes of 'The Buffs' and 'A Hundred Pipers', and the slow march was 'Men of Kent'. (For full details of these tunes see The Buffs and The Royal West Kent Regiment).

THE QUEEN'S OWN BUFFS, THE ROYAL KENT REGIMENT

1961 The Queen's Own Buffs, The Royal Kent Regiment
1966 re-designated 2nd Battalion, The Queen's Regiment

THE 2nd BATTALION THE QUEEN'S REGIMENT

1966 2nd Battalion, The Queen's Regiment
1992 The Princess of Wales' Royal Regiment (Queen's and Royal Hampshire)

When the two Kent regiments amalgamated in 1961, the incumbent Bandmaster of The Buffs, William Lynes, took over command of the new Band. The first two years were spent at home, the men kept busy with many military and civilian engagements, including successive performances in the Lord Mayor's Show. Equally celebrated, at least within the Band, was Corporal 'Fats' Fuller's 1962 appearance on the television game show *Double Your Money*; he won £32 answering questions on music.

1963 saw the first overseas trip of the new incarnation with a visit to Canada, followed the next year by several months in British Guiana. The latter posting was in the company of the Battalion and came in response to the disturbances that prefigured independence; there were regimental duties for the bandsmen as well as concerts and broadcasts.

The Band was equally busy in 1965, with a tour of Denmark and an appearance at the Memorial Service for Winston Churchill being the highpoints.

Towards the end of the year came the final overseas posting, this time to Hong Kong. Here the military and dance bands were augmented by two

The Queen's Regiment came into being on 31 December 1966 with The Queen's Own Buffs, The Royal Kent Regiment, then stationed in Hong Kong, becoming the 2nd Battalion. William Spry continued as Bandmaster, but retired just two years later.

Once it had returned home, the Band spent most of its existence in Colchester or in Germany, though it did have one posting further afield, with a trip to Gibraltar in 1978.

On 4 May 1974 the bands of the regiment massed when Queen Margarethe II of Denmark presented colours to the three regular battalions plus the 5th (Volunteer) Battalion.

When the Queen's Regiment restructured its bands in 1984, that of the 2nd Battalion was effectively disbanded. The incumbent Bandmaster, Mr Francis, moved to the Queen's Division Depot as a project officer.

Regimental Music

The quick march was an arrangement by Bandmaster Lynes of 'The Buffs' and 'A Hundred Pipers', and the slow march was 'Men of Kent'. (For full details of these tunes see The Buffs and The Royal West Kent Regiment).

BANDMASTERS OF
THE 1st BATTALION THE BUFFS
(The Royal East Kent Regiment)

1851-1853 GASSNER, Giovanni. Born 1828 died 1884. For full details see The Essex Regiment.

1853-1864 KENNEDY, William. Born 182? died 1875. Sgt (BM) 1/3 Ft 1853; Sgt (BM) 1/16 Ft 29/7/64; Died whilst serving 31/3/75.

1864-1872 Bandmaster(s) unknown.

1872-1876 DOUGLASS, James. Born 1840 died 1913. Enl 95 Ft 24/7/56; Sgt (BM) 1/3 Ft 16/8/72; Sgt (BM) 2/25 Ft 1/7/76; WO (BM) 1/7/81; BM Royal Hibernian School 30/11/92; retd 24/10/05.

1876-1885 VOLLER, George. Born 1844 died 1885. Enl 2/24 Ft 4/4/62; Sgt (BM) 1/3 Ft 1/7/76; WO (BM) 1/7/81; died whilst serving 9/4/85.

1885-1897 BIRKHEAD, Christopher. Born 1857 died 1938. Enl 2/13 Ft 25/5/71; WO (BM) 1 The Buffs 10/4/85; WO (BM) 2 Seaforth 17/2/97; retd 16/11/02.

1897-1904 HACKNEY, Charles Henry Richardson. Born 1865 died 1933. Enl 1 E Surr R 3/1/81; WO (BM) 1 The Buffs 17/2/97; retd 30/9/04.

1904-1923 ELVIN, George William. Born 1873 died 1936. Enl 1 S Wales Bord 11/1/89; WO (BM) 1 The Buffs 1/10/04; retd 5/10/23.

1923-1929 LEACH, Frank Luke ARCM. Born 1885 died 19??. Enl RA (Plym) 24/2/03; WO1 (BM) 1 The Buffs 6/10/23; retd 23/2/29.

1929-1947 SALMON, Wilfred Bruce MBE LRAM ARCM psm. Born 1900 died 1970. Enl 2 R Berks R 20/9/15; WO1 (BM) 1 The Buffs 24/2/29; Lt (DoM) RA (Port) 8/11/47; Capt (DoM) RA (BAOR) 25/8/53; Maj (DoM) RA (Plym) 15/9/58; retd 5/4/60.

1947-1950 FOSTER, Walter Benjamin MBE ARCM. Born 1902 died 1984. For full details see 2 Buffs.

1950-1959 SHARPE, Trevor Le Mare, LVO OBE (MBE) LRAM ARCM psm. Born 1921. Enl 1 Loyal R 2/9/35; WO1 (BM) The Buffs 4/4/50; WO1 (BM) RMSM 10/9/59; Lt (DoM) RAC Jnr Ldrs (badged RTR) 26/10/61; Lt (DoM) Coldm Gds 27/7/63; Lt-Col (DoM) RMSM 5/4/74; retd 11/3/78; Professor of Instrumentation RMSM 1978-1988.

1959-1961 LYNES, William Charles. Born 1928. For full details see The Queen's Royal Regiment.

BANDMASTERS OF
THE 2nd BATTALION THE BUFFS
(The Royal East Kent Regiment)

1863-1879 SWEENEY, R. Enl 79 Ft; Sgt (BM) or Civ BM 2/3 Ft 1863; retd 1879.

1879-1884 QUINN, Henry. Born 1851 died 1884. Enl 2/3 Ft 23/8/65; Sgt (BM) 2/3 Ft 5/4/79; WO (BM) 1/7/81; died whilst serving 12/11/84.

1884-1892 KELLY, Joseph. Born 1852 died 1914. Enl 2 Welsh R 8/3/67; WO (BM) 2 The Buffs 13/11/84; Retd 7/12/92.

1892-1902 GRIFFITHS, James. Born 1866 died 1944. Enl 23/4/78 Viceroy of India's Band; WO (BM) 2 The Buffs 8/12/92; WO (BM) 1 R Gar R 1/3/02; WO (BM) 1 Essex R 30/5/06; retd 22/4/08.

1902-1930 HEWITT, Charles Buckland MBE. Born 1876 died 1949. Enl 1 R Sussex R 4/2/91; WO (BM) 2 The Buffs 1/3/02; retd 21/6/30; Civ BM RASC 22/6/30; retd 23/8/38.

1930-1947 FOSTER, Walter Benjamin MBE ARCM. Born 1902 died 1984. Enl 15/19H 16/8/18; WO1 (BM) 2 Buffs 22/6/30; WO1 (BM) 1 Buffs 18/11/47; Retd 3/4/50; DoM Hong Kong Police 1950-1963.

Left: Bandmaster G W Elvin, 1st Bn The Buffs (RMSM)
Opposite page: Bandmaster T McKelvie, 2nd Bn R W Kent R (RMSM)

BANDMASTERS OF
THE 1st BATTALION THE QUEEN'S OWN ROYAL WEST KENT REGIMENT

1856-1884 **GASSNER**, Giovanni. Born 1828 died 1884. For full details see The Essex Regiment.

1884-1890 **BROSTER**, Richard. Born 1857 died 19??. Enl 45 Ft 17/6/71; WO (BM) 1 R W Kent R 23/7/84; retd 21/2/90.

1890-1899 **STEWART**, Andrew. Born 1856 died 1944. Enl 71 Ft 27/11/71; WO (BM) 1 R W Kent 22/2/90; retd 20/1/99.

1899-1918 **DAVIS**, George. Born 1866 died 1921. Enl 1 S Stafford R 24/2/82; WO (BM) 1 R W Kent R 21/1/99; retd 10/5/18.

1918-1922 **WALMSLEY**, Percival James. Born 1884 died 1937. Enl 1 Midd'x R 23/12/99; WO1 (BM) 1 R W Kent R 11/5/18; retd 25/4/22.

1922-1934 **BUTT**, Horace Lionel ARCM. Born 1892 died 19??. Enl 1 Gordons 31/1/08; WO1 (BM) 1 R W Kent R 26/4/22; retd 24/2/34.

1934-1948 **McKENNA**, John Robert ARCM. Born 1902. Enl 1 Seaforth 14/6/26; WO1 (BM) 1 R W Kent R 1/4/34; retd 1948.

1948-1950 **JACKSON**, George Edward ARCM. Born 1909. For full details see 2nd Battalion.

1950-1961 **WATKINS**, Roy Gordon MBE LRAM ARCM. Born 1919. Enl 2 KRRC 18/4/34; WO1 (BM) 1 R W Kent R 20/4/50; WO1 (BM) Home Counties Bde 3/7/61; Lt (DoM) RTR (Cambrai) 25/10/63; retd 18/1/69 rank of Capt.

BANDMASTERS OF
THE 2nd BATTALION THE QUEEN'S OWN ROYAL WEST KENT REGIMENT

1865-1887 **MANDEL**, Frederick. Born 1843 died 19??. Enl 97 Ft 22/9/64; Sgt (BM) 97 Ft 20/6/65; WO (BM) 1/7/81; retd 26/4/87.

1887-1897 **GRAHAM**, James. Born 1853 died 1922. Enl 1/101 Ft 8/11/65; WO (BM) 2 R W Kent R 27/4/87; retd 28/2/97.

1897-1902 **INGHAM**, Albert Edward. Born 1862 died 1939. Enl 1/18 Ft 2/10/76; WO1 (BM) 2 R W Kent R 1/3/97; retd 28/2/02.

1902-1914 **McKELVIE**, Thomas. Enl 1 Welsh R 26/10/82; WO (BM) 2 R W Kent R 1/3/02; retd 25/1/14.

1914-1928 **HUNT**, Alfred Daniel William. Born 1881 died 19??. Enl 2 Green Howards 10/8/95; WO (BM) 2 R W Kent R 26/1/14; retd 9/8/28.

1928-1938 **HALLOWAY**, Leslie John. Born 1896 died 19??. Enl 2 KRRC 12/1/11; WO1 (BM) 10/8/28; retd 7/5/38.

1938-1948 **JACKSON**, George Edward ARCM. Enl 1 R Innis Fus 21/3/24; WO1 (BM) 2 R W Kent R 8/5/38; WO1 (BM) 1 R W Kent R 1948; retd 19/4/50; BM North Rhodesian Police 1950-1953; DoM Royal Australian Air Force 1953.

BANDMASTERS OF
THE 1st BATTALION THE QUEEN'S OWN BUFFS, THE ROYAL KENT REGIMENT

1961-1965 **LYNES**, William Charles. Born 1928. For full details see The Queen's Royal Regiment.

1965-1966 **SPRY**, William Kenneth ARCM. Born 1934. Enl 1 R Berks R 11/11/50; WO1 (BM) QO Buffs 10/5/65; WO1 (BM) 2 Queens 31/12/66; retd 17/10/68.

BANDMASTERS OF
THE 2nd BATTALION THE QUEEN'S REGIMENT
(Queen's Own Buffs)

1966-1968 **SPRY**, William Kenneth ARCM. Born 1934. For full details see The Queen's Own Royal Buffs Regiment.

1968-1976 **GAME**, Daniel LGSM. Born 1936. Enl RA (Port) 21/8/51; WO1 (BM) 2 Queens 18/10/68; retd 1976.

1976-1984 **FRANCIS** Roger John. Born 1945. Enl 3 R Anglian 9/5/61; WO1 (BM) 2 Queens 23/7/76; WO1 (BM) Project Officer Queen's Division 1/4/84; retd 2/10/85.

BANDS OF THE

3RD BATTALION

THE QUEEN'S REGIMENT

THE ROYAL SUSSEX REGIMENT

1701	Earl of Donegall's Regiment of Foot	1853	East India Company's 3rd (Bengal European Light Infantry) Regiment
1751	35th Foot		
1782	35th (Dorsetshire) Foot	1858	3rd (Bengal Light Infantry) Regiment
1805	35th (Sussex) Foot		
1832	35th (Royal Sussex) Foot	1861	107th Bengal Infantry Regiment

1881	The Royal Sussex Regiment
1966	re-designated 3rd Battalion, The Queen's Regiment (Royal Sussex)
1968	re-designated 3rd Battalion, The Queen's Regiment

The first mention of the Band of the 35th Foot comes in an inspection report from June 1768, which states simply 'Has Band of Music'. Soon afterwards, the Regiment – which had originally been raised in Belfast – was given the county title of The Dorsetshire, a fact reflected in a report from 1790: 'Dorset Drums young – much dressed'. In 1805 this was changed to The Sussex Regiment, although the 35th did not visit that county until 1818 when, on its return from a posting in Malta, the Regiment marched with the Band and drums from Winchester to Brighton.

Two further battalions were formed in 1799 for service in the wars against Napoleon, but were disbanded after Waterloo, and it is not known whether they had any music beyond the usual fifes and drums.

In the infantry reforms of 1881, the surviving battalion of the 35th Foot was redesignated the 1st Battalion, The Royal Sussex Regiment, with the 107th Bengal Infantry forming the 2nd Battalion. This latter was the third regiment to be numbered the 107th, and had initially been raised for service with the Honourable East India Company.

By the time of the amalgamation, both constituent regiments had bandmasters appointed from Kneller Hall: Charles Hewitt of the 35th, and William Courtenay of the 107th – with whom he had previously served as a sergeant – were both appointed in 1875. Bandmaster Hewitt was to remain in his post for 22 years, and was held in such esteem that when the War Office decided at the turn of the century to have all regimental marches published by Messrs Boosey & Hawkes, he was one of just three musicians engaged to make the arrangements; the others were Mr M Retford and Mr J Kappey.

For much of his time with the 1st Sussex, however, Mr Hewitt had few enough opportunities to make music, and his immediate successors were not much more fortunate. The Battalion took part in the Nile campaigns of 1881-5, formed part of the detachment that vainly attempted to save General Gordon at Khartoum, and fought in the Boer War. During these conflicts, the bandsmen were on regimental duty, with no requirement for playing their instruments. And even though the Battalion was in India during the Great War, it was still involved in action, fighting in the Frontier Wars of 1915-17 and the Afghan War of 1919.

The 2nd Battalion Band enjoyed a more peaceful existence; despite twenty years of overseas postings from 1885 to 1906, it did at least function throughout this period as a Band. Then however came the Great War, and music ceased.

In the immediate post-war period, the bandsmen of the 2nd Sussex were again called upon to serve during the 1922 disturbances in the Middle East, but thereafter they returned home, and began to establish a fine concert reputation. This was enhanced with the arrival in 1935 of John Bailey as Bandmaster; under his baton, the Band increased its bookings and its status. The following programme, one of eighteen concerts given during the week of 11-17 July 1937 is characteristic of the period:

March	The Triumph of Right	Lovell
Overture	In Memoriam	Sullivan
Two Pieces	a) Humoreske	Dvorak
	b) Husarenitt	Spindler
Melodies from	The Belle of New York	Kerker

Interval

Cornet Solo	Ave Maria	Schubert
The Male Voice Choir in Part Songs and Novelties		
Excerpts from	The Maid of the Mountain	Fraser-Simpson
	Slavonic Rhapsody No 2	Friedmann
Regimental Marches	Sussex by the Sea	
	The Lass of Richmond Hill	
	Prince of Wales	
	National Anthem	

Mr Bailey stayed with the 2nd Sussex through the difficult war years, and was still Bandmaster

The Royal Sussex Regiment, c1910, Bandmaster C Hindmarsh   (RMSM)

2nd Battalion The Royal Sussex Regiment, 1942, Bandmaster J Bailey   (RMSM)

when the Battalion was disbanded in 1948, at which point he took over the amalgamated Band.

Following the upheavals of war and merger, came further disaster in 1950: a fire at Aqaba in Jordan destroyed the Band's complete library, its fanfare trumpets and virtually all its equipment, save for the marching band instruments. The resilience of the men in the face of such adversity, however, was remarkable, and the morning after the fire saw the Band on parade, playing 'Sussex by the Sea'.

The departure of Bandmaster Bailey in 1951 to become Director of Music of the Brigade of Gurkhas was a further blow to the Band, but fortunately his replacement was a suitable successor. Albert Kelly had a reputation not only as an excellent band trainer, but also as a gifted march composer; his most famous piece, 'Arromanches', is considered by many to be worthy of Kenneth Alford himself.

In 1959 the Regiment returned to Northern Ireland, the birth-place of the old 35th. Stationed in Lisburn, it was later awarded the Freedom of Belfast.

The same year saw Mr Kelly's appointment as Director of Music of the Pakistan Army. The new bandmaster, Donald Pryce, was also a composer of some note. His arrangement of 'Soldiers of the Queen' was adopted as the quick march of The Queen's Regiment in 1966, whilst an original piece,

'The Queensman', was much used as an unofficial second march, and ultimately became officially adopted as the quick march of The Queen's Division.

The Regiment had become part of the Home Counties Brigade in 1959, and in March 1966 Mr Pryce was appointed Bandmaster at the Brigade Depot.

Regimental Music

The quick march of the 1st Battalion was 'The Royal Sussex', a tune probably of French origin. Its association with The Sussex Regiment is believed to date from the battle of Quebec in 1775, when the 35th Foot routed the French Royal Roussillon Regiment of Grenadiers. In honour of that success, the white plume of the defeated French regiment was adopted; it is likely that the march was acquired at the same time, music often forming part of the spoils of victory.

The slow march was entitled 'Roussillon' in reference to the same event.

The quick march of the 2nd Battalion was 'The Lass of Richmond Hill', the words of which were written by a barrister, Leonard McNally, in praise of his future wife, Frances L'Anson, who lived at Hill House in Richmond, Yorkshire. The music was by James Hook, a prolific composer with more than two thousand songs to his credit.

A second march much used by the Regiment was 'Sussex by the Sea', a song composed in 1907 by W Ward-Higg, who gave a copy of it to Captain Roland Waitman, an officer of the 2nd Battalion who was engaged to his niece. The song was first performed in public at Ballykinlar Camp, Londonderry, where the Battalion was then stationed.

3rd BATTALION
THE QUEEN'S REGIMENT
(Royal Sussex)

1966	3rd Battalion, The Queen's Regiment (Royal Sussex)
1968	re-designated 3rd Battalion, The Queen's Regiment
1992	The Princess of Wales' Royal Regiment (Queen's and Royal Hampshire)

Roy Bedford was appointed Bandmaster of The Royal Sussex Regiment in March 1966; just a few months later, the Regiment became the 3rd Battalion, The Queen's Regiment. Under the leadership of both Mr Bedford and his successor, James Wood, the Band continued to maintain its high standards despite the organizational changes.

A six-month tour of Cyprus in 1972-3 proved a particular success, with the Band playing to contingents from the Commonwealth and Scandinavia. The performances of 'Soldiers of the Queen' and 'Sussex by the Sea' so impressed a Swedish officer, Lieutenant-Colonel Samelius, that he requested the two marches be played when his troops took over guard duties at the Royal Palace, Stockholm.

In 1978 Terence Davis, one of the most successful bandmasters of the Regiment, took over. The son of a former Army bandmaster – Arthur William Davies of the Royal Ulster Rifles – Mr Davis was later to rise to become Director of Music of the Royal Artillery, Woolwich.

The following year, however, saw the retirement of an equally distinguished figure, Band Sergeant Major George Beechey, who had joined The Middlesex Regiment in 1948 as a bandboy. Two years later, he had seen active service in the Korean War – one of the few British bandsmen involved in that conflict. When the 4th Battalion of The Queen's Regiment was disbanded in 1970, he was the Band Colour Sergeant, and transferred to the 3rd, where he completed 30 years of service.

With Mr Davis in command, the Band became a popular attraction in Germany in the early '80s; amongst the more prestigious engagements were three performances for Queen Margarethe II of Denmark within the space of eighteen months. During this period there was also a tour of Canada.

In 1982 Mr Davis was appointed Bandmaster to the Junior School of Music, The Queen's Division Depot, and was succeeded by Brian Cunningham. Under the reorganization of the music of The Queen's in 1984, the Band of the 3rd Battalion became the nucleus of the new Quebec Band, with Bandmaster Cunningham remaining in command.

Regimental Music

The quick march was 'Soldiers of the Queen' and the slow march was 'The Caledonian'. (For full details see 1st Battalion The Queen's Regiment.)

'The Royal Sussex March' and 'Sussex By The Sea' were still used as secondary marches. (For full details see The Royal Sussex Regiment.)

BANDMASTERS OF
THE 1st BATTALION
THE ROYAL SUSSEX REGIMENT

1875-1897 **HEWITT**, Charles William. Born 1848 died 1909. Enl 71 Ft 8/11/62; Sgt (BM) 35 Ft 1/7/75; retd 28/2/97.

1897-1904 **LEESON**, William Robert John. Born 1870 died 1931. Enl 1 King's Own R 23/4/84; WO (BM) 1 R Sussex R 1/3/97; retd 20/1/04.

1904-1909 **OLLERENSON**, Joseph. Born 1873 died 1940. Enl 2 Foresters 1/11/87; WO (BM) 1 R Sussex R 21/1/04; retd 25/3/09; BM 9 HLI (TA) 1922-1927.

1909-1922 **HINDMARSH**, Charles. Born 1873 died 1941. Enl R W Kent R 17/3/87; WO (BM) 1 R Sussex R 26/3/09; retd 21/1/22; WO1 (BM) 7 W York R (TA) 1922-1924; WO1 (BM) 6 E Surr R (TA) 1924-1929.

1922-1948 **GUILMANT**, Samuel Archibald. Born 1893 died 19??. Enl RA (Plym) 14/12/08; WO1 (BM) 1 R Sussex R 22/1/22; retd 1948.

1948-1951 **BAILEY**, John Patrick Curran LRAM ARCM. Born 1904 died 1986. For full details see 2nd Battalion.

1951-1959 **KELLY**, Albert Edward LRAM ARCM psm. Born 1914. Enl 3DG 24/9/29; tranf 4/7DG 29/9/44; WO1 (BM) 1 R Sussex R 7/1/51; retd 9/7/59; DoM Pakistan Army 1959-1963.

1959-1966 **PRYCE**, Donald Elwyn AmusTCL Born 1931. Enl RWF 11/6/46; WO1 (BM) R Sussex R 10/7/59; WO1 (BM) Home Counties Bde 10/3/66; WO1 (BM) Queen's Div Depot 31/12/66; WO1 (BM) Welsh Depot 1/5/70; Capt (DoM) Queen's Div (Queen's) 17/11/72; Capt (DoM) RE (Ald) 15/12/76; Capt (DoM) RE (Chat) 4/6/82; Maj (DoM) 17/11/84; retd 5/6/86; Maj (DoM) HAC 1986-9/92.

1966 **BEDFORD**, Roy. Born 1930. Enl 13/18H 12/3/45; WO1 (BM) 1 R Sussex R 10/3/66; WO1 (BM) 3 Queens 31/12/66; retd 18/8/71.

BANDMASTERS OF THE 2nd BATTALION THE ROYAL SUSSEX REGIMENT

1875-1887 **COURTNEY**, William. Born 1842 died 1927. Enl 107 Ft 9/1/57; Sgt (BM) 107 Ft 9/2/75; WO (BM) 1/7/81; retd 11/1/87.

1887-1898 **BUTLER**, Albert John. Born 1857 died 1950. Enl 68 Ft 16/3/72; WO (BM) 2 R Sussex R 21/1/87; retd 3/1/98.

1898-1903 **CROSSLEY**, John Gardiner. Born 1863 died 1932. Enl 83 Ft 27/3/77; WO (BM) 2 R Sussex R 1/1/98; retd 23/3/03.

1903-1914 **COLE**, John William. Born 1867 died 1946. Enl 1 R S Fus 12/1/83; WO (BM) 2 R Sussex R 24/3/03; retd 28/2/14. BM Duke of York's Royal Military School 1914-1932.

1914-1925 **MINNS**, Frederick Ernest. Born 1878 died 1950. Enl R Innis Fus 30/10/93; WO (BM) 2 R Sussex R 1/3/14; retd 31/5/25; BM Straits Settlements Police 1925-1935.

1925-1935 **POMPHREY**, Frank Harold. Born 1893 died 19??. Enl 20H 6/12/07; WO1 (BM) 2 R Sussex R 1/6/25; retd 5/12/35; DoM Governor of Madras Band 1935-1948.

1935-1948 **BAILEY**, John Patrick Curran LRAM ARCM. Born 1904 died 1986. Enl 1DCLI 25/5/19; WO1 (BM) 2 R Sussex R 15/12/35; WO1 (BM) 1 R Sussex R 1948; Capt (DoM) Gurkha Bde 1951; retd 10/60.

BANDMASTERS OF THE 3rd BATTALION THE QUEEN'S REGIMENT

1966-1971 **BEDFORD**, Roy. Born 1930. For full details see 1st Battalion The Royal Sussex Regiment.

1971-1978 **WOOD**, James. Born 1941. Enl KOYLI 27/7/57; WO1 (BM) 3 Queens 30/9/71; WO1 (BM) JLR badged 9/12L 1978; retd 2/8/81.

1978-1982 **DAVIS**, Terence Sean FTCL ARCM psm. Born 1951. Enl 2 R Anglian 24/10/66; WO1 (BM) 3 Queens 3/7/78; WO1 (BM) HQ Queen's Div 1/11/82; WO1 (BM) Queens (Alb) 9/85; Capt Deputy Chief Instructor RMSM 23/2/87; Capt (DoM) RAOC 15/1/90; Capt (DoM) RA (Wool) 3/5/92; Maj (DoM) 30/9/93.

1982-1984 **CUNNINGHAM**, Brian. Born 1951. Enl R U Rifles 26/9/66; trans IG 1976; WO1 (BM) 3 Queens 6/10/82; WO1 (BM) Queens (Queb) 1/5/84; WO1 (BM) serving with The Kohima (v) Band The Queen's Regiment TA 1990; retd 1/8/91.

The Royal Sussex Regiment, The Mall 1963   (RMSM)

THE MIDDLESEX REGIMENT
(Duke of Cambridge's Own)

1741	57th Foot	1787	77th Foot
1748	renumbered 46th Foot	1807	77th (East Middlesex) Foot
1756	59th Foot	1876	77th (East Middlesex) (Duke of Cambridge's) Foot
1757	57th Foot		
1782	57th (West Middlesex) Foot		

1881	The Middlesex Regiment (Duke of Cambridge's Own)
1966	re-designated 4th Battalion, The Queen's Regiment (Middlesex)

Raised in 1756, the 57th Foot had an establishment that included at the outset ten drummers. A review of the Regiment on 16 May 1771 by Lieutenant-General Dilkes in Phoenix Park, Dublin, recorded that this number had increased to a total of seventeen drummers and fifers, and refers to a newly formed 'Band of Musick', with musicians being employed at one shilling a day. By 1815, despite the usual fluctuations of wartime, the 57th had some 24 musicians, a total that probably includes drummers and fifers.

During the second Maori war in the 1860s the Band served with the Regiment in New Zealand, under the leadership of Italian bandmaster Philip Galea. Signor Galea won himself a reputation for, in the words of the *Taranaki Herald*, his 'vigorous exertions in promoting the cultivation of music among young people.' The same newspaper, however, had earlier found occasion to comment less favourably on the youthful exuberance of his charges: 'Such practical jokes as the throwing of hats and coats, and the squirting of liquids through an open window into a room full of ladies, show no wit, and are very unkind and ungentlemanly.'

The 77th Foot meanwhile had been raised in 1787 and could soon boast 26 drummers and two fifers. In the Crimean War 15-year-old Drummer MacGill won a French medal for valour for his capture of a Russian bugler.

When the military band of the 77th was formed is unclear, but it too followed the mid-19th century fashion for foreign bandmasters with the employment of Mr Cavallini, another Italian. Though he

BANDS OF THE

4TH BATTALION

THE QUEEN'S REGIMENT

2nd Battalion The Middlesex Regiment, India c1899, Bandmaster G Robertson (Eagles/Ogilby)

was later to serve with the 1st Worcesters, 2nd Borders and 2nd South Staffords, no record survives of his time with the Regiment, save for a water colour portrait.

The two regiments amalgamated to form The Middlesex Regiment in 1881. Shortly after, two further battalions were raised – the 3rd and the 4th – in response to the crisis of the South African War. Both had bands, though the battalions were disbanded in 1922. The two bandmasters were appointed to other bands, Mr Hudson to the 2nd Dorsets and Mr Mark to the 3rd Hussars.

In the early years of this century the Band of the 1st Battalion, under Bandmaster Imbusch, accompanied the men to India and Burma. Opportunities for serious music in the colonies were limited, but Mr Imbusch developed a series of novelty acts – parodies of village bands and of minstrels – that proved popular in regimental variety concerts. And, as ever, sport was also a key preoccupation of the musicians, with the Band's cricket team featuring several good players and achieving some local success.

Another distinguished athlete emerged from the 2nd Battalion Band during its overseas tour that lasted from 1919 to 1931. Bandsman F Turner, having won the Mile Championship of Malaya, went on in 1924 to win the All India Mile and Half-mile Championship in a record time.

That same year saw the departure of Bandmaster Cooke, who had been with the Battalion

since 1908 and who now took up a position as Director of Music of the Military Forces of His Highness The Sultan of Johore, serving in the rank of captain.

The 1st Middlesex had remained at home after the Great War, and the Band spent much of the '20s establishing itself as a popular fixture on the bandstands of such resorts as Southsea, Lowestoft, Brighton and Torquay. In 1925 it broadcast from Bournemouth and played at the British Empire Exhibition at Wembley, and in 1929 won press acclaim for its part in the Royal Tournament, when the Battalion recreated the Battle of Albuhera.

The 1st's only overseas service in this period was a one-year trip to China in 1927/28. Then 50 strong, the Band joined forces with the Band of the 1st Borderers for a tattoo in Shanghai in June 1927.

In 1931 the 2nd Battalion moved to Khartoum, where the Band found itself in more demand, as the regimental journal *The Die-Hards* notes:

In addition to the weekly Officers' Mess guest night we also play out here once a week in the NAAFI garden, on alternate Mondays at the Bristol Military Hospital, and once a month on the Officers' Mess lawn in the evening. So in spite of the lack of outside engagements . . . we are kept quite busy here.

Towards the end of the same year, the Battalion finally returned home, and for the remainder of the decade it remained in Britain. With greater opportunities for engagements, there evolved other combinations of musicians, including a dance-band in the style of Roy Fox and a male voice choir. Perhaps the most prestigious booking of the period came in July 1934 with a performance of the overture from *Die Meistersinger von Nürnberg* at Christ's College, Cambridge.

Within weeks of the 2nd's return, the 1st Middlesex had left for a long overseas tour of duty that took in Palestine, Egypt and Singapore before ending up in Hong Kong in 1937. Again the pursuit of sport was a crucial part of everyday life, though the Band Notes in *The Die-Hards* indicate that there were complicating factors:

> *The water polo season will be with us soon and if the cholera holds off this year, there is a strong possibility of us retaining the shield.*

The cholera, it appears, did hold off, but the Band's team was nonetheless knocked out in the second round of the competition. Success was instead found elsewhere, with the Band winning the platoon football and hockey tournaments and coming second in the cricket.

Despite these peaceful pursuits, the threat of conflict was growing, with Britain being dragged toward involvement in the Sino-Japanese war. The 1st Middlesex was amongst the battalions overrun in the valiant but doomed attempt to defend Hong Kong in December 1941. A memorial plaque in the chapel at Kneller Hall records that Bandmaster Kifford was killed in action at some point between 18 and 25 December 1941.

With the reorganization of the British Army in the aftermath of the Second World War, the 2nd Battalion disappeared in 1948. The Middlesex Band, however, remained a strong musical force; by the mid-'50s it could point to three of its former bandsmen having progressed to become bandmasters in their own right – Messrs Bayton, Plummer and Bently, then serving with the Lincolns, Glosters and Manchester Regiment respectively.

International commitments also continued. Stationed in Vienna, the Band played at various ceremonies in 1955 to mark the implementation of the Austrian State Treaty, and the handover from the International Guard. At the end of that year, a move was made to Cyprus, where terrorist activity was increasing. For the bandsmen there were military duties to be performed, as well as fortnightly concerts to be given at the NAAFI, these latter occasionally enlivened by celebrity visits from the likes of Professor Jimmy Edwards.

In the mid-'60s a tour of Northern Ireland enabled some bandsmen to broaden their musical experience by playing in the Belfast Studio Symphony Orchestra. Around the same time a trad jazz band – the Smoke City Stompers – became a regular and popular part of concert programmes. And the regimental tradition of male voice choirs survived also.

A more unusual musical combination was created in 1966, when the Band was stationed in British Guiana during the period when that country was achieving independence as Guyana. A local musician, Danny Sandiford from Georgetown, was recruited to create a steel band and proved such a success that, when the Regiment returned home, Lance-Corporal Sandiford – now a regular with the Corps of Drums – came with it. The Die-hards Steel Band soon became as popular with audiences in Britain as it had in Guyana.

Regimental Music

The quick march of the 1st Battalion was 'Sir Manley Power', named after a British General who, it is believed, found the march in a captured French position during the Peninsular War. Tradition has it

1st Battalion The Middlesex Regiment, 1952, Bandmaster F Jackson   (Eagles/Ogilby)

1st Battalion The Middlesex Regiment at Albuhera, 1964   (Eagles/Ogilby)

that the march was abandoned in 1851, whilst the 57th was in Dublin, on the orders of the General Officer Commanding, who considered it inappropriate for marching since it was 'all drum and damned noise'. Instead an arrangement of 'The Lass o' Gowrie' was adopted (for further details see The East Surrey Regiment), and this remained associated with the Regiment, though 'Sir Manley Power' did eventually return at the end of the century.

The 2nd Battalion used a quick step entitled 'Paddy's Resource'. It was written by the then Bandmaster of the 77th, Paddy O'Connor, whilst on active service during the Crimean War.

Other pieces used by the 57th included a slow march called 'The Highland March' – also known as 'The Gaelic March' – which was introduced in 1775

by a new Commanding Officer just arrived from the Argyll Highlanders, and a quick march 'The Jolly Die-hards', written by Bandmaster Moore.

A piece entitled 'The Caledonian March', or the March of the Die Hards 57th Regiment' was published in *The Gesto Book of Highland Music* in 1895. Despite its name, this has no connexion with 'The Caledonian' and is actually better known as 'Roussillon', the slow march of The Royal Sussex Regiment.

The 3rd Battalion used 'Sir Manley Power', and the 4th Battalion 'Paddy's Resource'.

When the 1st and 2nd Battalions amalgamated in 1948, an arrangement by Bandmaster Thirtle of 'Sir Manley Power' and 'Paddy's Resource' was authorized as the official quick march of the Regiment.

4th BATTALION
THE QUEEN'S REGIMENT
(Middlesex)

1966   redesignated 4th Battalion,
              The Queen's Regiment
1970   disbanded

In 1966 The Middlesex Regiment became the 4th Battalion (Middlesex) in the newly formed Queen's Regiment. John McShane, who had been Bandmaster for just five months at this stage, remained in his post until his retirement in 1969. His successor Peter Mallas, however, was the last bandmaster of the old Middlesex Regiment; the 4th Queen's was disbanded in 1970.

During its brief existence, the Band of the 4th Queen's served with its Battalion in Northern Ireland, shortly before the resurgence of the troubles in the province.

Keeping the Middlesex traditions alive, the Die-Hards Steel Band survived the disappearance of the battalion, moving to the 1st Battalion, The Queen's Regiment.

Regimental Music

The quick march was 'Soldiers of the Queen' and the slow march 'The Caledonian'. (For further details see 1st Battalion The Queen's Regiment.)

'Sir Manley Power', 'Paddy's Resource' and other tunes previously used by The Middlesex Regiment were still used as secondary marches. (For full details see The Middlesex Regiment).

BANDMASTERS OF
THE 1st BATTALION
THE MIDDLESEX REGIMENT

185?-1862 **GALEA**, Signor Philip. Sgt (BM) or Civ BM 57 Ft 185?; retd 1862.

1862-1865 **WALLACE**. Sgt (BM) 57 Ft (no other details known).

1865-1875 **MOORE**, Charles. Sgt (BM) 57 Ft 28/2/65; retd 31/7/75.

1875-1886 **COLEOPY**, Nicholas. Born 1848 died 1901. Enl 24 Ft 8/7/62; Sgt (BM) 57 Ft 1/8/75; retd 23/2/86.

1886-1887 **ROBERTSON**, George Pringle. Born 1860 died 1912. Enl 71 Ft 24/6/74; WO (BM) 1 Midd'x R 24/2/86; WO (BM) 2 Midd'x R 1887; retd 13/2/08.

1887-1890 **READ**, John. Born 1851 died 19??. For full details see 2nd Battalion.

1890-1897 **ALEXANDER**, George. Born 1861 died 1939. Enl 47 Ft 11/11/75; WO (BM) 1 Midd'x R 11/6/90; retd 18/2/97.

1897-1908 **IMBUSCH**, William James. Born 1865 died 1912. Enl 1 Dorset R 21/11/83; WO (BM) 1 Midd'x R 19/2/97; retd 20/11/08.

1908-1916 **HILLIER**, Thomas James. Born 1879 died 1948. Enl RA (Wool) 22/11/93; WO (BM) 1 Midd'x R 21/11/08; WO1 (BM) RA (Gib) 27/6/16; WO1 (BM) RA (Mtd) 3/6/20; retd 19/11/35.

1916-1931 **CLARK**, John William. Born 1886 died 19??. Enl 2 Cameronians 12/11/02; WO1 (BM) 1 Midd'x R 27/6/16; retd 11/4/31.

1931-1938 **JUDGE**, Albert Ernest. Born 1901 died 1964. Enl 1 Loyal R 4/8/15; WO1 (BM) 1 Midd'x R 12/4/31; retd 9/8/38.

1938-1941 **KIFFORD**, William Edward James ARCM. Born 1910 died 1941. Enl RWF 3/10/25; WO1 (BM) 1 Midd'x R 10/8/38; killed in action between 18-25/12/41.

1942-1949 **THIRTLE**, James Edward ARCM psm. Born 1913. Enl 8/11/28 R Scots; WO1 (BM) 1 Midd'x R 30/5/42; Lt (DoM) RMA (Sand) 9/4/49; Capt (DoM) RHG 24/2/54; retd 30/10/62 rank of Maj.

1949-1950 **BARNETT**, Louis Jack ARCM. Born 1914. For full details see The Black Watch.

1950-1960 **JACKSON**, Frederick Arthur LRAM ARCM. Enl 2 Ox & Bucks LI 4/12/35; WO1 (BM) 1 Midd'x R 26/4/50; retd 25/7/60.

1960-1966 **McSHANE**, John Henry ARCM. Born 1930. Enl 10H 16/6/47; WO1 (BM) 1 Midd'x R 26/7/60; WO1 (BM) 4 Queens 31/12/66; retd 13/1/69.

BANDMASTERS OF
THE 2nd BATTALION
THE MIDDLESEX REGIMENT

184?-184? **CAVALLINI**. Born 1807 died 1873. Civ BM 77 Ft 184?; Civ BM 29th Ft 184?; Civ BM 55 Ft 1854; Civ BM 80 Ft 1865; probably died in service.

184?-185? **O'CONNOR**, James. Born 182? died 1913. Enl 77 Ft 1836; Sgt (BM) 77 Ft 184?; retd 185?.

185?-186? **SERGEANT**, A. Sgt (BM) 77 Ft at some time during the 1850s/60s.

1863-1880 **PERRIE**, William. Enl 77 Ft 185?; Sgt (BM) 77 Ft 21/9/63; retd 19/7/80.

1880-1887 **READ**, John. Born 1851 died 19??. Enl 20H 11/9/66; Sgt (BM) 77 Ft 20/7/80; WO (BM) 1/7/81; WO (BM) 1 Midd'x R 1887; retd 10/6/90.

1887-1908 **ROBERTSON**, George Pringle. Born 1860 died 1912. For full details see 1st Battalion.

1908-1924 **COOKE**, Robert Arkley. Enl 2 KSLI 4/7/88; WO (BM) 2 Midd'x R 14/2/08; retd 21/2/24.

1924-1933 **CLIBBENS**, Herbert ARCM. Born 1893 died 19??. Enl Gren Gds 27/10/13; WO1 (BM) 2 Midd'x R 22/2/24; retd 24/3/33; WO1 (BM) 7 Midd'x R (TA) 1935-1939.

1933-1948 **DENNIS**, Carol Ernest ARCM. Born 1904. Enl WG 23/3/21; WO1 (BM) 2 Midd'x R 25/3/33; retd 1947.

Bandmaster G Robertson, 2 Midd'x

BANDMASTERS OF THE 3rd BATTALION THE MIDDLESEX REGIMENT

1901-1911 **CALTHORPE**, James Robert. Born 1870 died 1945. Enl 1 Lincoln R 16/4/84; WO1 (BM) 3 Kings 1/4/1900; WO1 (BM) 3 Midd'x R 1/11/01; retd 3/3/11.

1911-1922 **HUDSON**, George Edward. Born 1880 died 1942. Enl 2 KRRC 1/12/94; WO1 (BM) 3 Midd'x R 4/3/11; WO1 (BM) 2 Dorset R 6/11/22; retd 30/4/35.

BANDMASTERS OF THE 4th BATTALION THE MIDDLESEX REGIMENT

1900-1921 **HAWKINS**, William Frederick. Born 1870 died 19??. Enl 1 Loyal R 19/11/85; WO1 (BM) 4 Midd'x R 13/6/1900; retd 16/9/21.

1921-1922 **MARK**, Robert George. Born 1884 died 19??. Enl 3 R Fus 3/9/98; WO1 (BM) 4 Midd'x R 14/12/21; WO1(BM) 3H 22/5/22; retd 28/11/28; WO1 (BM) 4 Glosters (TA) 1928-1933.

BANDMASTERS OF THE 4th BATTALION THE QUEEN'S REGIMENT

1966-1969 **McSHANE**, John Henry ARCM. Born 1930. For full details see The Middlesex Regiment.

1969 **MALLAS**, Peter, ARCM. Born 1938. Enl RA (Wool) 4/9/59; WO1 (BM) 4 Queen's 15/1/69; QO Hldrs 1/7/70; WO1 (BM) Depot LI 15/6/77; Lt (L/Maj) (DoM) Sultan of Oman Land Force (badged LI) 4/2/80; retd 3/9/81; continued to serve as DoM Sultan of Oman Land Force, retiring 1982 in rank of Maj.

THE ALBUHERA AND QUEBEC BANDS OF THE QUEEN'S REGIMENT

On 31 March 1984 the Albuhera and Quebec Bands were formed to serve the three remaining battalions of The Queen's Regiment. Rather than amalgamate all three battalion bands and then split them into two, it was decided that the existing 1st Battalion Band under Bandmaster Phillip Hills would be renamed The Albuhera Band, and the 3rd Battalion Band under Bandmaster Brian Cunningham would become The Quebec Band.

All three bands paraded at Ebrington Barracks in Londonderry to mark the disbandment of the 2nd Battalion Band; the members were then transferred to the new bands.

THE ALBUHERA BAND

One of the first engagements of the new bands was a massed bands performance of the Queen's Division on Horse Guards Parade in the summer of 1985. The same year, The Albuhera Band began what was to become a restless process of touring with a move to Gibraltar. Whilst there, it also undertook two visits to Morocco. In 1986 members of the Band also visited the village of Albuhera on the Spanish/ Portuguese border, scene of the battle that gave the Band its name.

A posting to Minden followed in 1987, where the first Kneller Hall inspection of the new band, now under Bandmaster Ian Peaple, graded it as 'excellent'. The following year, the 70th anniversary commemorations of the Great War saw the men in Italy with a series of performances, parades and concerts. There were also trips to Bavaria, France and Denmark.

A return from Germany to Britain in 1991 did not prove an end to the Band's travels; there was still a tour of the Falklands to come.

In September 1992 The Queen's Regiment and The Royal Hampshire Regiment were amalgamated to become The Princess of Wales' Royal Regiment (Queen's and Royal Hampshire) with two battalions. The Albuhera Band with Bandmaster Jerry Young in command became the Band of the 2nd Battalion.

THE ALBUHERA AND QUEBEC BANDS OF THE QUEEN'S REGIMENT

THE QUEBEC BAND

The Quebec Band was also kept busy with international engagements, including a visit to Orleans in 1985 for a celebration of the life of Joan of Arc.

Following a tour of Denmark with the 1st Battalion, it was invited to the USA in 1989 for four weeks as part of a military exercise termed Exercise Trumpet Dance. During that time the musicians made a fleeting visit to Monterey in California, where they were the guests of 7th Infantry Division (Light). In April of that year they appeared on French Television and also gave concerts in Jersey.

The Band also made several appearances in military band spectaculars in Britain, in which Bandmaster Cunningham and his wife, Hildred, were featured as a vocal duo, singing songs from the war years.

1991 found the men in Cyprus, where for a time they became part of an Airfield Medical Reception Team. Their task was to unload casualities arriving from the Gulf War and either transport them to hospital or arrange to transport them back to the United Kingdom.

With the creation of The Princess of Wales' Royal Regiment (Queen's and Royal Hampshire) in 1992, the Quebec Band and the Band of The Royal Hampshire Regiment amalgamated to become the Band of the 1st Battalion, with Bandmaster Calum Gray in command.

BANDMASTERS OF THE ALBUHERA BAND

1984-1985 **HILLS**, Phillip Elvin, FLCM. Born 1947. For full details see 1 Queens.

1985-1987 **DAVIS**, Terence Sean FTCL ARCM psm. Born 1951. For full details see 3 Queens.

1987-1992 **PEAPLE**, Ian Roger. Born 1957. Enl RA (Mtd) 4/9/72; WO1(BM) Queens (Alb) 5/1/87; WO1 (BM) BW 1992; Capt (badged BW) Foundation Course Director RMSM 6/6/94.

BANDMASTERS OF THE QUEBEC BAND

1984-1990 **CUNNINGHAM**, Brian. Born 1951. For full details see 3 Queens.

1990-1992 **YOUNG**, Jeremy Rothwell BA BBCM. Born 1960. Enl DWR 1/10/82; WO1 (BM) Queens (Queb) 15/1/90; WP1 (BM) PWRR 1992; WO1 (BM) Queens (Norm) 1/8/94.

Right: The Quebec Band visit to Alamein   (RMSM)
Right below: 26th Battalion The Middlesex Regiment, Flixton Park 1916   (Turner)
Below: Bandmaster and Mrs B Cunningham
(B Cunningham)

26 Batt. Middlesex Band. Flixton Park. Aug. 1916.

THE ROYAL REGIMENT OF FUSILIERS

	1881	*1968*
5th Foot	Northumberland Fusiliers	1st Bn, Royal Regt of Fusiliers
6th Foot	Warwickshire Regiment	2nd Bn, Royal Regt of Fusiliers
7th Foot	Royal Fusiliers	3rd Bn, Royal Regt of Fusiliers
20th Foot	Lancashire Fusiliers	4th Bn, Royal Regt of Fusiliers

The 4th Battalion of The Royal Regiment of Fusiliers was disbanded in 1970.

In 1984 the Regiment chose to reduce from three bands to two, each with a larger establishment. The new bands were called the St George's Band and the Duke of Kent's Band.

The 3rd Battalion of The Royal Regiment of Fusiliers was disbanded in 1992.

THE ROYAL NORTHUMBERLAND FUSILIERS

1674	The Irish Regiment (also a 'Holland Regiment')
1751	5th Foot
1782	5th, or Northumberland Foot
1836	5th, or Northumberland Fusiliers
1881	The Northumberland Fusiliers
1935	The Royal Northumberland Fusiliers
1968	amalgamated to form The Royal Regiment of Fusiliers becoming 1st Battalion

When The Northumberland Fusiliers were inspected in 1755, it was reported that the 'Regiment has fifes'. Thirty years later there was still 'No Band', though it is believed that shortly afterwards a military band did come into existence.

There were certainly drums present at an early stage, with the establishment of the Regiment in the late 18th century including some 25 drummers. It was they who became responsible for upholding the regimental tradition of a third Colour: a green silk banner carried in celebration of the capture of a French Colour at the battle of Wilhelmstahl in 1762. When a royal order was issued in 1835 that 'no Regiment in His Majesty's service should be permitted to display a third Colour under any circumstances whatsoever,' a decision was taken to troop the banner only on St George's Day, with it being carried by the drums; it thus became known as the Drummer's Colour.

A further tradition born of the spoils of victory dates from the Indian Mutiny of 1857. The 1st Battalion of the Regiment had been on its way from Mauritius to Hong Kong when it was diverted to India to assist in the suppression of the rebellion. Following the relief of Lucknow, a bandmaster's baton was made from part of an ivory bedstead found in the Begum Kothee Palace, and a drummajor's staff from a silver stick in another palace.

Amongst those serving during the Mutiny was Thomas McGuire, who had joined the Band ten years earlier at the age of fourteen and who was awarded the campaign medal with two clasps. Also involved was a soldier named Ouzman, who was followed into the 5th by two sons, one of whom joined the Band whilst another – Thomas Ouzman –

BANDS OF THE

1ST BATTALION

THE ROYAL REGIMENT OF FUSILIERS

rose to be drum-major. Two of Thomas' sons extended the dynasty, with the elder also becoming drum-major.

A 2nd Battalion had been raised in 1799 and it too had a band. The earliest recorded bandmaster was Frederick Moran, appointed in 1861, though there are reports of a Mr Atkins serving as band sergeant from 1857 onwards.

The first known bandmaster of the 1st Battalion was William Dencer, who held the position from 1873 to 1896. During this time, the Battalion again spent much time in India and, with the recurring difficulties on the North-West Frontier, often found itself on the move at very short notice. The long marches were presumably borne by the men with the stoic endurance of the infantry, but contemporary accounts suggest that the Band's mascot – a dog named Mungo – was none too fond of this peripatetic existence. In 1883 the men marched 113 miles from Agra to Hapur, at which point Mungo disappeared, only to turn up back at base two days later; put on a train, Mungo again went AWOL, returning a further 135 miles back to Agra.

By 1889 the 1st Battalion was back in England, and the Band was giving concerts in Woolwich under the baton of a Mr Makepeace. Though he was not the bandmaster, Mr Makepeace was again conducting the orchestra two years later. It is possible that he was an officer or other member of the Regiment standing in for Mr Dencer, who we know was on sick leave during this period.

In 1891 the Band played for the visit to London of the German Emperor. After six hours on the steps of the Guildhall, the men marched more than ten miles back to Woolwich, playing wherever there was a sufficiently large crowd.

One of the most spectacular military band extravaganzas of the era was the Aldershot Torchlight Tattoo. In 1894 some fourteen bands, representing the four nations of the United Kingdom, played in the presence of Queen Victoria; Bandmaster Dencer conducted the Tattoo 'Zapfenstreich'.

Mr Dencer left in 1896 to become Bandmaster at Sandhurst and was replaced by Arthur Ivermee. Formerly a flautist in the Savoy orchestra under Arthur Sullivan, Mr Ivermee was also renowned as a xylophone-player and soon became a star turn in the battalion concert party known as St George's Minstrels.

1896 also saw the two battalions become the first in the Army to acquire the new aluminium bass drums from Messrs Potter of Aldershot.

When war broke out in South Africa, both bat-

Above: Bandmaster J Wallace, 2nd Battalion
The Northumberland Fusiliers, Aldershot 1905
(Eagles/Ogilby)
Right: 2nd Battalion The Royal Northumberland
Fusiliers, Bordon 1937, Bandmaster J Evans (RMSM)

talions were posted to that country, departing to the strains of 'British Grenadiers', 'Auld Lang Syne', 'Soldiers of the Queen' and 'The Girl I Left Behind Me'. It was a war that brought both casualties and honours: Band Sergeant J Hamilton of the 1st was killed at Modder River on 20 November 1899, whilst two weeks later Band Sergeant J Stone won the Distinguished Conduct Medal for his heroism in rescuing wounded soldiers under fire.

Also decorated was Mr Ivermee, who continued to command his Band despite being officially a non-combatant; he was awarded the Queen's South African Medal with the Cape Colony clasp. Though he survived the hostilities, however, Mr Ivermee was to fall victim to another of the hazards of Empire, dying of heat-stroke in Calcutta in 1906.

During the South African crisis, the Regiment raised a 3rd and a 4th Battalion. Though both disappeared in 1906, they did have bands, with the 3rd stationed in Blomfontein and the 4th in Limerick.

In 1914 the men again returned to active duty; in the words of Bandmaster Windram: 'Upon the outbreak of war the band, as such, of course ceased to exist. The NCO's and Bandsmen took their places as Regimental stretcher bearers, the boys and young men under age coming to the Depot at Newcastle.' One 2nd Battalion bandsman later wrote of the band playing for the troops as they left India for the war; '[then] we ourselves paraded to leave but there was no band to play us off.'

Under the leadership of Mr Windram, a Band was gradually rebuilt at the depot. Its rapid growth in confidence and competence was demonstrated in a concert given in February 1915, which opened with the national anthems of Belgium, France, Japan, Serbia and Russia, and went on to include:

March	Entry of the Gladiators	Fucik
Overture	The Jolly Bandits	Suppé
Waltz	Donna Wellen	Ivanovici
Selection	HMS Pinafore	Sullivan
Echo Novelty	Sizilietta	von Blon
Descriptive	Mill In The Forest	Eulenberg
	Three Light Pieces	Fletcher
Fantasia	Songs of Scotland	arr Godfrey
	National Anthem	

By June of the same year, the Band could boast 39 musicians and was giving promenade concerts. Meanwhile in France, some of the bandsmen were playing in the Brigade Band whenever suitable opportunities arose.

Between the wars, the 2nd Battalion was stationed for some years in Mesopotamia, before returning to York and – for the Band – the familiar round of seaside engagements. The 1st Battalion saw more of the world during this period, with postings in Germany, England, Bermuda, Jamaica and Egypt.

Bermuda, in particular, was a triumph for the Band, as a local newspaper reported:

The first appearance in Hamilton of the Band of the 1st Battalion The Northumberland Fusiliers was made on Thursday evening on the Terrace Roof, Hamilton Hotel, and an excellent impression was made by their playing . . . . The Band plays in tune and has a good tone. Beginning with Sousa's 'Stars and Stripes Forever', Mr Hollick led his men through a varied and popular list of old favourites, even to selections from that old Broadway hit of years ago, 'The Belle of New York'. Another favourite which he gave was the 'Blue Danube' waltz.

The Bandmaster of the 2nd Battalion from 1932 onwards was John Evans. It was he who, during the Second World War, had the task of creating a new band at the depot. Soon after the end of hostilities, he took the Band on a tour of the Far East, visiting Japan, Hong Kong and Singapore. When the 2nd Battalion was disbanded in 1947, Mr Evans transferred to the 1st, where he remained until his retirement in 1953. Few bandmasters this century could boast over two decades of service with a single regiment.

In 1954 the Regiment was posted to Kenya, then still troubled by the Mau Mau rebellion. On this occasion the Band was left behind, but the Corps of Drums formed a dance band to keep the troops entertained in its absence.

The '60s saw a variety of overseas postings, including Hong Kong, West Germany, Aden and Ethiopia. Amongst the more prestigious engagements in Germany were the Tattoo at the Berlin International Industries Exhibition (1962), the Berlin International Radio Exhibition (1963), the 20th Anniversary of the Liberation of Europe (1964) and several Berlin Military Tattoos.

Regimental Music

As with all Fusilier regiments, the quick march was 'The British Grenadiers' (For full details see Grenadier Guards).

In 1959 the Regiment also adopted 'Blaydon Races' as a second quick march. The earliest known use of the tune was in an 1862 pantomime, though it may well have originated prior to that date.

The slow marches were a troop entitled 'St George', believed to have been written by a former band-sergeant, and the patriotic song 'Rule Britannia'. The music for the latter was written by Thomas

Arne, with words by James Thompson and David Mallet, for a Masque titled 'Alfred', first performed in 1740. Its rapid popularity is partly attributable to its London premiere coming in 1745, when patriotic sentiments were being stirred up by the Jacobite rebellion.

1st BATTALION THE ROYAL REGIMENT OF FUSILIERS

1968   1st Battalion, The Royal Regiment of Fusiliers

In 1968 the Northumberland Fusiliers became the 1st Battalion of The Royal Regiment of Fusiliers. For the Band there was no major upheaval in the change; John Pope remained as Bandmaster for a further four years, and the close association with the county of Northumberland was fiercely preserved.

Historical connexions were further invoked with a posting to Gibraltar in the early '70s; The Irish Regiment, precursors of the 5th Foot, had been in the first garrison of the Rock back in 1713, when it was originally ceded to Britain under the Treaty of Utrecht.

In 1984 the Regiment decided that the establishment of 66 musicians could be more effectively organized in two bands rather than the existing three. The 1st Battalion Band was absorbed into the newly-formed St George's Band.

Regimental Music

The regimental quick march of the new regiment was originally 'The British Grenadiers' (for further details see Grenadier Guards). A specially commissioned march 'The New Fusilier', written by Derek Kimberley, then Bandmaster at the Fusilier Depot was introduced but it failed to replace 'The British Grenadiers' and became a second regimental march.

Top right: Bandmaster A Hollick 1st Bn R North'd Fus
(RMSM)

Right: Bandsmen of 1st Battalion The Royal Northumberland Fusiliers engaged on decontamination drill, Mersa Matruh 1936   (RMSM)

BANDMASTERS OF THE 1st BATTALION THE ROYAL NORTHUMBERLAND FUSILIERS

1873-1896 **DENCER**, William H. Born 1849 died 1907. Enl 1/79 Ft 26/8/69; Sgt (BM) 1/5 Ft 1/11/73; WO (BM) 1/7/81; WO (BM) RMC (Sand) 22/1/96; retd 23/8/99.

1896-1906 **IVERMEE**, Arthur. Born 1863 died 1906. Enl Gren Gds 12/2/76; WO (BM) 1 North'd Fus 22/1/96; died whilst serving 25/4/06.

1906-1914 **MOSS**, Arthur Napier. Born 1868 died 1930. Enl 1 Wilts R 23/8/83; WO (BM) 1 North'd Fus 26/4/06; retd 17/1/14.

1914-1930 **WINDRAM**, James Causley, LRAM psm. Born 1886 died 1944. Enl 1 Gordons 9/8/1900; WO (BM) 1 North'd Fus 18/1/14; Lt (DoM) Coldm Gds 23/11/30; Major Snr DoM Bde Gds 1942; killed in enemy action 18/6/44.

1930-1946 **HOLLICK**, Alexander, MBE LRAM. Born 1903 died 19??. Enl The Greys 17/1/17; WO1 (BM) 1 North'd Fus 23/11/30; retd 18/8/46; DoM Belfast Police 1946-1971.

1947-1953 **EVANS**, John Lionel ARCM. Born 1901 died 19??. For full details see 2nd Battalion.

1953-1959 **STONE**, Henry Francis. Born 1917. Enl 2 N Stafford R 4/7/32; transf 2 S Stafford R 22/8/40; WO1 (BM) Gold Coast Regt RWAFF 30/1/50; WO1 (BM) 1 R North'd Fus 28/12/53; retd 20/1/59.

1959-1963 **ALLEN**, William MBE ARCM psm. Born 1921 died 1987. For full details see 1 R S Fus.

1963-1968 **POPE**, John ARCM. Born 1933. Enl QDG 21/11/49; WO1 (BM) R North'd Fus 25/10/63; WO1 (BM) 1 RRF 23/4/68; WO1 (BM) RAC Jnr Ldrs 5/4/72; retd 4/73.

BANDMASTERS OF
THE 2nd BATTALION THE ROYAL
NORTHUMBERLAND FUSILIERS

1861-1878 **MORAN**, Frederick. Born 18?? died 1878. Enl 4 DG 18??; Sgt (BM) 2/5 Ft 1/12/61; died whilst serving 30/9/78.

1878-1886 **QUIGLEY**, Thomas John. Born 1849. Enl 1/19 Ft 24/11/63; Sgt (BM) 2/5 Ft 1/10/78; WO (BM) 1/7/81; retd 14/4/86.

1886-1906 **WALLACE**, Lewis. Born 1852 died 1918. Enl 1/5 Ft 16/3/66; WO (BM) 2 North'd Fus 15/4/86; retd 28/2/06.

1906-1916 **COOPER**, William Frederick. Born 1866 died 1937. Enl 1 HLI 5/1/81; WO (BM) 1 KOSB 1/12/92; WO (BM) 5 R Gar R 8/6/02; WO1 (BM) 2 North'd Fus 1/3/06; retd 3/1/16; BM Halifax Police 1916-1928; BM Royal Jersey Militia 1929-1936.

1916-1932 **STEFFEN**, Walter. Born 1886 died 19??. Enl 2 KRRC 14/11/1900; WO1 (BM) 2 North'd Fus 4/1/16; retd 13/11/32.

1932-1947 **EVANS**, John Lionel ARCM. Born 1901 died 19??. Enl 2 Welsh R 10/5/15; WO1 (BM) 2 North'd Fus 14/11/32; WO1 (BM) 1 North'd Fus 1947; retd 27/12/53.

BANDMASTERS OF
THE 3rd BATTALION THE ROYAL
NORTHUMBERLAND FUSILIERS

1900-1903 **SHEPHERD**, Richard James. Born 1872 died 1940. Enl 2 Dorset R 24/1/88; WO (BM) 3 North'd Fus 9/5/1900; WO (BM) 1 Dorset R 14/12/03; retd 31/7/10.

1903-1906 **STRONG**, George. Born 1861 died 1926. Enl 2 R Scots Fus 31/8/76; WO (BM) 1 Dorset R 17/12/98; WO (BM) 3 North'd Fus 14/12/03; retd 1/9/06.

Bandmaster R J Shepherd, 3rd Bn R North'd Fus

(RMSM)

BANDMASTERS OF
THE 4th BATTALION THE ROYAL
NORTHUMBERLAND FUSILIERS

1900-1906 **SMITH**, Albert Oscar. Born 1863 died 1936. Enl 14H 21/11/78; WO (BM) 4 North'd Fus 1/4/1900; WO (BM) King's Own R 28/11/06; retd 26/1/19; Professor saxophone and clarinet RMSM 1919-36.

BANDMASTERS OF
THE 1st BATTALION THE ROYAL
REGIMENT OF FUSILIERS

1968-1972 **POPE**, John ARCM. Born 1933. For full details see 1st Battalion.

1972-1977 **DOTT**, James. Born 1938. Enl 1 R Fus 7/3/53; WO1 (BM) 1 RRF 5/4/72; retd 14/1/78.

1977-1984 **MULKERN**, Timothy Paschal. Born 1944. Enl D and D 8/10/63; WO1 (BM) 1 RRF 20/11/77; retd 8/4/84.

THE ROYAL
WARWICKSHIRE FUSILIERS

1675	Vane's Regiment (in Dutch service)
1685	taken on the English establishment
1751	6th Foot
1782	6th (1st Warwickshire) Foot
1832	6th (Royal Warwickshire) Foot
1881	The Royal Warwickshire Regiment
1963	The Royal Warwickshire Fusiliers
1968	amalgamated to form The Royal Regiment of Fusiliers becoming 2nd Battalion

The date of the creation of the Band of the 6th Foot can be placed between 23 August 1771 and 19 May 1784; Inspection reports from those years comment respectively: 'No Band of Music' and 'Very good Band'. There had, of course, been drummers for some time before.

The size of the Band in its first years is unclear, but the demands placed upon the men – in terms of both military action and repeated upheaval – must have made it difficult to maintain any stability, let alone a reasonable standard of music. The men served in the ranks and as stretcher bearers in the Napoleonic Wars, and during the first quarter of the 19th century saw postings in England, Scotland, Ireland, Gibraltar, Spain, Portugal, Holland, France, Canada, the Cape, India and the East Indies.

The first known bandmaster was not appointed until Herr Claus in 1858, though he was certainly not the first, for the post is mentioned in the Standing Orders of 1846:

Section LIII
Band, Drums and Drummers

1 The band master has the immediate direction of the band, and reports to the president of the band committee, whenever any instrument is broken, or out of order.

2 No musician is ever to engage himself to play anywhere, without the consent of the President of the Band Committee.

3 When the band is directed to play at the mess, or at any public assembly, they are to be dressed regimentally.

4 The band master reports direct to the adjutant on all points connected with duty.

BANDS OF THE

2ND BATTALION

THE ROYAL REGIMENT OF FUSILIERS

1st Battalion The Royal Warwickshire Regiment, Quetta 1907, Bandmaster H Bradley   (Eagles/Ogilby)

5 The band master is considered the sole instructor of the band, subject only to the directions of the Commanding Officer and committee; no others are to interfere either in the practice, or public playing of the band.

6 The drum-major is to be obeyed as a sergeant, he is to keep the roster of the drummers and fifers.

Born in Germany in 1833, Herr Claus came to England with his father – Bandmaster of the 10th Hussars – and obtained his first position with an East India regiment at the age of just 19. It was when the Warwicks were posted to India in 1858 that he joined the Regiment, though it is probable that he remained a civilian throughout his career.

In common with the other senior regiments of foot, the 6th had a 2nd Battalion with its own Band, and in 1869 the first recorded bandmaster was appointed: Sergeant Mangelsdorf was a Kneller Hall graduate who had previously served with the 1st Battalion.

The first Bandmaster of the senior battalion to be appointed by Kneller Hall was Sergeant Wilcox.

He replaced Herr Claus in 1878, joining in time to accompany the Regiment from India to Aden, before it returned to Britain. The 1st's history of travelling continued – by the end of the century they had been posted to Malta and Egypt and again to India. One of the bandmasters to serve during this period was Edward Stebbing, who retired in 1891; thirty years later his son took up the baton of the 2nd Battalion.

For a brief period between 1898 and 1906, the Regiment had a 3rd and a 4th Battalion. Both had bands, with that of the 3rd being stationed in Malta and Bermuda. Meanwhile the bandsmen of the 2nd Warwicks were engaged upon more active service, acting as stretcher-bearers in the Boer War.

The Great War saw the musicians of the two surviving battalions join the ranks; with them disappeared the string sections that had been a feature of both.

After the War, the 2nd Battalion left for India, where it was visited in 1922 at Landi Kotal by the Prince of Wales. The following year Sidney Henwood took over as Bandmaster; one of his first tasks was to organize a Remembrance Day commemoration in Nasirabad, as described in the regimental magazine *The Antelope*:

> After dark, under the baton of Bandmaster S W Henwood, the band of the 10/6th Rajputana Rifles joined our band and the concerted piece – The Battle of Waterloo – drew applause from all. The scene was impressive. Above, the quiet sky – below, the band of the Rajputana Rifles massed in the centre of the square and then, appearing from the four corners in turns, we saw the Band and Drums of the 6th Royal Regiment march into the centre lit up by torches carried by Indian torch-bearers. The crack of blank ammunition, the whistle of rockets, and the roar of cheers, ended a memorable day – a day of great sounds and a greater silence.

India in the '20s provided opportunities for a variety of engagements, and both the military and dance bands were employed at venues such as the Royal Bombay Yacht Club, the Japanese Legation and the Royal Western India Golf Club at Nasik. Somewhat less formal was a booking reported by the *Times of India* in December 1929:

> The Band of the 2nd Battalion The Royal Warwickshire Regiment, which has been playing under the direction of Mr S W Henwood at the Capital Cinema, Bombay, since Saturday, has proved a wonderful attraction. The Regimental Band is known and deservedly popular among music lovers of this city. No more suitable prologue to Tommy Atkins we think could have been selected than The Battle of Waterloo.
>
> During the screening of the film the Band played various British Regimental airs.

The same newspaper suggests elsewhere the repertoire of the era, mentioning the second movement of Beethoven's 'Moonlight Sonata' and the suite from Greig's *Sigurd Jorsalfar*. For the Kneller Hall inspection of 1929, the pieces chosen were Drysdale's overture 'Tam O'Shanter' and a selection from Wagner's *Rienzi*.

The 1st Battalion, meanwhile, was stationed at Woking during the '20s, playing at the Aldershot Searchlight Tattoo and various holiday resorts.

In 1931 the two battalions effectively exchanged postings, with the 2nd returning home and the 1st journeying to India. The musicians of the latter were reportedly far from impressed by the local standard of repair, having been used to the service provided by Boosey & Hawkes; they were particularly bemused by an invoice for the following instruments:

1 slight trum bum, 2 claronut, 1 carnut, 1 bess, 1 E.Phoniaum, 1 Clarionut, 1 B Phlat Saxiphone, half dozen O.B.Reads.

Back home the Band of the 2nd Battalion interrupted its schedule of seaside engagements to play at the 1937 Coronation Procession. According to *The Antelope*, 55 members of the Band and Drums travelled from Tidworth to London by train, each carrying by way of sustenance 'two packets of marching chocolate, two packets of Horlicks tablets and four cubes of Tate's sugar.' The following year the Band appeared at the Empire Exhibition at Ibrox Stadium.

During the Second World War the 2nd Battalion, accompanied by most of its bandsmen, fought in the retreat to Dunkirk, suffering heavy casualties. The 1st remained in India.

Following the reduction to a single battalion, a need for more musicians was answered with the re-forming in 1949 of the 7th Battalion Band. Though strictly a volunteer affair, the standard reached was so high that within a few months the men were carrying out official regimental duties.

The 1st Battalion was stationed for a while in Austria, proving a great success with the inhabitants of Graz, before returning to England. For a short period all four bands of the Midland Brigade were home at the same time, and the Warwicks joined forces with the Lincolns, the Leicesters and the Sherwood Foresters for massed performances at a number of venues throughout the Midlands.

From 1954 the Band was again on the move, with a series of postings to Suez, Cyprus, Hong Kong and Germany.

A single day in May 1962 saw the Band undertake two prestigious engagements, playing when the Queen opened the Civic Centre in Birmingham and then moving on to Coventry for the opening ceremony of the new Cathedral.

That same year the Midland Brigade was renamed the Forester Brigade, but it was a short-lived designation and, following one last massed band parade at the Royal Show in Newcastle in 1963, the Warwicks became part of the Fusilier Brigade. Five years later The Royal Regiment of Fusiliers brought together the four existing regiments, with the Warwicks becoming the 2nd Battalion.

Regimental Music

As the Royal Warwickshire Regiment did not become Fusiliers until 1963, they did not use 'The British Grenadiers' but had their own quick march 'The Warwickshire Lads'. This march was an adaptation of a song of the same name, composed for the Shakespeare Jubilee celebrations at Stratford-upon-Avon in 1769. The music was written by Charles Dibben and the words are attributed to David Garrick. The opening two verses are:

Ye Warwickshire lads and ye lasses
See what at our Jubilee passes,
Come revel away, rejoice and be glad
For the lad of all lads was a Warwickshire lad
  Warwickshire lad
  Ever be glad,
For the lad of all lads was a Warwickshire lad.

Be proud of the charms of your country,
When nature has lavished her bounty;
Where much she has given, and some to be spared,
For the bard of all bards was a Warwickshire bard
  Warwickshire bard,
  Never paired,
For the bard of all bards was a Warwickshire bard.

An officer of the regiment, Lieutenant W F MacBean (or McBean) composed a slow and quick march around 1782. These were known simply as 'MacBean's Slow March' and 'MacBean's Quick March'; the former became the official slow march for the regiment.

Fanfare trumpeters of 1st Battalion The Royal Warwickshire Regiment, Egypt 1955   (Eagles/Ogilby)

2nd BATTALION, THE REGIMENT OF FUSILIERS

1968   2nd Battalion, The Royal Regiment of Fusiliers

The 1968 re-organization did not impact directly upon the Band, and WO1 Roy Fitch remained as Bandmaster for a further two years, before moving to the Light Infantry.

His replacement was Rodney Parker, who took the Band to Canada in 1973 for six weeks as guests of Princess Patricia's Light Infantry Band.

With the re-structuring of the Fusilier Bands in 1984, the musicians of the 2nd Battalion were absorbed into the St George's Band.

Regimental Music

The regimental quick march of the new regiment was originally 'The British Grenadiers' (for further details see Grenadier Guards). A specially commissioned march 'The New Fusilier', written by Derek Kimberley, then Bandmaster at the Fusilier Depot was introduced but it failed to replace 'The British Grenadiers' and became a second regimental march.

Bandmaster D McNeil, 1st Battalion, The Royal Warwickshire Regiment (RMSM)

BANDMASTERS OF THE 1st BATTALION THE ROYAL WARWICKSHIRE REGIMENT/FUSILIERS

1858-1878 **CLAUS**. Born 1833. German Civ BM East India Regt 1852; Civ BM 1/6 Ft 1858; retd 1878.

1878-1880 **WILCOX**, William H. Sgt (BM) 100 Ft 9/2/75; Sgt (BM) 100 Ft 9/2/75; Sgt (BM) 1/6 Ft 1/6/78; retd 29/1/80.

1880-1891 **STEBBING**, Edward R. Born 1845 died 1933. Enl 2/11 Ft 30/6/59; Sgt (BM) 1/6 Ft 1/3/80; WO (BM) 1/7/81; retd 1/11/91.

1891-1898 **McNEIL**, Duncan. Born 1863 died 1915. Enl Camerons 7/12/87; WO (BM) 1 R Warwicks 2/11/91; retd 1/12/98.

1898-1910 **BRADLEY**, Henry. Born 1864 died 1935. Enl 44 Ft 30/11/78; WO (BM) 1 R War R 7/12/98; retd 8/2/10; BM 5/6 R War R (TA) 1910-1928.

1910-1931 **HARTMANN**, Cecil August. Born 1874 died 1953. Enl 1 R Sussex R 24/8/91; WO (BM) 1 R Warwick R 9/2/10; retd 8/2/31; BM 1 Hertfordshire Regt (TA) 1932-1939.

1931-1937 **LAWTON**, William Henry ARCM. Born 1901 died 19??. Enl 1 Foresters 20/3/17; WO1 (BM) 1 R Warwick R 9/2/31; retd 17/9/37.

1937-1948 **PARKER**, Charles Owen ARCM. Born 1905 died 1982. Enl 2 KOSB 11/5/19; WO1 (BM) 1 R Warwick R 18/9/37; retd 1948.

1948-1950 **SAVAGE**, George LRAM ARCM. Born 1907. For full details see 2nd Battalion.

1950-1959 **HILLING**, Robert Frederick ARCM. Born 1914. Enl 2 KRRC 14/8/28; WO1 (BM) 1 R Warwick R 9/8/50; WO1 (BM) Forester Bde 16/2/59; retd 9/6/59.

1959-1965 **KIMBERLEY**, Derek Richard MBE FTCL LRAM LGSM ARCM psm. Born 1931. Enl 1 R Hamps 6/11/45; WO1 (BM) 1 R War R 16/2/59; WO1 (BM) Fus Bde 14/3/65; WO1 (BM) Fus Depot (badged RRF) 23/4/68; Capt (DoM) RTR (Alamein) 14/12/69; Maj (DoM) Gren Gds 28/3/77; Lt Col (DoM) 27/11/84; Snr DoM Household Division 1986; retd 30/4/87.

1965-1967 **PARKINSON**, James Munro ARCM. Born 1933. Enl RTR 12/7/50; WO1(BM) 1 R Warwick R 14/3/65; retd 4/9/67.

1967-1968 **FITCH**, Frederick Roy LRAM ARCM psm. Born 1930 died 1988. Enl 15/19H 11/2/46; WO1 (BM) 10H 26/5/59; WO1 (BM) 1st King's African Rifles (Malawi) 23/6/64; WO1 (BM) 2 RRF 9/2/67; WO1 (BM) LI Depot 2/11/70; Capt (DoM) 1/2/74; Capt (DoM) RTR (Alamein) 31/3/77; Maj Snr DoM BAOR Apr 84; retd 17/4/85.

BANDMASTERS OF
THE 2nd BATTALION THE ROYAL
WARWICKSHIRE REGIMENT/FUSILIERS

1869-1878 **MANGELSDORF**, C. Enl 1/6 Ft 18??; Sgt (BM) 2/6 Ft 8/6/69; retd 30/4/78.

1878-1883 **MORELLI**, Albert. Sgt (BM) 76 Ft 28/2/65; Sgt (BM) 2/6 Ft 1/5/78; WO (BM) 1/7/81; retd 29/5/83.

1883-1894 **MALLANDAINE**, Alfred. Born 1851 died 1936. Enl 1/20 Ft 11/12/65; WO (BM) 2 R Warwick R 30/5/83; retd 24/5/94.

1894-1911 **COCKING**, John Thomas. Born 1867 died 1929. Enl 1 Wilts R 30/10/81; WO (BM) 2 R Warwick R 25/5/94; retd 31/7/11; BM 79th Royal Canadian Highlanders 1911-1927; BM Royal Jersey Militia 1927-1929.

1911-1923 **STEBBING**, Edwin Armstrong DCM. Born 1876 died 19??. Enl 2 Devon R 30/4/91; WO (BM) 2 R Warwick R 1/8/11; retd 24/1/23; DoM Governor of Bombay's Band 1925-1935.

1923-1935 **HENWOOD**, Sidney William MBE. Born 1898 died 19??. Enl 1 RWF 17/10/13; WO1 (BM) 2 R Warwicks R 25/1/23; DoM British Guiana Militia 4/35; retd 1965.

1935-1948 **SAVAGE**, George LRAM ARCM. Born 1907. Enl 8H 15/11/23; WO1 (BM) 2 R Warwicks R 5/4/35; WO1 (BM) 1 R Warwicks R 1948; retd 8/8/50.

BANDMASTERS OF
THE 3rd BATTALION THE ROYAL
WARWICKSHIRE REGIMENT

1898-1907 **HAYWARD**, Joseph Henry. Born 1864 died 1912. Enl 2 R Hamps 4/2/80; WO (BM) 3 R Warwick R 1/4/98; WO (BM) 2 Leicester R 23/3/07; retd 18/2/08.

BANDMASTERS OF
THE 4th BATTALION THE ROYAL
WARWICKSHIRE REGIMENT

1900-1906 **MATTHEWS**, John. Born 1872 died 19??. Enl 1 Welsh R 2/2/87; WO (BM) 4 R Warwick R 1/4/1900; WO (BM) 1 Queen's R 13/11/06; retd 31/12/14.

BANDMASTERS OF
THE 2nd BATTALION THE ROYAL
REGIMENT OF FUSILIERS

1968-1970 **FITCH**, Frederick Roy LRAM ARCM psm. Born 1930 died 1988. For full details see 1st Battalion.

1970-1976 **PARKER**, Rodney James FTCL ARCM psm. Born 1941. Enl Wilts R 26/8/57; WO1 (BM) 2 RRF 2/11/70; WO1 (BM) Depot Queen's Div 26/7/76; Capt (DoM) PoW Div (badged DERR) 7/11/77; Capt (DoM) RAOC 16/3/81; Capt (DoM) Gurkhas (badged 2 GR) 9/12/83; Maj (DoM) Gren Gds 16/2/87; Maj Snr DoM BAOR 13/6/88; Maj i/c Jnr Trg RMSM 17/2/91; retd 1/9/92; DoM Royal Yeomanry 1993/93; Lt Col (DoM) 1/4/94.

1976-1984 **DODD**, John H. Born 1945. Enl Coldm Gds; WO1 (BM) 2 RRF 26/7/76; retd 10/12/85.

The Royal Warwickshire Regiment,
Bandmaster D R Kimberley 1962 (RMSM)

THE ROYAL FUSILIERS
(City of London Regiment)

1685	Our Royal Regiment of Fuziliers; also Our Ordnance Regiment
1689	7th (Royal Fusiliers)
1881 (May)	The City of London Regiment (Royal Fusiliers)
1881 (July)	The Royal Fusiliers (City of London Regiment)
1898	3rd Battalion raised
1900	4th Battalion raised
1922	3rd & 4th Battalions disbanded
1968	amalgamated to form The Royal Regiment of Fusiliers becoming 3rd Battalion

Raised at the time of Monmouth's rebellion, The Royal Fusiliers had drums and fifes from the outset, and there are reports of hautboys in use from as early as 1686. The first definite mention of a band, however, dates from 1769, when an inspection report commented: 'Music but indifferent.' A similar report three years later makes no judgement on quality and confines itself to a simple statement of fact: 'Band of Music'.

In 1789 the Duke of Kent (the son of George III and father of Queen Victoria) became Colonel of the Regiment, and when he was subsequently appointed Governor of Gibraltar, the Fusiliers formed part of the garrison. Under his leadership, the Band acquired a reputation of being the most ornately dressed musicians in the Army, with a specially designed uniform of white with blue facings richly laced with gold. Swords were worn in brass scabbards, and the bass drum, cymbals and Jingling Johnny were played by black percussionists wearing turbans.

The musical instrumentation of the period is referred to in a 1790 letter written by the Duke of Kent: 'The plan for the harmony of the Regiment according to the Orders of His Britannic Majesty is of four Clarinettes, 4 Cors, 4 Bassoons and un [sic] Serpent.'

An unusual record survives of one of the characters from the early 19th century, in the form of a memorial tablet in the churchyard of St George's, Mossley, Lancashire. Beneath a long list of battle honours is the inscription:

BANDS OF THE

3RD BATTALION

THE ROYAL REGIMENT OF FUSILIERS

'BAND' 1ˢᵗ BATTN: ROYAL FUSILIERS. 1920.

SACRED TO THE MEMORY OF
John Whitworth

of Mossley, late of Manchester, who departed this life on the second day of August, AD 1848, in the 64th year of his age. He entered the Service as a drummer in the year MDCCCIV, and was discharged in MDCCCXXV. He was a Field Bugler during the Peninsular and Pyrenees Wars, and late Drum Major to the 7th Royal Fusiliers.

There follows a six-verse poem that includes the lines:

*His drum and bugle's voice with warlike cheers
To action roused the Royal Fusiliers,
And by his valour gained his countries love
In glorious battles, as inscribed above.*

REST, WARRIOR, REST.

The first recorded bandmaster is Henry Winterbottom, who served with the 1st Battalion between 1845 and 1850 before moving on to the 18th Foot. During his incumbency the Regiment spent some time in Africa, and a report from 1847 talks of the famous chief Macomo listening intently as the Band played polkas and a selection from Donizetti's opera *Lucrezia Borgia.*

Following Mr Winterbottom's departure, there is a gap in the records before the arrival in 1865 of the first Kneller Hall appointee, Sergeant Croker, formerly a musician in the Regiment. Meanwhile the 2nd Battalion had sent Sergeant Cleary to Kneller Hall to be trained as a bandmaster; he completed his course and returned to the Regiment in 1862.

A later bandmaster of the 2nd Battalion was Frederick James Colman, who took over in 1880. His father had held a similar position with the 3rd Battalion, King's Royal Rifle Corps in the 1860s, and – it is believed – his grandfather with the 1st Battalion of the 4th Foot in the 1830s. Mr Coleman upheld the family tradition in impressive fashion, remaining in his post until his retirement in 1907 at the age of 51; he subsequently took over the Band of the Royal Guernsey Militia.

The Coleman era, of course, included the Boer War, and the bandsmen of the 2nd Battalion served as stretcher-bearers and as rank-and-file soldiers. The 1st Battalion, meanwhile, was stationed in Nasirabad, India.

In 1898 a 3rd Battalion was formed, to be followed two years later by a 4th. Both had Bands from the outset and, unlike most of the new battalions raised at the time, both survived through to 1922. The 3rd

Battalion existed long enough to develop a string band. Even beyond these four regular battalions, both the 5th and 6th Battalions – comprising volunteers – had Bands capable of taking on regimental engagements when required.

The 2nd Battalion took part in the famous 1911 Delhi Durbar to celebrate the accession of George V, and Coronation Durbar Medals were presented to Bandmaster Vickers, Band Corporal A Tuersley and Bandsman A Hole.

Following the upheavals of the Great War, and the disbandment of the 3rd and 4th Battalions, the two surviving regular Bands returned to a succession of postings through the Empire. The 2nd Battalion was in Aden in the early '20s, the men playing for the visit of the Prince of Wales and giving a series of classical concerts and Beating Retreats; these latter proved especially popular and gained the Drums the nickname 'Tom Tom Wallahs' from the local population.

The 1st Battalion was in Ireland and then India, where Bandmaster Wood had the idea of dressing the small orchestra in old Fusiliers' uniforms of the Napoleonic era. Music had to be re-written to allow for the modern line-up, but the venture was hugely successful and proved more popular than the military band itself.

The Band, of course, continued to fulfil its official engagements, and a typical weekly routine comprised:

Sunday	1000-1100	Church
	1115-1215	Playing to troops
Monday	1700-1800	Playing to troops
Tuesday	2000-2230	Officers Mess
Friday	1500-1900	Playing at Dog Meeting

In 1926 the Band of the 2nd Battalion was invited for the first time to play in the Lord Mayor's Procession, a surprisingly late debut for the City of London Regiment. Many years later, in 1993, the combined St George's and Duke of Kent's Bands would play in the procession for the last time before Fusilier bands finally disappeared from the Army.

Other engagements back home were undertaken by the Band in the late '20s, including ten days at Bognor Regis playing for the King, but most of the time it remained with the 2nd Battalion, then stationed in Germany. When the troops were pulled out of that country in 1929, the Fusiliers were appropriately the last to leave: in 1918 they had been the first infantry to cross the Rhine. At a ceremony in Weisbaden, Bandmaster Tulip conducted the last

Bandmaster G Quick, 1st Battalion The Royal Fusiliers, 1941 (Eagles/Ogilby)

British Band to play on German soil until 1945.

Further memories of the Great War were stirred on 21 May 1938, when King Leopold III of Belgium unveiled a Rose Window and Tablet at St Martin's Cathedral in Ypres. The 2nd Battalion Band played at the ceremony and later at the civic function in the Town Hall, with the following programme:

March	Amporita Roca	Texidor
Selection	Cavalcade	Coward
Suite	Othello	Coleridge-Taylor
Selection	Merrie England	German
Xylophone Duet	Two Imps	Alford
Waltz Medley	The Golden Waltz	arr Winter
Echo Cornet	Sizilietta	von Blon
Selection	Frederica	Lehar
Song March	Tipperary	Judge
	Marche de Normande	
	British Grenadiers	
	Rule Britannia	
	La Brabanconne	
	God Save the Queen	

By late 1938 war was becoming inevitable and the bandsmen of the 2nd Battalion were kept busy digging air raid shelters, whilst those of the 1st were training to become the Intelligence Section of their Battalion. When war did come and the men went off to regimental duties, Dick Tulip returned to the depot at Hounslow to build a new Band. The level of activity is indicated in his diary, which includes the following typical week from February 1944:

6 Sunday	08.40	Free Church
	09.50	Church of England followed by march past
	11.15	Passing-out parade
7 Monday	15.30	Concert Cadet Recruiting Centre, Wrotham
	20.00	Ensa Concert, NAAFI
8 Tuesday	13.00	Concert, Brigade Headquarters
	20.00	Concert, RASC Remsing
9 Wednesday	10.00	Concert, Royal Artillery
	13.00	Concert, Royal Artillery
	15.30	Concert, Royal Signals
	18.30	Boxing, Central Hall
10 Thursday	13.00	Concert, Sherwood Foresters
11 Friday	09.00	Drill Parade
	13.00	Dance Band
12 Saturday	10.00	Passing-out parade rehearsal, Royal Berkshire Regiment
	12.00	Passing-out parade, Royal Berkshire Regiment
	14.45	Play draft off, Sherwood Foresters

With the disbandment of the 2nd Battalion in 1947, Mr Tulip moved to Kneller Hall to become Professor of Piano. The surviving Band, under Bandmasters Quick, Blaber and Hicks, had considerable success at home and abroad as a concert band and as a marching combination.

Regimental Music

'The British Grenadiers' became the official quick march for all Fusilier regiments in 1882, though the 7th Foot had been using it since around 1835. (For further details see Grenadier Guards).

George Le Brunn composed the music-hall song 'Fighting with the 7th Fusiliers' around 1882 and it soon became a favourite of the Regiment. It was used as a second match for many years and in 1966 an arrangement by Bandmaster Brian Hicks was published as the official march to be played before 'British Grenadiers'.

The slow march was 'Normandie', a piece composed in Canada in 1791.

It was customary for the Band to play the patriotic song 'Rule Britannia' before the National Anthem to commemorate the fact that companies of the Royal Fusiliers served as marines in 1688 and 1756. (For further details see Royal Northumberland Fusiliers).

3rd BATTALION THE ROYAL REGIMENT OF FUSILIERS

1968   3rd Battalion, The Royal Regiment of Fusiliers

On St George's Day 1968 The Royal Fusiliers (City of London Regiment) became the 3rd Battalion, The Royal Regiment of Fusiliers. The following year, Bandmaster Brian Hicks left, ultimately to become Major Hicks of the Scots Guards. His replacement, Peter Hannam, was to have an equally distinguished career, rising to the rank of Lieutenant-Colonel and becoming the Senior Director of Music of the Household Division.

When the Regiment decided to re-structure its music in 1984, most of the 3rd Battalion Band joined the new Duke of Kent's Band.

Regimental Music

The regimental quick march of the new regiment was originally 'The British Grenadiers' (for further details see Grenadier Guards). A specially commissioned march 'The New Fusilier', written by Derek Kimberley, then Bandmaster at the Fusilier Depot was introduced but it failed to replace 'The British Grenadiers' and became a second Regimental march.

Top: The Royal Fusiliers' farewell march through London prior to amalgamation. Bandmaster B Hicks
(Eagles/Ogilby)

Above: 2nd Battalion The Royal Fusiliers, c1946, Bandmaster R Tulip (Tulip)

BANDMASTERS OF THE 1st BATTALION THE ROYAL FUSILIERS

1845-1850 **WINTERBOTTOM**, Henry. Born 18?? died 1856. Civ BM 1/7 Ft 1845; Civ BM 1/18 Ft 1850; MoB RM (Wool) 1854; retd 1856.

1850-1865 Bandmaster(s) not known

1865-1869 **CROKER**, J. Enl 1/7 Ft 185?; Sgt (BM) 1/7 Ft 1/5/65; retd 9/8/69.

1869-1889 **MORAN**, Thomas. Born 1836 died 1911. Enl 1/21 Ft 8/11/54; Sgt (BM) 1/7 Ft 10/8/69; retd 16/4/89.

1889-1902 **MILLMAN**, Frederick. Born 1856 died 1916. Enl 2/22 Ft 19/1/71; WO (BM) 1 R Fus 17/4/89; retd 2/5/02.

1902-1909 **O'KEEFE**, Ernest Arthur Hugh. Born 1876 died 1909. Enl 2 R Ir Fus 19/3/92; WO (BM) 1 R Fus 3/5/02; died whilst serving 22/1/09.

1909-1914 **WALLACE**, Arthur Leonard. Born 1878 died 1947. Enl 2 York & Lanc R 30/5/93; WO (BM) 1 R Fus 23/1/09; retd 29/5/14; BM Trinidad Police 1914-1936.

1914-1926 **WOOD**, Frederick Lewis. Born 1886 died 1933. Enl 4 KRRC 27/11/06; WO (BM) 1 R Fus 30/5/14; retd 23/2/26; BM North Rhodesian Police 5/29; retd 6/2/33.

1926-1928 **BUTT**, Albert James. Born 1897 died 1928. Enl 2 Essex R 12/4/17; WO1 (BM) 1 R Fus 24/2/26; died 29/6/28 whilst still serving.

1928-1937 **HULL**, Harold Ernest. Born 1894 died 1953. Enl 1 E York R 10/1/10; WO1 (BM) 1 R Fus 30/6/28; retd 14/10/37; DoM Zanzibar Police 1939-1953.

1937-1952 **QUICK**, George Bertram Charles CD LRAM ARCM. Born 1910 died 1990. Enl 11H 22/2/27; WO1 (BM) 1 R Fus 15/10/37; retd 12/7/52; BM Assistant Inspector Canadian Army 1952; DoM The Toronto Regiment (Militia).

1952-1958 **BLABER**, Frederick John ARCM. Born 1925. Enl 1 RS 19/6/39; WO1 (BM) 1 R Fus 13/7/52; WO1 (BM) Fusiliers Bde 20/8/58; retd 13/3/65.

1958-1962 **FULLER**, Peter John. Born 1929. Enl 13/18H 17/7/47; WO1 (BM) 1 R Fus 16/6/58; retd 6/4/62.

1962-1968 **HICKS**, Brian Erwin FVCM LRAM ARCM psm. Born 1935. Enl RE (Chat) 9/10/50; WO1 (BM) R Fus 7/4/62; WO1 (BM) 3 RRF 23/4/68; WO1 (BM) HQ Para 20/5/69; Capt (DoM) Para 14/3/74; Capt (DoM) RA Mtd 30/6/78; Maj (DoM) SG 22/11/82; retd 1/10/84.

BANDMASTERS OF
THE 2nd BATTALION
THE ROYAL FUSILIERS

1862-1873 **CLEARY**, William. Enl 2/7 Ft 185?; Sgt (BM) 1/10/62; retd 31/5/73.

1873-1880 **FORD**, Thomas William. Born 1845 died 1880. Enl 89 Ft 18??; Sgt (BM) 2/7 Ft 1/6/73; died whilst serving 3/8/80.

1880-1907 **COLEMAN**, Frederick James. Born 1852 died 19??. Enl 3 Rifle Bde 10/11/66; Sgt (BM) 25/11/80; WO (BM) 1/7/81; retd 25/11/07; BM Royal Guernsey Militia 1907-19??.

1907-1925 **VICKERS**, James. Born 1877 died 19??. Enl 11H 3/8/92; WO (BM) 2 R Fus 26/11/07; retd 2/8/25.

1925-1947 **TULIP**, Richard William. Born 1897 died 1974. Enl 4 DLI 7/6/16; transf 2 DLI 10/2/19: WO1 (BM) 2 R Fus 3/8/25; Professor of Piano RMSM 1947; retd 12/10/52; Civilian Professor of Piano RMSM 1952-1974.

BANDMASTERS OF
THE 3rd BATTALION
THE ROYAL FUSILIERS

1898-1919 **KEEFE**, William Henry LRAM. Born 1872 died 1942. Enl 2 R Fus 20/4/87; WO (BM) 3 R Fus 1/4/98; retd 21/10/19.

1919 **COMPTON**, William Cyril. Born 1891 died 19??. Enl 1 DCLI 19/1/09; WO1 (BM) 3 R Fus 22/10/19; WO1 (BM) 4 R Fus 25/11/19; WO1 (BM) Bedfs & Herts R 1/9/22; retd 18/1/33.

1919-1921 **WRIGHT**, Edward. Born 1871 died 1951. For full details see 4th Battalion.

1921-1922 **FROUD**, George James. Born 1890 died 19??. Enl 8H 18/8/05; WO1 (BM) 3 R Fus 24/8/21; WO1 (BM) 17/21L 12/5/22; retd 24/8/25.

BANDMASTERS OF
THE 4th BATTALION
THE ROYAL FUSILIERS

1900-1919 **WRIGHT**, Edward. Born 1871 died 1951. Enl S Wales Bord 24/8/85; WO (BM) 4 R Fus 9/5/1900; WO1 (BM) 3 R Fus 25/11/19; retd 23/8/21.

1919-1922 **COMPTON**, William Cyril. Born 1891 died 19??. For full details see 3rd Battalion.

BANDMASTERS OF
THE 3rd BATTALION
THE ROYAL REGIMENT OF FUSILIERS

1968-1969 **HICKS**, Brian Erwin FVCM LRAM ARCM psm. Born 1935. For full details see 1st Battalion.

1969-1974 **HANNAM**, Peter MBE BEM psm. Born 1938. Enl 1 Glosters 8/4/57; WO1 (BM) 3 RRF 19/5/69; WO1 (BM) PoW Mercian Depot (badged Glosters) 4/11/74; Capt (DoM) Queens Div (badged RRF) 2/7/79; Capt (DoM) REME 20/8/84; Capt (DoM) WG 6/1/86; Lt-Col Snr DoM Household Division 1989; retd 24/4/93.

1974-1980 **ROAD-NIGHT**, Peter Charles. Born 1945. Enl RA (Alan) 11/1/61; WO1 (BM) 3 RRF 4/11/74; WO1 (BM) LI Depot 20/2/80; WO1 (BM) 2 RGJ 23/6/82; retd 17/9/85.

1980-1981 **COOMBER**, Ronald Leslie. Born 1944. Enl R Signals 11/1/62; WO1 (BM) 3 RRF 20/2/80; WO1 (BM) 1 Para 16/2/81; retd 21/9/84.

1981-1984 **SMITH**, Stephen John ARCM psm. Born 1954. Enl R Anglian 18/9/69; WO1 (BM) 3 RRF 14/1/81; WO1 (BM) Duke of Kent's Band 1/5/84; Capt DoM Inf (South) 23/11/87; Capt (DoM) RAOC 1/6/92; Capt (DoM) RLC (Deepcut) 5/4/93; Capt (DoM) RLC 10/1/94.

THE LANCASHIRE FUSILIERS

1688   Peyton's Regiment of Foot
1751   20th Foot (also XXth Foot)
1782   20th (East Devonshire) Foot
1881   The Lancashire Fusiliers
1968   amalgamated to form The Royal
        Regiment of Fusiliers
        becoming 4th Battalion
1969   disbanded as 4th Battalion.

From its inception the 20th Foot had drums and possibly fifes, though typically the military band did not evolve until the second half of the 18th century. As is so often the case, our first glimpse comes from the Inspection Reports of the period, which note as early as 1769 the existence of a 'Band of Music'. Five years later, this is fleshed out with a reference to eight musicians and the presence of 'a German post-horn'.

In those first years the Band served with the Regiment in Gibraltar and Quebec, with postings in the early 19th century taking it even further afield to Minorca, Alexandria, Malta, Naples, Portugal, Bombay, Ireland and Bermuda.

In 1854 the Regiment departed on the P&O steamship *Colombo* for Turkey to join the Crimean War. The bandsmen served as medical orderlies and stretcher bearers at the Battle of Inkerman that year.

Soon afterwards, a 2nd Battalion was raised at Clonmel in County Tipperary, and efforts were made to form a new Band.

The first bandmaster to be traced in the regiment is Sergeant Oliver, who served with the 1st Battalion from 1857. It is assumed that he remained until 1873 when the first Kneller Hall graduate, Michael Troy, arrived from the 73rd Foot. Meanwhile, Sergeant Thomas Berry, previously with the 4th Foot, had been appointed to the 2nd Battalion in 1870.

Although the Kneller Hall system of appointments had thus already begun to establish itself, there were still occasionally those who rose through the ranks in their original regiment. One such was Robert Tucker, who joined the 1st Battalion in 1863 at the age of eleven, and remained for 30 years, eventually becoming Bandmaster in 1885.

Both Battalions were posted to India at various

BANDS OF THE

4TH BATTALION

THE ROYAL REGIMENT OF FUSILIERS

2nd Battalion The Lancashire Fusiliers, Rizalpur 1921, Bandmaster E Haywood (RMSM)

points in the second half of the 19th century, where conditions for men and musicians alike were often extremely arduous. Indeed the bandsmen were expected to be as fit as the rest of the regiment, and to participate in the long marches that were then the Army's favoured means of moving units around the country. In 1858 the 1st Battalion marched 130 miles to Lucknow, fighting three battles en route, whilst in 1881 the 2nd Battalion marched from Mhow to Nasirabad, a total of 476 miles, in just over a month.

At a time when sport was often the major pre-occupation of the Army, the Band of the 1st Battalion distinguished itself, particularly in hockey, becoming champions of Aldershot and District. Also much vaunted were the achievements of Edward Rogers, the 1st Battalion Bandmaster from 1893 to 1905; apart from being a first-class musician, Mr Rogers was also a leading light in the regimental cricket team, and regularly topped the bowling averages.

It was he too who led the Band in the 1895 competition at the Arts and Crafts Society Exhibition in Dublin. Six bands competed in a programme carefully chosen by Lieutenant Griffiths, Director of Music at Kneller Hall, to test the various soloists:

March	Pomposo	Ord-Hume
Valse	Soldaten Leider	Gung'l
	Own choice selection	
Overture	William Tell	Rossini
Fantasia	Erin	Basquit

The result was a victory for the Fusiliers, winning a prize of £21 and an Eb Alto Saxophone valued at 18 guineas.

A more typical programme of the era, however, was played at a swimming gala in 1896:

March	Lynwood	Ord Hume
Overture	Les Cloches de Corneville	Planquette
Selection	The Grand Duke	Sullivan
Japanese Mazurka	La Mousme	Ganne
La Serenata	Der Engel Lied	Braga
Selection	Carnavalia	Williams
Waltz	Santiaga	Corbin
Aria	Che Faro	Gluck
Selection	Little Christopher Columbus	Caryll
Galop	Vivat	Zikoff
Extras		
Dance	Anne Boleyn	Ball

Song	Whisper and I shall Hear	Piccolomini
Selection	A Gaiety Girl	Jones

In 1898 a 3rd Battalion was raised and a new band formed. A government grant of £150 was provided, to be split between the Officers' Mess and the Band; the officers unanimously voted to give the whole sum to the Band, though this still fell far short of the estimated start-up costs of at least £500.

Two years later a 4th Battalion was also raised. Though both the new bands were short-lived, they did form string sections, and a note in the regimental journal tells of a moonlight birthday picnic given in honour of the Commanding Officer's wife, for which the strings of the 3rd Battalion provided musical accompaniment.

Less pleasant duties still demanded the attention of the musicians, however. In 1899 the 2nd Battalion sailed for South Africa, with the bandsmen acting as stretcher bearers. And the industrial action on the railways in 1911 saw the same Band on strike duty with the Battalion.

During the Great War, most of the bandsmen were absorbed into the ranks, though many took their instruments with them for use whenever possible. Even in the midst of war, the regimental day was celebrated in 1917 with a ceremony of Trooping the Colour.

The upheavals of the war, together with the uncertainty generated by the Army reforms immediately afterwards, were eased somewhat by the presence of long-serving Bandmasters. Ernest Miles was with the 1st Battalion for 27 years from 1905, whilst George Pitt transferred to the 2nd when the 4th was disbanded in 1907, and stayed until 1920; his replacement, Talbot Haywood remained in his post for 20 years.

The '20s and '30s were thus a period of some stability in the Bands' lives, and both were much in demand, both at home and abroad. A further period of success came during the eight-year incumbency of Tony Richards (later to become Director of Music of The Life Guards) in the late '50s, but for the most part the years after the Second World War were troubled ones for the Regiment.

The 2nd Battalion was disbanded in 1948, though unusually it was to return briefly in 1953, with Bandmaster Leo Marks having the unenviable task of forming and then disbanding the Band. And though The Lancashire Fusiliers were amalgamated into the new Royal Regiment of Fusiliers in 1968, becoming the 4th Battalion, it too was a short-lived arrangement; the following year the Battalion was disbanded.

Fanfare trumpeters of The Lancashire Fusiliers
(Eagles/Ogilby)

Regimental Music

As with all Fusilier regiments, the quick march was 'The British Grenadiers' (for further details see Grenadier Guards).

The Regiment also adopted 'The Minden March' as a second quick march. This is an adaptation of an old hymn-tune known as 'Lammas Day'; the 20th Foot were one of the six regiments who fought at the Battle of Minden on Lammas Day.

The slow march was 'The Lancashire Fusiliers Slow March', adapted from 'The Minden Waltzes' composed by an unknown bandmaster of the regiment.

For the short time that the 4th Battalion of The Royal Regiment of Fusiliers was in existence, it used the same music as the other three battalions.

BANDMASTERS OF
THE 1st BATTALION
THE LANCASHIRE FUSILIERS

1857-1873 **OLIVER**, R. Sgt (BM) 1/20 Ft 1857; retd 1873?

1873-1880 **TROY**, Michael. Born 18?? died 1880. Enl 73 Ft; Sgt (BM) 1/20 Ft 1/11/73; died 7/6/80 whilst still serving.

1880-1885 **FAIRBAIRN**, James. Born 1845 died 1905. Enl RHA 17/9/66; Sgt (BM) 1/20 Ft 8/6/80; WO (BM) 1/7/81; retd 7/6/85.

1885-1893 **TUCKER**, Robert William. Born 1852 died 1920. Enl 1/20 Ft 13/2/63; WO (BM) 1 Lan Fus 8/6/85; retd 6/3/93.

1893-1905 **ROGERS**, Edward. Born 1861 died 1938. Enl 100 Ft 13/3/77; WO (BM) 1 Lan Fus 7/3/93; WO (BM) Royal Hibernian Military School 24/10/05; retd 17/4/07.

1905-1932 **MILES**, Ernest Norton. Born 1877 died 1950. Enl 1 HLI 4/2/92; WO (BM) 1 Lan Fus 25/10/05; retd 4/11/32.

1932-1948 **ELLIOTT**, William Albert LRAM ARCM. Born 1902. Enl 1 DWR 27/10/18; WO1 (BM) 1 Lan Fus 5/11/32; retd 1948.

1948-1949 **WRIGHT**, Frederick L ARCM. Born 1905. For full details see 2nd Battalion.

1949-1956 **HAWORTH**, James ARCM. Born 1910. Enl 2 Manch R 8/7/26; WO1 (BM) 2 E Lan R 14/8/45; WO1 (BM) 1 Lan Fus 12/3/49; WO1 (BM) Midland Bde 2/5/56; retd 15/2/59.

1956-1964 **RICHARDS**, Antony John FTCL LRAM LGSM ARCM psm. Born 1930. Enl 13/18 H 31/12/46; WO1 (BM) 1 Lan Fus 2/5/56; Lt (DoM) RTR (Alamein) 2/4/64; Capt (DoM) LG 24/6/70; retd 1984 rank of Maj; Lt-Col (DoM) Royal Oman Police 1984.

1964-1968 **MUTLOW**, Jack Cyril ARCM. Born 1921 died 1974. Enl REME 8/2/46; WO1 (BM) Sierra Leone Regiment 28/4/59; WO1 (BM) 1 Lan Fus 2/4/64; WO1 (BM) 4 RRF 23/4/68; WO1 (BM) 3 RGJ 13/8/69; retd 7/8/71.

BANDMASTERS OF
THE 2nd BATTALION
THE LANCASHIRE FUSILIERS

1870-1877 **BERRY**, Thomas. Enl 62 Ft 185?; Sgt (BM) 2/20 Ft 8/4/70; retd 31/3/77.

1877-1884 **DIMMER**, Hyam. Born 1843 died 1917. Enl 2/20 Ft 16/6/58; Sgt (BM) 2/20 Ft 1/4/77; retd 13/3/84.

1884-1893 **BISHOP**, Luke. Born 1849 died 1913. Enl 1/16 Ft 17/9/67; WO (BM) 2 Ldn Fus 14/5/84; retd 16/5/93.

1893-1907 **COLLINS**, Henry Leonard. Born 1863 died 1939. Enl 1/7 Ft 28/2/77; WO (BM) 2 Lan Fus 17/5/93; retd 27/2/07.

1907-1920 **PITT**, George Ernest. Born 1876 died 1948. For full details see 4th Battalion.

1920-1940 **HAYWOOD**, Ernest John Talbot. Born 1887 died 19??. Enl 3 E York R 17/11/02; WO1 (BM) 2 Lan Fus 25/10/20; retd 1/3/40.

1940-1948 **WRIGHT**, Frederick L ARCM. Born 1905. Enl 1 R W Kent R 7/7/20; WO1 (BM) 2 Lan Fus 2/3/40; WO1 (BM) 1 Lan Fus 1948; retd 11/3/49.

1948-1953 Battalion disbanded.

1953-1955 **MARKS**, Leo Franklin. Born 1925. Enl 2 Queens R 14/10/40; WO1 (BM) 2 Lan Fus 8/6/53; WO1 (BM) 1 R Ir Fus 18/7/55; WO1 (BM) North Irish Bde 8/1/65; WO1 (BM) R Irish Rang Depot; retd 12/12/68.

BANDMASTERS OF
THE 3rd BATTALION
THE LANCASHIRE FUSILIERS

1898-1906 **WORMS**, Joseph George. Born 1864 died 19??. Enl 49 Ft 30/10/79; WO (BM) 3 Lan Fus 1/4/98; WO (BM) 3 Worc R 5/12/06; retd 3/2/19.

BANDMASTERS OF
THE 4th BATTALION
THE LANCASHIRE FUSILIERS

1900-1907 **PITT**, George Ernest. Born 1876 died 1948. Enl 2 E York R 21/6/90; WO (BM) 4 Lan Fus 5/5/1900; WO (BM) 2 Lan Fus 18/2/07; retd 28/6/20.

BANDMASTERS OF
THE 4th BATTALION THE ROYAL
REGIMENT OF FUSILIERS

1968-1969 **MUTLOW**, Jack Cyril ARCM. Born 1921 died 1974. For full details see Lancashire Fusiliers.

THE ST GEORGE'S BAND OF THE ROYAL REGIMENT OF FUSILIERS

The St George's Band was formed on 1 May 1984 from the old 1st and 2nd Battalion Bands. With little or no time to settle down, it went straight into a busy season, ending the year in Northern Ireland with the 1st Battalion and participating in the Londonderry Tattoo.

The following year visits were made to Kenya and Northern Ireland before a move to Cyprus, where the men stayed until February 1988.

Returning home, they travelled to Denmark and Norway, where they won friends with both their musical and medical expertise: during a concert in the Tivoli Gardens in Copenhagen, a lady in the audience collapsed and without hesitation Corporal Wakeford left the stage to give resuscitation. A hospital spokesman claimed that the prompt action had probably saved her life.

As the first step towards implementing the Options for Change policy, the two bands moved together with the 1st Battalion at Warminster. Although they were still officially two separate establishments, most of the time they practised and performed together.

In 1992 the two bands, conducted by Bandmaster Chris Attrill, performed as a male voice choir at the Festival of Remembrance held at the Royal Albert Hall, and in December 1993 the massed bands visited Canada.

THE DUKE OF KENT'S BAND OF THE ROYAL REGIMENT OF FUSILIERS

The Duke of Kent's Band was formed on 1 May 1984, with its nucleus coming from the old 3rd Battalion Band. The tradition of wearing replicas of the brass swords and scabbards presented by HRH The Duke of Kent to the Band of the 7th Foot in the 18th century was continued by The Duke of Kent's Band.

On Spring Bank Holiday 1988 the Band gave a spectacular performance at Castle Howard of the

THE ST GEORGE'S BAND AND THE DUKE OF KENT'S BAND OF

THE ROYAL REGIMENT OF FUSILIERS

1812 Overture, which was televised by Yorkshire Television.

In 1990 they visited Nanyuki, Kenya with the 1st Battalion and later massed with a Russian Band at the Passau Military Show, near the Austrian/Czechoslovakian border.

BANDMASTERS OF THE ST GEORGE'S BAND OF THE ROYAL REGIMENT OF FUSILIERS

1984-1985 DODD, John H. Born 1945. Enl Coldm Gds; WO1 (BM) 2 RRF 26/7/76; WO1 (BM) St George's Band RRF 1/5/84; retd 10/12/85.

1985-1994 ATTRILL, Christopher Charles. Born 1956. Enl Para 9/5/72; WO1 (BM) St George's Band RRF 18/12/85; Capt (DoM) R Irish 1/4/94.

BANDMASTERS OF THE DUKE OF KENT'S BAND OF THE ROYAL REGIMENT OF FUSILIERS

1984-1987 SMITH, Stephen John ARCM psm. Born 1954. Enl R Anglian 18/9/69; WO1 (BM) 3 RRF 14/1/81; WO1 (BM) Duke of Kent's Band 1/5/84; Capt DoM Inf (South) 23/11/87; Capt (DoM) RAOC 1/6/92; Capt (DoM) RLC (Deepcut) 5/4/93; Capt (DoM) RLC 10/1/94; Maj (DoM) 3/9/94.

1987-1994 CLARK, Peter Robert ARCM. Born 1957. Enl RE (Ald) 5/7/72; WO1 (BM) Duke of Kent's Band 16/11/87; WO1 (BM) RE 1994; Capt TDT RMSM 15/2/95.

Combined bands of The Royal Regiment of Fusiliers, London 1985   (Colin Dean)

THE ROYAL ANGLIAN REGIMENT

	1881	*1958-60*	*1964*
9th Foot	Norfolk Regt)	1st East Anglian Regt	1st Bn Royal Anglian Regt
12th Foot	Suffolk Regt)		
10th Foot	Lincs Regt)	2nd East Anglian Regt	2nd Bn Royal Anglian Regt
48th Foot) 58th Foot)	Northants Regt		
16th Foot	Beds & Herts Regt)	3rd East Anglian Regt	3rd Bn Royal Anglian Regt
44th Foot) 56th Foot)	Essex Regt)		
17th Foot	Leics Regt		4th Bn Royal Anglian Regt

The 4th Battalion, The Royal Anglian Regiment was disbanded in 1968.

The 3rd Battalion, The Royal Anglian Regiment was disbanded in 1992.

BANDS OF THE

1ST BATTALION

THE ROYAL ANGLIAN REGIMENT

THE ROYAL NORFOLK REGIMENT

1685	Cornwell's Regiment of Foot
1751	9th Foot
1782	9th (East Norfolk) Foot
1881	The Norfolk Regiment
1935	The Royal Norfolk Regiment
1959	amalgamated with The Suffolk Regiment to form The 1st East Anglian Regiment (Royal Norfolk and Suffolk)

The advent of music into the Norfolk Regiment is obscure, with no mention even of fifes until 1771. The following year, however, an inspection report mentions a 'Band of Music' for the first time, and by 1798 the Regiment, then stationed at Yarmouth, is noted as having 'Two Sergeants and nine Privates clothed as musicians', a not inconsiderable band for the infantry of the time.

A 2nd Battalion was raised and disbanded on several occasions over the years, with the only durable incarnation being in existence from 1857 through until 1947. It too had a Band, though when it was formed is unsure.

The first known Bandmaster in the Regiment served for just one year, but his tenure was nonetheless significant. William van den Heuvel was the first British Army bandmaster to come from Kneller Hall, and his arrival at the 9th Foot in 1858 thus inaugurated the system of appointments that remains in effect to this day.

For the Band itself, a perhaps more important date was 1865, when Chevalier V Bonicoli, said to have been one of the best clarinet players in London, became Bandmaster. He was to remain in his post for twenty years, during which time the 1st Norfolks acquired the reputation of possessing one of the finest bands in the Army. A year earlier the 2nd Battalion had also appointed its first known Bandmaster.

The beginning of this century saw another long-serving bandmaster take up the baton of the 1st Norfolks: George Dean served for eighteen years, including the duration of the Great War. His first engagement was a fortnight at an exhibition in Cape Town in 1905/6 which proved so successful that the booking was extended for another two weeks.

The war years were as traumatic and disruptive for the bands of The Norfolk Regiment as they were for others, with most of the musicians being co-opted into the ranks. The '20s and '30s, in contrast, were a time of stability, particularly for the 2nd Battalion, which was stationed at home throughout, save for a brief stint in Gibraltar.

These were the glory days of British military music, when every seaside resort seemed to have a bandstand, and every bandstand to have been surrounded by enthusiastic audiences. The 2nd Norfolks played the circuit each summer, including a concert in the presence of the Duke and Duchess of York at Weston-Super-Mare in 1928, and another at Lowestoft the same year to a crowd of 3000 people.

The winter months were less busy, with sport and practice the only ways to relieve the boredom of barracks life. An extract from the regimental magazine gives a glimpse of the winter routine:

We are on parade every Tuesday and Thursday for an hour which consists of musketry drills. For a quarter of an hour daily we parade for individual training. Naturally we attend route marches, but the bulk of our time is occupied by practice.

For the Band of the 1st Battalion, there were more exotic locations, with postings in Bermuda, Egypt, Shanghai and India. Here, even more, sport was the centre of social activity, and the bandsmen as ever played their full part. Particularly celebrated was Bandsman W Nugent, whose successes at an athletics meeting in 1932 featured victories in both the three mile and the one mile races, the latter in an unofficial Punjab record of 4'15" (the world record at the time stood at 4'09").

Musical engagements came in a variety of forms. Concerts featured not only the military band, but also community singing, a male voice choir and xylophone solos, whilst the dance band was kept busy entertaining troops and the public, including a booking at a Hindu wedding. Equally popular were The Jazz Maniacs, a five-piece band featuring piano, trumpet, trombone, clarinet and alto saxophone, who secured regular bookings in Calcutta.

Back home, the Depression was starting to take its toll, and the 1932 season saw many seaside resorts forced into cost-cutting exercises that left the bandstands empty. Nonetheless, the Band of the 2nd Norfolks played a fortnight at Lowestoft and kept itself busy with regular weekly concerts in Plymouth, where the Battalion was based.

The quality of the musicianship was attested to by no less an authority than F J Ricketts; when the Band joined the Royal Marines for the King's Birthday Parade at Plymouth Hoe in 1934, the famous composer of 'Colonel Bogey' wrote to Bandmaster Burgess:

1st Battalion The Norfolk Regiment, Aldershot 1912, Bandmaster G Dean   (RMSM)

1st Battalion The Norfolk Regiment, 1929, Bandmaster R Howard (RMSM)

Your men were excellent. The delightful restrained playing during the inspection was a real pleasure . . . . The keen attention throughout and obvious sincerity of purpose of your Band appealed to me very much.

He later added: 'Massed Bands are invariably a source of annoyance; on this occasion it was a most pleasant and successful association.'

The initial experiences in the Second World War were particularly costly for the 2nd Battalion, when an heroic rearguard stand at La Bassée ended with the capture of the 100 men still left. Amongst the casualties and captured were many bandsmen.

Meanwhile a new band was being formed in Norwich by a few regulars and a handful of conscripts. Their number was augmented in 1944 by the arrival back home of eight prisoners of war repatriated from Germany. These latter were, of course, unable to travel abroad, but a band of 27 men did visit Italy, where it spent a year playing for the troops, covering a total of 12,000 miles. VE Day was celebrated with a Thanksgiving Service in

the Piazza Signoria in Florence. Soon after, still in Florence, the Band broadcast direct to New York.

With the large number of retirements at the end of hostilities, the 2nd Battalion Band was reduced to just seven men. A slow process of rebuilding to full strength was followed almost immediately by the Battalion's disbandment.

The 1st Battalion survived barely a decade more as a discrete formation, being amalgamated with The Suffolk Regiment in 1959. During that final period, however, the Band was kept busy, both at home and on postings in Hong Kong and Germany. Also active during the '50s were a dance band and chamber group.

Regimental Music

The badge of the 9th Foot was the figure of Britannia, in celebration of which 'Rule Britannia' was adopted as the regimental march (see 1st Battalion, The Royal Regiment of Fusiliers).

THE SUFFOLK REGIMENT

1685	Duke of Norfolk's Regiment of Foot
1686	Earl of Lichfield's Regiment of Foot
1751	12th Foot
1782	12th (East Suffolk) Foot
1881	The Suffolk Regiment
1959	amalgamated with The Royal Norfolk Regiment to form The 1st East Anglian Regiment (Royal Norfolk and Suffolk)

Raised in 1685, the 12th Foot was augmented by a 2nd Battalion in 1759, but this soon evolved into a regiment in its own right, and was re-numbered the 65th Foot (later to become the 1st Battalion of The York & Lancaster Regiment). Another 2nd Battalion existed for a brief period during the Napoleonic crisis, but it was not until 1858 that a more durable incarnation was born. The new formation was accompanied by a band, which acquired the services of a German Bandmaster, Herr Richs.

The senior battalion, of course, had had a band for some considerable time by this stage, though when it came into existence is uncertain. An Inspection Report dated 11 October 1756 makes no mention of musicians, though it does note:

Drum & Fifes good. Uniform – red, lapelled, faced and lined with yellow – bound and looped with a mixed binding of white and yellow.

The first reference to a band comes in a later report from August 1792: '13 Drums, 12 Music = 25 (4 little boys).'

Presumably this band, in keeping with the fashions of the time, also employed foreign bandmasters during much of the 19th century, though no records even of their names survive. The first known Bandmaster was Mr W Hutchinson, appointed in 1870.

Both Bands seem to have performed their imperial duties, serving in a variety of British territories throughout the world. In 1890, for example, the 1st Suffolks were in Jhansi in India, while the following year the 2nd Battalion arrived in the same country from Alexandria.

During this era of the *pax Britannica*, one of the most valuable contributions a band could make to servicemen and their families, stranded thousands of miles from home, was simply to relieve boredom.

Concerts therefore often relied more on songs than on military music. A typical performance came with an outdoor concert by the Band of the 2nd Battalion in May 1893; the pieces included such comic and sentimental songs as 'Little Peach in an Orchard Grew', 'Bang Upon the Big Drum' and 'My Sweetheart When a Boy'. Perhaps the most spectacular contribution was made by the weather: it was so windy that the stage was blown away during the last song.

There were also, however, more traditional engagements for the musicians. The programme has survived of a massed band concert given the same month, in conjunction with the 2nd Battalion, The Welsh Regiment and the 21st Hussars:

Quick March	The War	Griffiths
Overture	Haydée	Auber
Valse	Eldorado	Royle
Selection	Tannhauser	Wagner
Gavotte	Stephanie	Czibulka
Descriptive Quadrille	British Army	Jullien
Ballet Music	William Tell	Rossini
	God Save The Queen	

At a time when bandmasters often remained in their posts for many years, the 2nd Suffolks had a particularly unstable history; in the space of just thirty years between 1865 and 1895, there were no fewer than six bandmasters. Three of these died whilst in service: Mr Wallace, the second incumbent, after little more than a year in the job, his successor, Mr Emmings, and then later Edmond O'Neill, who died of Bright's Disease in Secunderabad, again the year after his appointment.

Despite these setbacks, the Band continued to serve its Battalion, and to diversify its repertoire; in 1896 it added a Minstrel Troupe, such features then being highly popular in the Raj. A concert that year in Rangoon drew the following notice from the regimental journal:

Undoubtedly the great success of the evening, judging from the thundering applause with which it was received, was the singing of 'Little Birds are Sleeping' by Boy Chandler of the Band, in whom the Company have found a most valuable member, who is certain of a welcome whenever he sings to us . . . . Well done little man.

The versatility of the Band was further demonstrated in 1899, when it formed an orchestra for a four-night production of *Bluebeard Re-Trimmed or The Lottery of Modern Wedlock: A Burlesque Extravaganza in 3 Acts.*

In 1912 a Smoking Concert was held in Cairo to say farewell to various members of the Regiment who were leaving, amongst them the highly popular Bandmaster Varnfield. In the privacy of the Sergeants' Mess, more risqué material was clearly permissible, and songs performed included 'The Gay Drum Major', 'Naughty Boy', 'Has Anybody Seen My Tiddler?' and 'What Did I Do?'

Mr Varnfield's reputation was testified to in a letter signed by 'A Music Lover', which appeared in the *Egyptian Morning News* remembering the 'excellent programmes he has conducted in the Ezbekieh Gardens and other places, where his music was most popular, and also the splendid concerts we have had the pleasure of attending at the Citadel.'

His replacement was Mr Beale, who took the Band through the Great War and later served in India. A composer and arranger of some accomplishment, his pieces included 'Le Corps d'Elite' and several locally inspired works such as 'Punkah Wallah' and 'Marche Orientale', the latter featuring drums and cymbals. He also introduced fortnightly concerts dedicated to classical music by the likes of Tchaikovsky, Puccini, Schubert, Kalman, Sibelius and the inevitable Wagner.

Further contributions to regimental life came from Mrs Beale, who acted in sketches and gave recitations, and Band Sergeant Double, who provided musicians for the Dance Club, an association that immediately attracted over 200 members. A male voice choir was later formed from within the Band, under the leadership of Mr Gubbins, who arranged Beethoven's anthem 'Creation' for the choir's debut performance.

The 2nd Battalion, meanwhile, was stationed in Britain and Ireland in the post-war years, its bandmaster being the famous Hector Adkins. He left in 1921 to become Director of Music at Kneller Hall, with perhaps his most spectacular moment coming in 1923 when he conducted more than a thousand bandsmen in eight days of concerts at Wembley Stadium. He was eventually to retire in the rank of Lieutenant-Colonel.

1st Battalion The Suffolk Regiment, Devonport 1939, Bandmaster H Gubbins   (Eagles/Ogilby)

In 1926 both Bands were together for a rare combined Trooping the Colour in Gibraltar, scene of the Regiment's greatest battle honour. The 1st then returned home to play at the usual seaside resorts in Britain, and a successful stint at the 1932 Henley Regatta, where Mr Gubbins was personally congratulated by The Duke of Connaught. The 2nd proceeded to China, where the dance band played a season at the Majestic Hotel in Shanghai, and then on to India.

Following the Second World War, in which bandsmen of both battalions served as medical orderlies and in the ranks, the 2nd Battalion was disbanded. The Band of the 1st, however, survived to lead the Regiment through Ipswich, when the Suffolks were granted the freedom of the city.

Later postings included Germany and Cyprus. In the latter there was little to do in the way of concerts, but the Regiment's skiffle group, The Eastenders, scored a major triumph in winning the island's Inter Services Skiffle Competition in 1958.

In 1958 The Suffolk Regiment was amalgamated with The Royal Norfolk Regiment.

Regimental Music

The quick march of the 1st Battalion was 'Speed the Plough', an East Anglian air that dates back to at least the 17th century. In Scotland it is known as 'The Inverness Country Dance'.

The 2nd Battalion went through a succession of marches, starting with a German quickstep introduced by Herr Richs in 1858, and then moving through 'Milanollo', 'The Men of Harlech', 'The Dashing White Sergeant' and 'The White Cockade', before settling on 'The Duchess'. Following an extensive debate in the regimental journal, 'The Duchess' was finally supplanted by 'Speed the Plough' in 1898.

The slow marches were 'The 1st Suffolk Regimental Slow March' and, for the 2nd Battalion, 'The Druids' Chorus' from *Norma*.

1st BATTALION, THE ROYAL ANGLIAN REGIMENT

1959   The 1st East Anglian Regiment (Royal Norfolk and Suffolk)
1964   1st (Royal Norfolk and Suffolk) Battalion, The Royal Anglian Regiment
1968   1st Battalion, The Royal Anglian Regiment
1980   1st Battalion (Norfolk, Suffolk and Cambridgeshire), The Royal Anglian Regiment

On amalgamation, the strength of the Band stood at 46 musicians under the leadership of Mr Holben, formerly the Bandmaster of the 1st Battalion, The Suffolk Regiment.

Posted to Berlin in 1960, the Band retained its historical association with East Anglia, returning there for a summer tour that year.

In 1962 the Battalion was sent to British Guiana, but the Band remained at home, performing guard duties in addition to its musical responsibilities. Later in the year, however, the Band did join the rest of the Battalion in the Caribbean.

A subsequent posting saw the Band in the Middle East and in Aden in the mid '60s.

More pleasant was a two-year spell in Gibraltar during the '80s. Some of the highlights were playing on board the cruise ships *QE2* and *Canberra*, both frequent visitors to the Rock. The Band also travelled to Morocco in 1988 to play for the birthday celebrations of King Hassan.

In November 1990 the men left Colchester for Saudi Arabia, where they were attached to 33 Field Hospital in their secondary role as medical orderlies. In March 1991 with Gulf hostilities ended, they returned home.

In October 1992 the 3rd Battalion of The Anglian Regiment was disbanded, and Bandmaster Tim Parkinson and many of his band were transferred to the 1st. In 1993 the newly rejuvenated Band made a three-month tour of Canada and America; it was to be the last major overseas visit of the Band before it disappeared into the new musical structure of the Queen's Division.

Regimental Music

The quick march is a combination of 'Rule Britannia' and 'Speed the Plough', arranged by Bandmaster George Holben and authorized in 1965.

The slow march is 'The Devonshire Rose'. (For further details see The Northamptonshire Regiment.)

BANDMASTERS OF
THE 1st BATTALION THE ROYAL
NORFOLK REGIMENT

1858-1859 **HEUVEL**, William van den. Born 1836 died ????. Enl 7H; Sgt (BM) 1/9 Ft 1858; retd 1859; Sgt (BM) 7H 19/7/73; Sgt (BM) 1LG 25/9/79; WO1 (BM) 1/7/81; retd 31/10/90.

1859-1865 **FOSTER**, William M. Sgt (BM) 1/9 Ft 1859; retd 11/7/65.

1865-1885 **BONICOLI**, Vincelas. Born 1830 died 18??. Enl 1/9 Ft 4/2/65; Sgt (BM) 1/9 Ft 12/7/65; retd 24/3/85.

1885-1896 **SHARPE**, Edward. Born 1856 died 1934. Enl 56 Ft 19/5/70; WO (BM) 1/9 Ft 25/3/85; retd 12/5/96.

1896-1904 **BARTLETT**, George B. Born 1869 died 1946. Enl 1 KRRC 15/5/83; WO (BM) 1 R Norfolk R 13/5/96; retd 4/4/04.

1904-1922 **DEAN**, George. Born 1867 died 19??. Enl 1 Devon R 13/11/82; WO (BM) 1 R Norfolk R 5/5/04; retd 29/6/22.

1922-1923 **ABBOTT**, William Henry. Born 1874 died 1956. For full details see Queen's Own Cameron Highlanders.

1923-1928 **COOMBES**, Henry Joseph. Born 1888 died 19??. Enl 2 R W Kent R 27/9/07; WO1 (BM) 1 R Norfolk R 30/7/23; retd 26/10/28; WO1 (BM) 7 W York R (TA) 1929-1937; WO1 (BM) 8 W York R (TA) 1937-1939.

1928-1941 **HOWARD** Reginald Francis Adolphus LRAM ARCM. Enl 1 R S Fus 7/7/14; WO1 (BM) 1 R Norfolk R 27/10/28; retd 2/3/41.

1941-1948 **SMYTHE**, Edwin S ARCM. Born 1910. Enl 2 North'n R 28/10/25; WO1 (BM) 1 R Norfolk R 19/12/41; WO1 (BM) 1 Kings 1/8/48; WO1 (BM) East Anglian Brigade 5/3/60; retd 19/8/65.

1948-1954 **HARVEY**, Daniel ARCM. Born 1915. For full details see 2nd Battalion.

1954-1959 **THOMPSON**, Eric. Born 1921. Enl 2 Green Howards 6/11/35; WO1 (BM) 1 R Norfolk R 27/1/54; WO1 (BM) RMSM 30/8/59; WO1 (BM) Foresters Brigade 26/1/62; WO1 (BM) JLR 24/10/63; retd 8/66.

BANDMASTERS OF
THE 2nd BATTALION THE ROYAL
NORFOLK REGIMENT

1864-1874 **VLACCO**, Antonio. Sgt (BM) 2/9 Ft 1/8/74; Sgt (BM) 1 The Buffs 1/7/76; retd 9/4/85.

1874-1877 **NEUZERLING**, Albert. Enl 68 Ft; Sgt (BM) 2/9 Ft 30/4/74; retd 31/3/77.

1877-1887 **SAGE**, George. Born 1844 died 1887. Enl 68 Ft 12/9/66; Sgt (BM) 2/9 Ft 1/4/77; WO (BM) 1/7/81; retd 26/9/87.

1887-1894 **BROWN**, William John. Born 1855 died 19??. Enl 95 Ft 29/1/69; WO (BM) 2 R Norfolk R 27/9/87; retd 28/1/94.

1894-1918 **ELFORD**, Edward. Born 1863 died 19??. Enl 2 DWR 25/11/82; WO (BM) 2 Norfolk R 29/1/94; WO1 (BM) RMC 22/7/18; retd 31/7/23.

1918-1945 **BURGESS**, Edward Charles Henry. Born 1885 died 1949. Enl 2 KSLI 25/10/1900; WO1 (BM) 2 R Norfolk R 22/7/18; retd 30/5/45.

1945-1948 **HARVEY**, Daniel ARCM. Born 1915. Enl RA (Sal Pl) 23/5/30; WO1 (BM) 2 R Norfolk R 1/6/45; WO1 (BM) 1 R Norfolk R 31/5/48; retd 26/1/54.

BANDMASTERS OF
THE 1st BATTALION THE SUFFOLK
REGIMENT

1870-1879 **HUTCHINSON**, William. Enl 1/12 Ft; Sgt (BM) St Helena Regt 1/1/63; Sgt (BM) 1/12 Ft 2/8/70; Sgt (BM) 63 Ft 16/1/79; WO (BM) 1/7/81; retd 7/3/82.

1879-1885 **WALKER**, William. Born 1847 died 1906. For full details see 2nd Battalion The Essex Regiment.

1885-1900 **THOMAS**, Charles. Born 1854 died 1911. Enl 32 Ft 5/8/69; WO (BM) 1 Suffolk R 19/8/85; retd 15/12/1900.

1900-1912 **VARNFIELD**, Alfred George. Born 1868 died 1929. Enl 2 Ox & Bucks LI 31/1/82; WO (BM) 1 Suffolk R 16/12/1900; retd 16/10/12; WO (BM) 5 HLI (TA) 1912-1929.

1912-1924 **BEALE**, Bertram. Born 1882 died 19??. Enl 2 Gordons 22/2/98; WO (BM) 1 Suffolk R 17/10/12; retd 24/4/24.

1924-1940 **GUBBINS**, Bertie Henry LRAM ARCM. Born 1899 died 19??. Enl 1 Seaforth 24/4/15; WO1 (BM) 1 Suffolk R 25/4/24; retd 2/1/40.

1940-1949 **STUNELL**, George Herbert ARCM psm. Born 1910 died 1981. Enl 1 R Sussex R 24/2/27; WO1 (BM) 1 Suffolk R 3/1/40; WO1 Instructor RAEC (att RMSM) 29/9/49; WO1 (BM) RMSM 29/5/51; Lt (DoM) RMA 25/2/54; retd 30/12/64 rank of Maj.

1949-1955 **MITCHENHALL**, Albert ARCM. Born 1913 died 1987. Enl 1 R Norfolk R 8/5/28; WO1 (BM) 2 S Lan R 2/9/45; WO1 (BM) 1 Suffolk 30/9/49; retd 31/8/55.

1955-1959 **HOLBEN**, George Arthur ARCM. Born 1923. Enl 1 Rifle Bde 13/7/37; WO1 (BM) 1 Suffolk R 1/9/55; WO1 (BM) 1 E Anglian 29/8/59; WO1 (BM) 1 R Anglian 1/9/64; retd 1/4/65.

BANDMASTERS OF
THE 2nd BATTALION THE SUFFOLK REGIMENT

1858-1864 RICHS, Herr. No details known other than in main text.

1864-1865 WALLACE, William. Born 1814 died 1865. Enl 2/12 Ft; Sgt (BM) 1/4/64; died whilst serving 30/11/65.

1865-1874 EMMINGS, J. Sgt (BM) 2/12 Ft 1/12/65; died whilst serving 23/10/74.

1874-1883 CLARKE, George. Enl 2/12 Ft; Sgt (BM) 2/12 Ft 24/10/74; retd 22/5/83.

1883-1884 SYKES, John Henry. Born 1845 died 1923. Enl 2/12 Ft 29/3/58; WO (BM) 2 Suffolk R 23/5/83; retd 26/8/84.

1884-1893 ANCLIFFE, John. Born 1854 died 1916. Enl 38 Ft 15/6/69; WO (BM) 2 Suffolk R 27/8/84; WO (BM) 2 SLI 1/1/94; retd 31/10/08.

1894-1895 O'NEILL, Edmond. Born 1862 died 1895. Enl 57 Ft 5/9/76; WO (BM) 2 Suffolk R 1/1/94; died whilst serving 21/8/95.

1895-1913 FROUD, William. Born 1863 died 19??. Enl 10H 13/11/77; WO (BM) 2 Suffolk R 22/8/95; retd 7/3/13.

1913-1921 ADKINS, Hector Ernest Mus Doc LRAM ARCM psm. Born 1885 died 1963. Enl 2 Glosters 8/5/1900; WO (BM) 2 Suffolk R 8/3/13; Lt (DoM) RMSM 22/9/21; Lt-Col (DoM) 20/1/42; retd 14/4/43.

1921-1933 LEWIS, Frederick George ARCM. Born 1861 died 19??. Enl 21 L 20/9/10; WO1 (BM) 2 Suffolk R 12/12/21; WO1 (BM) 2 BW 12/11/33; retd 14/3/38; BM 66 RA (TA) 1938-39.

1933-1943 LONGSTAFF, Joseph. Born 1902. Enl 1 R North'd Fus 18/7/18; WO1 (BM) 2 Suffolk 12/11/33; retd 14/5/42.

1943-1946 SELLEY, Robert Eric ARCM. Born 1915. Enl 1 RWF 16/8/32; WO1 (BM) 2 Suffolk R 30/5/42; retd 23/10/46.

BANDMASTERS OF
THE 1st BATTALION THE EAST ANGLIAN REGIMENT

1959-1964 HOLBEN, George Arthur ARCM. Born 1923. For full details see The Suffolk Regiment.

BANDMASTERS OF
THE 1st BATTALION THE ROYAL ANGLIAN REGIMENT

1964-1965 HOLBEN, George Arthur ARCM. Born 1923. For full details see The Suffolk Regiment.

1965-1969 CUNNELL, Thomas Anthony Woods. Born 1929. Enl 1 Border R 24/7/47; WO1 (BM) Aden Protectorate Levies 29/1/62; WO1 (BM) 1 R Anglian 2/4/65; retd 16/6/69.

1969-1973 GOMERSALL, Anthony LGSM AmusLCM. Born 1939 died 1990. Enl RE(Chat) 5/1/55; WO1 (BM) 1 E Anglian 17/6/69; retd 20/4/73.

1973-1978 CHERRY, John. Born 1938. Enl DWR 4/10/56; WO1 (BM) 1 R Anglian 21/4/73; retd 14/1/79.

1978-1983 LINES, Stephen Philip W. Born 1949. Enl 2 R Anglian 27/4/65; WO1 (BM) 1 R Anglian 13/11/78; retd 27/12/83.

1983-1993 WALLIS, Niall Charles. Born 1954. Enl 3 RGJ 14/9/70; WO1 (BM) 1 R Anglian 27/12/83; retd 8/8/94.

1993-1994 PARKINSON, Timothy John ARCM ALCM. Born 1955. For full details see 3rd Battalion The Royal Anglian Regiment.

Bandmaster C Thomas, 1st Battalion, The Suffolk Regiment, c1885 (RMSM)

BANDS OF THE

2ND BATTALION

THE ROYAL ANGLIAN REGIMENT

THE ROYAL LINCOLNSHIRE REGIMENT

1685	Granville's Regiment of Foot
1751	10th Foot
1782	10th (North Lincolnshire) Foot
1881	The Lincolnshire Regiment
1946	The Royal Lincolnshire Regiment
1960	amalgamated with The Northamptonshire Regiment to form The 2nd East Anglian Regiment (Duchess of Gloucester's Own Royal Lincolnshire and Northamptonshire)

The first mention of a band in the Inspection Reports of the 10th Foot comes 99 years after the Regiment's formation; on 9 June 1784 it is noted that there is a 'Very good Band'. Despite this early praise, very little is known of the Band for some considerable time afterwards.

A 2nd Battalion was formed in 1858, and furnished with a band almost immediately, with the officers appointing a German musician, Mr J Rubel, as Bandmaster the following year. The terms of his contract are worth quoting at some length, since it is typical of the kind of agreements prevalent in the days before Kneller Hall, as well as giving an insight into the standard of living in the early Victorian Army:

1st   Mr Rubel to be enlisted as a Soldier in the 2nd Battalion 10th Regiment and to have the rank of Sergeant to enable him to assume the necessary control over the musicians but not to be subject to Military Regulations in other respects.

2nd   Mr Rubel in addition to his Regimental pay as Sergeant to receive the following Salary to be paid to him by the Band Committee monthly in arrears; One hundred and fifty pounds per annum and also the following allowances; Suitable quarters in Barracks or compensation in lieu thereof. A subaltern's allowance of Fuel and Candles or the regulated compensation in lieu thereof, and Twelve Cwt weight of Baggage carried free of expense on a march or remove taking place.

4th   Mr Rubel also undertakes . . . to arrange any music that may be required for the use of the Band free of expense to the Regiment, but it shall be the duty of the Band Committee to furnish Mr Rubel

1st Battalion The Lincolnshire Regiment, Dover 1928, Bandmaster C Trowt (RMSM)

with the necessary supply of Music Paper for that purpose.

6th   No Persons to interfere with or give any directions to Mr Rubel except the Commanding Officer or Band Committee.

These Articles of Agreement were signed by Captain J E Waites, the President of the Band Committee, and must have proved a satisfactory basis for Mr Rubel's employment, for he stayed with the Battalion through to 1882, when it left for India.

The 1st Battalion, meanwhile, had acquired its first Kneller Hall-trained Bandmaster in 1864. Mr J Fenton served with the Regiment during the occupation of Japan, and remained in that country on his retirement.

His successor was Mr C Young, who joined the Battalion in Japan and eventually accompanied it home, via a posting in Malaya. With the restructuring of the infantry in 1881, Sgt Young was promoted to the rank of Warrant Officer Class I. The same year he inaugurated a series of Sunday concerts at the Landport Hippodrome in Portsmouth, for which he engaged many of the leading singers of the era from London.

A posting to Ireland in 1882 saw the ranks of the 1st Lincolns augmented by the Band-Sergeant and ten bandsmen from the 2nd Battalion, whilst the remainder of that Band departed for India under its new Bandmaster, Mr Grainger. The 1st Battalion, too, soon had a new Bandmaster, Mr F A Marks, whose first task – the day after his arrival – was to conduct the men in a Military Band Contest in Cork; despite the short notice, the Lincolns won a creditable Bronze Medal.

Both Bandmasters Grainger and Marks were renowned in their day as march composers, with Mr Marks also taking a particular interest in church music, and even in arranging minstrel songs for brass and voices; these latter proved especially popular during the long route marches that characterized the period.

Mr Grainger's departure in 1890 brought the appointment of Mr A Hurst, who remained with the Battalion for some 19 years, before passing the baton on to a series of other long-serving Bandmasters – Messrs Carbury, Stringer and Williams. Between them, these four men presided over the final 58 years of the Band's existence, during which time it toured many of the outposts of Empire, being stationed in India, Singapore, Gibraltar, Bermuda, the Sudan and Malta.

It also served in Palestine in the '30s, where the Regiment was awarded the Palestine Medal for combatant duties.

At the outbreak of the Second World War a new band was formed by Mr Williams, developing so quickly that it was playing on parade even before the men came back to England, having been evacuated from Dunkirk. Some of the regular bandsmen were permitted to return from the ranks to strengthen it further, and the outfit was granted official recognition, becoming the Regimental Band of The Lincolnshire Regiment.

During the first half of this century, the experience of the 1st Battalion was similar to that of the 2nd: Bandmasters stayed in their post for extended periods, and the Battalion toured the colonies.

In 1943 W T Brown was appointed Bandmaster of the 1st Lincolns. The youngest of four brothers who were all Army bandmasters, Mr Brown had the task of re-building the 1st Band, and then steering it through the difficult post-war period when the 2nd Battalion was disbanded.

His replacement was Dennis Bayton, an outstanding musician who subsequently became Professor of Trombone at Kneller Hall. He also played trombone with the BBC Symphony Orchestra and BBC Concert Orchestra, and could often be seen on such television programmes as Granada's *Spot the Tune*. He later emigrated to the USA where he continues to play as a professional musician.

Regimental Music

The regimental quick march of all the Lincolnshire battalions was 'The Poacher', officially adopted in 1881 but in use for many years before. An old English folk song, it was common to several other regiments since the words could be adapted for different counties:

When I was bound apprentice in famous Lincolnshire,
Full well I served my master for more than seven year,
Till I took up to poaching, as you shall quickly hear:
Oh, 'tis my delight on a shining night, in the season of
the year.

Amongst those using the song was The South Lincoln Regiment (the 69th Foot). When Mr Young transferred from that regiment to the 1st Lincolns via Kneller Hall, he added the regimental call at the beginning and a coda in order to distinguish the Lincolns' version.

The emotional power of the song, and of music in the Army, was attested to by Rudyard Kipling in a speech at the Mansion House, reported by *The Times* on 28 January 1915:

I remember in India in a cholera camp, where the men were suffering very badly, the band of the 10th Lincolns started a regimental sing-song and went on with that queer, defiant tune 'The Lincolnshire Poacher' . . . . There was nothing in it – nothing except all England, all the East Coast, all the fun and daring and horseplay of young men bucketing about big pastures in the moonlight. But as it was given very softly at that bad time in that terrible camp of death, it was the one thing in the world that could have restored as it did restore shaken men back to their pride, humour and self-control.

Other marches associated with the Regiment were 'The Royal Windsor' and 'The Maple Leaf'.

2nd Battalion The Lincolnshire Regiment, Lincoln 1935, Bandmaster R Williams   (Eagles/Ogilby)

1st Battalion The Royal Lincolnshire Regiment, Malaya c1955, Bandmaster D Bayton (RMSM)

THE NORTHAMPTONSHIRE REGIMENT

1740	Cholmondley's Regiment of Foot	1740	58th Foot
1751	48th Foot	1748	renumbered 47th Foot
1782	48th (Northamptonshire) Foot	1755	renumbered 60th Foot
		1782	58th (Rutlandshire) Foot

1881	The Northamptonshire Regiment
1960	amalgamated with The Royal Lincolnshire Regiment to form The 2nd East Anglian Regiment (Duchess of Gloucester's Own Royal Lincolnshire and Northamptonshire)

Both the Regiments that were to amalgamate in 1881 to form The Northamptonshire Regiment had bands at an early stage. An inspection report dated 14 April 1767 notes of the 48th Foot: 'Fifers and a large Band of Music'. The next day, the 58th was inspected and a similar comment made: 'Fifers and a Band of Music'.

The Band of the 48th was involved in military action almost from its inception. It was present during the four-year siege of Gibraltar, from 1779 to 1783, and accompanied the Regiment through the Peninsular Campaign, reportedly playing the men into action at Talavera.

The first mention of a bandmaster is also considerably earlier than in most infantry regiments; there is a reference that a German was employed for this function in 1798, though his name is not recorded. At the same time six boys were enlisted for the Band, and it appears that the strength then stood at thirteen musicians, bandmaster and drum-major; this figure may have included drummers.

The vogue for continental musicians was still strong in the mid-19th century, when the first known bandmaster, Signore Tamplini of the 48th Foot, was appointed. His Italianate influence on the repertoire of the Band can be clearly seen in a programme that has survived of a concert given in Corfu:

1.	*The Ladies' March* (*four Neopolitan melodies expressly composed for this occasion*)	*Tamplini*
2.	*Grand Overture from 'La Favorita'* (*first performance*)	*Donizetti*
3.	*Brindisi: Il segrato per esser felice* (*The supper song from Lucrezia Borgia*)	*Donizetti*
4.	*Selection from 'Robert le Diable'* *Clarinet, Oboe and Cornet Obligato*	*Meyerbeer*
5.	*Le Zephir et la Belle Greque Waltz* (*first performance*)	*Sig. Manzaroeli*

1st Battalion The Northamptonshire Regiment, India 1896, Bandmaster W Pepperill (Eagles/Ogilby)

Meanwhile the Band of the 58th Foot was also functioning successfully, acquiring its first known bandmaster, Mr H Basquit, in 1846. When the two Regiments amalgamated in 1881, the serving Bandmasters, Messrs Holland and Moran, continued in their posts, and there is no evidence to suggest that the merger had too great an impact on the musicians.

Perhaps the greatest disruption faced by either Band came in 1936 when the Bandmaster of the 2nd Battalion, Mr Trayton Adams, left to take up a position as Musical Adviser to the Aldershot Tattoo. He had been with the Battalion for twenty years, rebuilding the Band in the midst of the Great War. Most of his career had been spent at home, playing the usual round of seaside resorts and becoming a regular feature at Aldershot long before he took up his new post. His departure coincided with that of Band Sergeant W Overy, who went on to become Bandmaster of the Birmingham Tramways Band.

Despite this double loss, the Band of the 2nd Northants continued to go from strength to strength, and made its first broadcast on the BBC in 1939, under its new leader, Mr Marriott.

Meanwhile, the Band of the senior Battalion was abroad, stationed in Palestine, Egypt, Iraq and India. In the latter posting, the bandsmen were called upon to serve as stretcher-bearers in the frontier struggles against the Fakir of Ipi in Waziristan.

At the outbreak of the Second World War, the 2nd Northants Band had a strength of 53, including a dozen boys. All those old enough joined the Battalion in the British Expeditionary Force in France, also fulfilling their wartime function as stretcher-bearers. It was a costly campaign for the regiment; two companies were over-run by the enemy and by the time of the evacuation from Dunkirk, just 150 men were left fighting fit. Amongst the casualties were one bandsman killed and ten captured. Also lost were many instruments and a considerable amount of music.

During the later years of the war, the Regimental Band was stationed at the depot in Northampton, under the guidance of Bandmaster Marriott and Band Sergeant 'Chink' Holland.

The war ended with the 1st Battalion in India – following an involvement in the Burma campaign of 1944-45 – and the 2nd in Germany. In 1947 the 1st Battalion was reduced to a token cadre, and the following year the two battalions were officially amalgamated at a ceremony in Austria.

The Band that survived was under the command of Mr Ord Hume, Bandmaster of the 1st Battalion since 1938, and the son of the famous march composer from the Territorial Army. The degree of musicianship attained under his leadership was attested to by a local Austrian newspaper, which reported a 'never-to-be-forgotten concert' given in Judenburg Town Square in 1951:

In open-mouthed astonishment [the townspeople] listened to Austrian marches, waltzes and operatic selections. Many of our own musicians who have been saying for years that the British had no ear for music, had to confess that they were wrong. They were transported by a concert of such rare character of their own native music played by people from another land.

Further evidence of Mr Ord Hume's ability can be found in the fact that by 1956 five ex-members of his Band had become bandmasters in their own right.

Other postings in the 1950s included Italy, Germany, Korea, Hong Kong and Aden. In Hong Kong many of the bandsmen, in addition to their regular commitments, also played in other ensembles, including the Sino British Orchestra and a film orchestra. There was less time for such extra-curricular activities in Aden, where the Northants had the only band, which was consequently kept very busy.

In 1960, The Northamptonshire Regiment was amalgamated with The Royal Lincolnshire Regiment.

Regimental Music

Around 1800 the regimental march of the 48th Foot was 'Wilke's Release', which – despite the existence of a band – was scored for fifes. In the early 1850s, however, William Allen, then Bandmaster of the Northampton Militia, wrote 'The Northamptonshire', a piece also known as 'Hard Up'. It was officially adopted by the 48th in 1879, and subsequently also became the regimental march of the 2nd Battalion, replacing 'The Lincolnshire Poacher'.

A long-standing regimental tradition for guest nights in the Officers' Mess called for the playing of three particular pieces: 'Rule Britannia', because the 48th supposedly once served as Marines; 'God Bless the Prince of Wales', in honour of the future Edward VII who dined with the Regiment at the Tower of London in 1889; and 'Bon Soir', as a none-too-subtle hint to the Commanding Officer that it was time to go home to bed.

Dance band, 1st Battalion The Northamptonshire Regiment c1932, Bandmaster H Hope (RMSM)

Band and Drums, 2nd Battalion The Royal Anglian Regiment, Berlin, Bandmaster G Joseph (RMSM)

2nd BATTALION, THE ROYAL ANGLIAN REGIMENT

1960	The 2nd East Anglian Regiment (Duchess of Gloucester's Own Royal Lincolnshire and Northamptonshire)
1964	The 2nd (Duchess of Gloucester's Own Royal Lincolnshire and Northamptonshire) Battalion, The Royal Anglian Regiment
1968	2nd Battalion, The Royal Anglian Regiment
1980	2nd Battalion (Lincolnshire, Leicestershire and Northamptonshire), The Royal Anglian Regiment

On amalgamation Mr Colin Blackburn of the Northants was appointed Bandmaster, acquiring a Band that was well over strength.

Though the county titles were dropped from the various battalion titles in 1968, the 2nd Battalion Band continued to make visits to the two home counties whenever time and funds permitted, and emphasised still further the nickname of 'The Poachers' in an attempt to keep the old traditions alive.

In 1987 the Band was invited by the government of Barbados to represent Britain at celebrations of the 21st anniversary of independence, thus renewing an association with the island that had started in the late 17th century when the Leicestershire Regiment had served there. One of the key ceremonies was the Trooping of the Colours of the Barbados Defence Force, a parade for which the 2nd Anglians were joined by the Bands of the Barbados Defence Force and of the Jamaican Army.

In 1990 the men flew to Saudi Arabia to do their bit as medical assistants. Hostilities over, it was back to Germany and a punishing series of tours that included concerts as far afield as Denmark and Luxembourg.

The last year before the Regiment was reduced to two bands saw the 2nd playing in Vienna, Bonn, Denmark, Belgium, Holland and even in the UK. It also appeared on French and German television.

Regimental Music

The quick march is a combination of 'Rule Britannia' and 'Speed the Plough', arranged by Bandmaster George Holben and authorized in 1965.

The slow march is 'The Devonshire Rose'. (For further details see The Northamptonshire Regiment.)

BANDMASTERS OF THE 2nd BATTALION THE ROYAL LINCOLNSHIRE REGIMENT

1873-1882 **RUBEL**, John B. Sgt (BM) 2 Lincoln R 3/7/73; WO (BM) 1/7/81; retd 17/1/82.

1882-1890 **GRAINGER**, Samuel. Born 1851 died 19??. Enl 39 Ft 1/6/67; WO (BM) 2 Lincoln R 10/1/82; retd 18/3/90.

1890-1909 **HURST**, Alfred. Born 1857 died 1934. Enl 47 Ft 28/11/70; WO (BM) 2 Lincoln R 19/3/90; retd 31/1/09.

1909-1923 **CARBURY**, William. Born 1875 died 1950. Enl 1 Foresters 5/1/89; WO (BM) 2 Lincoln R 1/2/09; WO1 (BM) RMC 1/8/23; retd 4/1/36.

1923-1934 **STRINGER**, Arthur ARCM. Born 1890 died 19??. Enl 2 Lan Fus 26/10/04; WO1 (BM) 2 Lincoln R 1/8/23; retd 25/2/34.

1934-1946 **WILLIAMS**, Ralph LRAM ARCM. Born 1904. Enl The Greys 28/10/19; WO1 (BM) 2 Lincoln R 1/4/34; retd 1946; BM Sheffield Transport 1946.

BANDMASTERS OF THE 1st BATTALION THE ROYAL LINCOLNSHIRE REGIMENT

1864-1872 **FENTON**, J T. Sgt (BM) 1/10 FT 1/8/64; retd 3/6/72.

1872-1883 **YOUNG**, Charles. Sgt (BM) 1/10 Ft 1/6/72; retd 14/8/83.

1883-1896 **MARKS**, Frederick August. Born 1857 died 19??. Enl 83 Ft 4/9/72; WO (BM) 1 Lincoln R 15/8/83; retd 30/9/96.

1896-1920 **WRIGHT**, Christopher. Born 1865 died 1937. Enl 31 Ft 9/7/79; WO (BM) 1 Lincoln R 1/10/96; retd 1/7/20.

1920-1935 **TROWT**, Charles Stanley. Born 1882 died 1971. Enl 2 Midd'x R 13/8/09; WO1 (BM) 1 Lincoln R 30/11/20; retd 23/4/35.

1935-1943 **GRIFFETT**, Robert William ARCM. Born 1905. Enl 1 S Lan R 9/5/21; WO1 (BM) 1 R Lincoln R 24/4/35; retd 25/10/43.

1943-1955 **BROWN**, William Thomas ARCM. Born 1914. Enl 2 S Wales Bord 1/8/30; WO1 (BM 1 Lincoln R 26/10/43; WO1 (BM) Lancastrian Bde 20/7/55; retd 7/4/62.

1955-1960 **BAYTON**, Dennis Arthur. Born 1928. Enl 1 Midd'x R 11/10/42; WO1 (BM) 1 R Lincoln R 21/7/55; WO1 (BM) 1 KOSB 10/8/60; WO1 (BM) Welsh Bde 27/7/63; DoM (Capt) Kenya Regiment 21/11/65; retd 10/8/69.

BANDMASTERS OF THE 1st BATTALION THE NORTHAMPTONSHIRE REGIMENT

185?-1865 **ALLEN**, William. Born 1831 died 189?. Sgt (BM) or Civ BM 48 Ft 7/7/65; Sgt (BM) or Civ BM 2/15 Ft 8/7/65; retd 18/5/86.

1865-1867 Bandmaster(s) not known.

1867-1878 **TAMPLINI**, Guiseppe. Sgt (BM) or Civ BM 96 Ft 1856; retd 30/4/66; Sgt (BM) or Civ BM 48 Ft 1867; Sgt (BM) or Civ BM 1/24 Ft 8/1/78; retd 4/8/82; BM HAC 1882.

1878-1887 **HOLLAND**, Edward. Born 1850 died 1933. Enl 1 Rifle Bde 17/9/65; Sgt (BM) 48 Ft 8/2/78; WO (BM) 1/7/81; WO (BM) SG 29/6/87; retd 26/8/93; BM Norfolk Artillery (TA).

1887-1898 **PEPPERILL**, William Arthur. Born 1856 died 1904. Enl 11H 23/5/71; WO (BM) 1 North'n R 29/6/87; retd 2/5/98.

1898-1914 **WEYER**, Albert. Born 1864 died 1941. Enl 8H 22/7/79; WO (BM) 1 North'n R 3/5/98; retd 3/5/14.

1914-1928 **CRESSWELL**, William LRAM. Born 1883 died 19??. Enl RGA 15/3/99; WO (BM) 2 North'n R 21/1/14; retd 31/10/69.

1928-1938 **HOPE**, Harold ARCM. Born 1899 died 19??. Enl 2 Worc R 28/8/14; WO1 (BM) 1 North'n R 3/6/28; retd 27/4/38; BM 5 Green Howards (TA) 1938-1939.

1938-1955 **ORD HUME**, Sidney Wilson ARCM. Born 1908. Enl RHG 18/7/26; WO1 (BM) 1 North'n R 28/4/38; WO1 (BM) East Anglian Bde 20/7/55; retd 4/3/60.

1955-1956 **PRITCHARD**, Reginald Arthur John. Born 1920. Enl 2 E Yorks R 17/9/34; WO1 (BM) 1 North'n R 20/7/55; WO1 (BM) Nigeria Regt 27/4/56; WO1 (BM) LIBde 30/1/60; retd 30/6/68.

1956-1960 **BLACKBURN**, Colin ARCM. Born 1930 died 1991. Enl Rifle Bde 8/3/45; WO1 (BM) 1 North'n R 27/4/56; WO1 (BM) 2 E Anglian 11/7/60; WO1 (BM) 2 R Anglian 1/9/64; WO1 (BM) R Anglian Regt (Bde) 20/8/65; retd 28/7/69.

Bandmaster J Adams, 2nd Battalion The Northamptonshire Regiment, Aldershot 1933
(Eagles/Ogilby)

BANDMASTERS OF THE 2nd BATTALION THE NORTHAMPTONSHIRE REGIMENT

1846-1864 **BASQUIT**, Heinrich. Born 18?? died 1877. Civ BM 58 Ft 20/9/46; retd 20/1 64.

1864-1869 **CREIGHTON**, William. Enl 31 Ft; Sgt (BM) 58 Ft 21/1/64; retd 31/10/69.

1869-1891 **MORAN**, John. Born 1835 died 1916. Enl 2/5 Ft 15/10/49; Sgt (BM) 58 Ft 1/11/69; WO (BM) 1/7/81; retd 10/4/91.

1891-1905 **GALLWAY**, Edward. Born 1865 died 1949. Enl 101 Ft 26/9/79; WO (BM) 2 North'n R 11/4/91; retd 18/2/05.

1905-1907 **BEECHEY**, Ernest Edward. Born 1875 died 19??. Enl 2 Leins R 19/11/90; WO (BM) 2 North'n R 19/2/05; WO (BM) 1 Leins R 1/11/07; WO1 (BM) 2 N Stafford R 16/9/22; retd 27/7/25.

1907-1916 **WALKER**, George Ostlere. Born 1872 died 19??. Enl RA 6/11/93; WO (BM) 2 North'n R 1/11/07; retd 6/2/16.

1916-1936 **ADAMS**, Trayton. Born 1884 died 1943. Enl 1 Durham LI 22/7/99; WO1 (BM) 2 North'n R 7/2/16; retd 7/2/36; Musical adviser Aldershot Tattoo 1936-1939.

1936-1946 **MARRIOTT**, Charles Edward Francis ARCM. Enl 8H 22/12/20; WO1 (BM) 2 North'n R 8/2/36; retd 1946; BM Liverpool Police 1946-71.

BANDMASTERS OF THE 2nd BATTALION THE ROYAL ANGLIAN REGIMENT

1960-1965 **BLACKBURN**, Colin ARCM. Born 1930 died 1991. For full details see The Northamptonshire Regiment.

1965-1973 **O'CONNELL**, Peter Michael LTCL. Born 1933. Enl R U Rifles 25/6/48; WO1 (BM) 2 R Anglian 20/8/65; retd 6/6/73.

1973-1984 **JOSEPH**, Gordon Edward ARCM. Born 1944. Enl R War R 11/1/60; WO1 (BM) 2 R Anglian 7/6/73; retd 10/9/84.

1984-1991 **McCRUM**, David. Born 1955. Enl 1 R Irish 6/11/72; WO1 (BM) 2 R Anglian 24/5/84; Regt Commission 1/6/87; Capt 1/6/93.

1991 **SHEARER**, Christopher ARCM AmusLCM BBCM MISM. Born 1959. Enl 13/18 H 12/9/76; WO1 (BM) 2 R Anglian 27/5/91; retd 31/10/94.

THE BEDFORDSHIRE AND HERTFORDSHIRE REGIMENT

1688	Douglas's Regiment of Foot
1751	16th Foot
1782	16th (Buckinghamshire) Foot
1809	16th (Bedfordshire) Foot
1919	The Bedfordshire and Hertfordshire Regiment
1958	amalgamated with The Essex Regiment to form The 3rd East Anglian Regiment (16th/44th Foot)

For many years after its formation, the 16th Foot had only a drum and fife band, though this was at least a considerable establishment, reported to include fourteen drummers by 1760. The military band probably did not come into existence until the beginning of the 19th century, and the earliest definite report of its activities comes from a parade on Southsea Common in 1842, when Lady Pakenham presented new colours to the Regiment.

The first bandmasters to be mentioned are Sergeant William Kennedy, who came to the 1st Battalion from the 3rd Foot in 1864, and Signor Deconni, a civilian attached to the 2nd Battalion around the same time. The latter retired in 1871 and was succeeded by Sergeant Boehmer, a member of the Band who had completed a course at Kneller Hall. After four years in the post, he transferred to the 1st Battalion, handing over to George Miller.

Sergeant Miller was the son of a bandmaster of the 63rd Foot, and father of a future Director of Music of the Grenadier Guards; all three shared the same name, George John Miller (see 'Musical Families' in *Volume One*). He was later to become Bandmaster of the Royal Military College and Director of Music of the Royal Marines, and was a respected musician, passing the Bachelor of Music examination at Cambridge. Amongst his compositions was the epic 'A Voyage on a Troopship', written whilst travelling to India with the 16th in 1876.

The Standing Orders of the Regiment published in 1885 lay down the rules and requirements governing the Band:

1 The Band-master is entrusted with and is responsible for the instruction of the Bandsmen and

BANDS OF THE

3RD BATTALION

THE ROYAL ANGLIAN REGIMENT

Boys; he reports to the president of the Band Committee all requirements, and whenever any instrument is broken, damaged or out of order; and to the Adjutant on all questions of discipline arising whilst he is present, and actually on duty with the Band.

2   He is to make a weekly inspection of all Band property.

3   The sergeant and men of the Band are under the orders of the Adjutant in respect to their discipline, and under the direction and control of the Band Committee and the Band-master, as musicians.

4   The Band-sergeant is to co-operate with, and assist the Band-master; he is to bring to prompt notice any loss of, or damage done to instruments or property; he is responsible for the manner in which the Bandsmen turn out, and for their punctual attendance; for the cleanliness of their barracks, and their interior economy and discipline.

The Boer War saw the bandsmen employed as stretcher-bearers, but there were better times to come in South Africa; a photograph taken in East London in 1912 shows the 2nd Battalion Band to be 45 strong.

One of the popular hits of the Edwardian era, the waltz 'Destiny', was to acquire special significance for the Beds & Herts. When news of the declaration of war was received in August 1914, the 1st Battalion was holding an Officers' Ball in Mullingar, Ireland – the last dance that evening was 'Destiny'. Thereafter it was regarded almost as a sacred work, and was played as a voluntary at Old Comrades' Services and on Remembrance Day.

A further tradition dates from the Great War. When the 1st Battalion's position came under threat at Mons in 1914, Drummer Smith left his instrument with a Belgian woman for safe-keeping; it remained in her house for the duration, serving as a hat-stand, and escaped notice even by the German soldiers billeted upon her. All the other drums were lost, save this one, which was recovered when the Battalion returned to the area in 1918. A Trooping the Colour ceremony at Namur – scene of the Regiment's first battle honour in 1785 – saw the 'Mons Drum' back on parade with Drummer Smith. It remained a feature of important parades in later years.

For the bands of the Beds & Herts, as for most others, the '20s were a period of relative security. The 1st was stationed at home, and when the Band

and Drums played for the King's Birthday Parade, they were reported to be at a strength of 50 musicians. Soon after, in January 1925, the string section of the Band made its first public appearance, and was acclaimed a success. There were, however, more ominous signs for the long term, with the bandsmen receiving weapons training, a development that, according to the regimental journal *The Wasp*, left some baffled: 'Imagine the plight of the oboe player when confronted with the body locking-pin, or the bass player with an escape of Army pattern Lewis-gun gas.'

The 2nd Battalion, meanwhile, was abroad, stationed in India and Iraq, and was acquiring a reputation as one of the best bands in the Service. Performances in Iraq included regular appearances at the National Cinema and a massed band memorial service for the Queen Mother.

In 1926 the two bands crossed paths in Malta, the 2nd on its way home, and the 1st *en route* for China. The latter was still led by the long-serving Bandmaster Vince, whose abilities were recognized even on the other side of the world. He conducted a performance in Shanghai by the massed bands of the 13th and 14th Infantry Brigades and the 9th Jhanis Indian Brigade to rapturous reviews; the *North China News* enthused:

The playing of Tchaikovsky's '1812' Overture has left an indelible impression on the writer. Never has this overture been better played by massed military musicians, and never will it be, in all likelihood. Mr Vince's conducting of this was exceptionally able; the response of his musicians remarkable.

The Battalion moved on to India, and in 1929 Mr Vince retired, to be succeeded by the extremely capable 'Paddy' Purcell. The demands of the period can be seen in a report that, at the end of a 21-mile march from the Sakrauda, the Band were still playing as the men entered Ghangara. In the same town a Memorial Service for George V was held in January 1936, at which Bandmaster Purcell and a choir of bandboys sang Psalm 130.

Mr Purcell did not restrict his talents to such sacred ceremonies, as a report from *The New Statesman* of India made clear in a review of a 1934 concert party: 'Bandmaster Purcell was indefatigable in his singing and step dancing . . . . [He] also conducted the Dance Band and appeared with Corporals Hulme and Stone as the Three Brigands.' In addition to this variety of entertainment, the 56-strong Band could still field a string band.

The Commanding Officer of the Eastern Frontier Forces presented the Bandmaster with a kukri in recognition of services to the EFF Band, and a similar gift was made to Bandsman Garham for composing a regimental march for the EFF.

Back home, the 2nd Battalion Band was busy playing the circuit of parks and seaside resorts. It was also required to keep prepared for action, as the Band Notes in *The Wasp* of December 1937 record:

In the near future we start our real vocations – motor-cyclists, Bren gunners, snipers and anti-aircraft defence on one side; and stretcher bearing on the other. The idea being that if in the next war we hurt the enemy too much, we shall be able to patch him up for another go.

When war came in 1939, the 1st Battalion was in the Middle East, while the 2nd formed part of the British Expeditionary Force. Both bandmasters returned to the depot to build anew; Mr Goddard of the 1st later took a band overseas to serve in Gibraltar and then Palestine, whilst Mr Thorpe of the 2nd was kept busy playing for fund-raising campaigns, parades, factory concerts, troops entertainments and the like. Strengthened by the return of seven bandsmen from the BEF, the new 2nd Battalion Band made more than 30 broadcasts on the BBC from 1942 onwards. It also had the honour of playing at Buckingham Palace.

In November 1946 the Band of the 2nd left for a five-month tour of Greece. Two years later the Battalion was disbanded; Bandmaster Elloway moved on to the 1st for a brief spell before emigrating to Canada, where he pursued his musical career.

Regimental Music

The quick march was 'La Mandolinata', adapted from a serenade from a French opera *Le Passant* composed in 1872 by Emile Paladilhe. Another quick march used was 'The Mountain Rose' the

Bedfordshire & Hertfordshire Regiment, Bedford 1952, Bandmaster A Underwood (Eagles/Ogilby)

regimental quick march of the former Bedfordshire Regiment. Very little is known of the origin of the tune, but it is thought to have been arranged by Bandmaster George Miller.

The slow march was 'Scipio'. (For further details see the Grenadier Guards.)

THE ESSEX REGIMENT

1741	55th Foot	1755	58th Foot
1748	renumbered 44th Foot	1756	renumbered 56th Foot
1782	44th (East Essex) Foot	1782	56th (West Essex) Foot

1881	The Essex Regiment
1958	amalgamated with The Bedfordshire and Hertfordshire Regiment to form The 3rd East Anglian Regiment (16th/44th Foot)
1968	redesignated 3rd Battalion, The Royal Anglian Regiment

A succession of inspection reports tells the story of the early days of the Band of the 55th Foot. In 1768, the only musicians mentioned are six fifers, but on 20 May 1772 there is a reference to a 'Band of Music'. Further reports tell us 'Fifers are quite boys; Band very young' (1787), and that there are '12 Drums, 10 Music' in 1792.

A 2nd Battalion was raised in Ireland in 1805, but was disbanded in 1816 following the defeat of Napoleon, and it is not known whether any music existed. Similarly the 56th Foot had a 2nd Battalion in those years, and even for a short spell in 1813/14 a 3rd Battalion; again no record survives of music in these battalions.

That the regular Battalion of the 56th had a band, however, is clear from an 1805 letter written by the central authorities at Horse Guards in response to a query about recruiting:

His Royal Highness will not object to you receiving into the Band of the 56th Regiment any Swiss, German or Italian Musicians alluded to in your letter, but it is His Royal Highness's pleasure that French men are on no account to be admitted.

The first mention of a bandmaster in either regiment comes with the appointment of Giovanni Gassner to the 44th in 1848. Signor Gassner had come from the Swiss Guards and was one of the most successful of the mid-19th century foreign bandmasters, later serving with the 3rd Foot and the 50th; fuller details of his career can be found above in the West Kents.

The first known bandmaster of the 56th is more obscure, with the only reference coming in the shape of a memorial stone in the parish church of St George in Bermuda. On the stone are recorded a number of regimental personnel who died in 1853 during a yellow fever epidemic; amongst the names is that of 'J H Thompson, bandmaster'. Given the period, it is probable that Mr Thompson was a civilian, though if so, he was one of the relatively few prepared to accompany his battalion on a posting overseas.

There is a gap in the available information after both Signor Gassner and Mr Thompson. When records resume both battalions had sergeant bandmasters: Sgt Farrugid in the 44th and Sgt McNerney in the 56th.

In 1872 the Band of the 44th Foot under Sergeant William Beyers accompanied the Regiment on a thirteen-year overseas tour that commenced in India, and was to take in Tonga, Burma and Aden before returning home. The following decade, it was again on its travels, serving in the Boer War. The 3rd Battalion of the regiment, better known as the Essex Regimental Militia, also fought in that conflict, along with what was known as its Permanent Staff Band.

The 2nd Battalion, too, spent time abroad in the 1880s and '90s, stationed in Egypt and then in Malta, of which a former bandboy, Colour Sergeant Richard Motley, was later to write:

This was a particularly busy time for the Band, with divisional parades, guards of honour (to our own royalty and foreign potentates), and massed band rehearsals for the Diamond Jubilee festivities

Despite this full schedule, time was also found to organize a minstrel troupe.

The 1881 Cardwell reforms, that brought The Essex Regiment into existence, also swept away the extraordinary cornucopia of facings that characterized the British Army; virtually every regiment had adopted a different colour facing for its uniform, amongst the most distinctive of which was that of the 56th. The particular shade of crimson used was named after the notorious Marquise de Pompadour (1721-64), mistress of Louis XV, and the regiment consequently acquired the nickname 'The Pompadours'.

Despite the 1881 amalgamation, the regimental tradition of the new 2nd Essex was fiercely protected, and the name 'The Pompadours' was used as the title to one of the best known of Leo Stanley's marches. Leo Stanley, of course, was the pseudonym of Randolph Ricketts, the most celebrated bandmaster to serve with the Battalion, holding the post from 1913 to 1925.

During the same era the 1st Battalion had an even longer-serving Bandmaster with Henry Facer, who spent 21 years with the Essex. Mr Facer joined the Battalion in 1908, shortly after it had returned from several years in India; under his predecessor, 'Sammy' Harmon, a successful orchestra had also been formed and it is believed this survived through to the Great War. Even though Bandmaster Facer's time with the Essex included the trauma of the war years, he was still able to claim at a Sergeants' Mess smoking concert on his retirement in 1929 that this period was 'the happiest of my life'. At the same event, the RSM paid tribute to 'his cheeriness and lightheartedness, sociability and capacity for hard work'.

Mr Ricketts' successor in the 2nd Battalion was Ronald Botting, a veteran of the Great War who had won a Distinguished Conduct Medal and a Military Medal whilst serving with the Royal Fusiliers. He was also an accomplished musician; stationed in

2nd Battalion The Essex Regiment, 1899 (Eagles/Ogilby)

Right: Programme of 1884 benefit concert for the widow of Bandmaster J Hansen, 2nd Battalion The Essex Regiment featuring the Duke of Edinburgh on violin (RMSM)

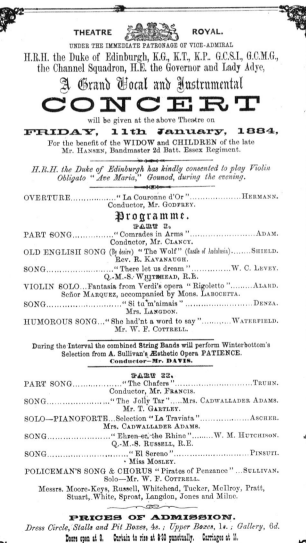

1st Battalion The Essex Regiment, Colchester 1929, Bandmaster B Howe   (Eagles/Ogilby)

India in the late '20s, he inaugurated a series of classical concerts and led the Band in a Torchlight Tattoo to celebrate the Silver Jubilee of 1935. His greatest challenge, however, was to come in the Second World War.

With the 1st Battalion in Egypt in 1939, where the bandsmen were employed on guard and driving duties rather than music, it was left to Mr Botting to create a wartime band at the depot. Within a short time it was playing throughout Southern England, and in October 1944 ventured across the Channel for a six-month tour of north France and the Low Countries. Amongst its more memorable moments were a performance at the Opera House in Ghent, and two weeks spent with the 2nd Battalion in Nijmegen.

The immediate post-war years saw a series of celebratory parades as The Essex Regiment was awarded the freedom of various towns in the county, including Southend, Chelmsford, Colchester, East Ham, Ilford and Romford. Then in November 1948 came the official amalgamation parade of the 1st and 2nd Battalions.

In fact, the two bands had come together the previous year, when Bandmaster Botting finally retired. Horace Monk, who had become Bandmaster of the 1st Battalion, took over a merged Band of some 67 men and boys. Within six months, this had fallen to just a dozen bandsmen and a few boys, as post-war demobilization took its toll. At the same time, however, the sudden reduction in the numbers of bands in the Army ensured that there were more engagements to play than ever before; inexperienced boys were given an intense course of what was known as 'play as you learn'.

A posting in Germany in the early '50s followed, though the Band still returned each year for the summer season. In 1954 Bandmaster Monk retired after 37 years of service; his successor, Reginald Brown, had no sooner joined than he was accompanying the Regiment to Hong Kong. Two years in that colony saw the musicians kept busy with military engagements, with dance band bookings and with a noted band choir. Broadcasts on local radio were also made.

The Regiment returned in 1956, and was amalgamated with the Beds & Herts two years later. The final Kneller Hall inspection of the Band of The Essex Regiment saw it achieve the very rare grade of 'Outstanding'.

Regimental Music

The official quick march of The Essex Regiment was 'The Essex'; it opens with a fanfare and the regimental bugle call, whilst the tune that follows is similar to Weber's 'Lutzow's Wild Hunt'. In the early years of this century, however, the Regiment chose to use 'The Hampshire', an adaptation of the Scottish tune 'The Highland Piper', in preference, and 'The Essex' largely dropped out of use. In 1944 a new march, 'The Essex Regiment', written by Bandmaster Botting of the 2nd Battalion, was officially adopted, but failed to displace 'The Hampshire' in the Regiment's affections.

The 1st Battalion also used the Scottish march, 'We'll Gang Nae Muir to Yon Toun', which was also the quick march of The Queen's Royal Regiment. The 2nd had an old march, 'Pompadour', dating from its earlier incarnation: 'Pompadour! Pompadour! The old Fifty-Sixth!'

3rd BATTALION
THE ROYAL ANGLIAN REGIMENT

1959	The 3rd East Anglian Regiment (16th/44th Foot)
1964	3rd (16th/44th Foot) Battalion, The Royal Anglian Regiment
1968	3rd Battalion, The Royal Anglian Regiment
1980	3rd Battalion (Bedfordshire, Hertfordshire and Essex), The Royal Anglian Regiment
1992	disbanded as 3rd Battalion

The Beds & Herts and The Essex Regiment were amalgamated in 1959, with Reg Brown taking over the merged Band.

Later that year it made the first of its many overseas tours, to Malaya and Singapore, where both the military band and dance band found plenty of work. Highlights included a trip into the jungle to play for the troops on exercise and a television appearance in Bangkok. Further visits were subsequently undertaken to Spain and North America, the latter centring on the 1964 New York World Fair.

In 1968 Robert Smith was appointed Bandmaster. Whilst with the Regiment, he married Captain Zara Bowness, the Director of Music of the WRAC, at a ceremony in the Kneller Hall chapel. Shortly after, the two appeared together at the Wembley Military Music Pageant with their respective bands.

One of the most symbolic performances of the 3rd Anglians occurred at a ceremony in Happy Valley, Cyprus in 1976 to mark the closure of Headquarters British Forces Near East. For the Regiment, an equally significant moment was the celebration in 1988 of the tercentenary of the 16th Foot. But for the public, the most memorable contribution was surely in 1989 when the Band appeared in the opening titles and closing credits of the classic BBC TV series *Blackadder Goes Forth*, complete with Bandsman Baldrick (played by Mr Tony Robinson) on triangle.

Military duties still continued, however, and in 1990 the bandsmen were called upon in their medical capacity, answering emergencies during the ambulance workers' dispute. For his outstanding work during the four-month strike, Lance Corporal Guy Burrows was awarded the BEM in the 1991 New Year Honours List.

One of the most widely travelled of bands in recent years, the 3rd Anglians made one last trip overseas in 1991 with a five-week tour of Canada. The following year, the Battalion was disbanded, as noted in the Kneller Hall magazine, *Fanfare*:

> The Pompadours Band will cease to exist on 4 October 1992. On this day the 3rd Battalion's colours are to be laid up at Warley Chapel and the three battalions of The Royal Anglian Regiment will merge to form two new battalions. The Pompadours' musicians will disperse to the two other battalion bands and 'Mandolinata' will be heard no more (well, less often anyway).

Regimental Music

The quick march is a combination of 'Rule Britannia' and 'Speed the Plough'. (For further details see 1st Battalion, The Royal Anglian Regiment).

The slow march is 'The Devonshire Rose'. (For further details see The Northamptonshire Regiment.)

BANDMASTERS OF THE 1st BATTALION THE BEDFORDSHIRE AND HERTFORDSHIRE REGIMENT

1864-1875 **KENNEDY**, William. Born 182? died 1875. Sgt (BM) 1/3 Ft 1853; Sgt (BM) 1/16 Ft 29/7/64; died whilst serving 31/3/75.

1875-1885 **BOEHMER**, H C. For full details see 2nd Battalion.

1885-1895 **POCOCK**, Richard. Born 1855 died 1907. Enl 2/3 Ft 28/2/70; WO (BM) 1 Bedfs & Herts R 24/12/85; retd 10/12/95.

1895-1907 **KIRWAN**, John. Born 1863 died 1951. Enl 64 Ft 17/10/78; WO (BM) 1 Bedfs & Herts 11/12/95; retd 18/4/07.

1907-1912 **BORLAND**, Hugh. Enl 1/3 Ft 4/8/83; WO (BM) 1 Bedfs & Herts R 19/4/07; retd 18/4/12.

1912-1929 **VINCE**, John Erwin Seymour. Born 1879 died 1940. Enl 38 Ft 20/5/93; WO (BM) 1 Bedfs & Herts 19/4/12; retd 9/5/29.

1929-1938 **PURCELL**, Patrick Ambrose ARAM LRAM ARCM. Born 1902 died 1972. Enl RA 10/7/18; WO1 (BM) 1 Bedfs & Herts R 10/5/29; WO1 (BM) 2 E York R 9/4/38; retd 20/7/45.

1938-1948 **GODDARD**, Frederick Albert George LRAM ARCM. Born 1908. Enl RA (Mtd) 13/6/23; WO1 (BM) 1 Bedfs & Herts R 10/4/38; WO1 (BM) WRAC 1/7/49; Lt (DoM) WRAC 5/1/53; Capt (DoM) RAOC 17/11/54; retd 6/2/62 rank of Maj. (During the war years he served as Bandmaster with not only the 1st but also the 2nd and the 5th Bns and the Army Apprentice College.)

1948-1955 **UNDERWOOD**, Arthur ARCM. Born 1912 died 1962. Enl 2 N Stafford R 14/9/28; WO1 (BM) 1 W York R 24/2/45; WO1 (BM) 1 Bedfs & Herts R 25/11/48; WO1 (BM) RA (Plym) 6/7/55; Lt (DoM) RA (BAOR) 15/9/58; died whilst serving 30/7/62.

1955-1958 **PEARSON**, James William. Born 1919. Enl 2 E York R 13/9/34; transf 2 Foresters 7/2/46; WO1 (BM) Sierra Leone Regt 8/2/50; WO1 (BM) 2 Foresters 10/2/53; WO1 (BM) 1 Bedfs & Herts R 6/7/55; WO1 (BM) British Military Mission, Libya 1958; retd 1961.

BANDMASTERS OF THE 2nd BATTALION THE BEDFORDSHIRE AND HERTFORDSHIRE REGIMENT

18??-1871 **DECONNI**, Signor. Civ BM 2/16 Ft; retd 28/3/71.

1871-1875 **BOEHMER**, H C. Enl 2/16 Ft; Sgt (BM) 2/16 Ft 29/3/71; Sgt (BM) 1/16 Ft 1/4/75; WO (BM) 1/7/81; retd 23/12/85.

1875-1880 **MILLER**, George John MVO BMus (Cantab) LRAM. Born 1853 died 1928. Enl RM (Plym) 7/8/72; Sgt (BM) 2/16 Ft 1/4/75; Sgt (BM) RMC 17/7/80; W1 (BM) 1/7/81; WO (BM) RMLI (Port) 18/11/84; Lt (BM) 12/98; retd 3/3/17 rank of Maj.

1880-1891 **KELLY**, William. Born 1846 died 19??. Enl 91 Ft 19/1/69; Sgt (BM) 2/16 Ft 17/7/80; WO (BM) 1/7/81; retd 10/3/91.

1891-1903 **WILLIS**, Robert. Born 1865 died 1907. Enl 7 H 4/2/79; WO (BM) 2 Bedfs & Herts 19/3/91; retd 10/6/03.

1903-1922 **BAXTER**, Ernest Arthur. Born 1869 died 1927. Enl 1 R S Fus 3/1/83; WO (BM) 2 Bedfs & Herts R 11/6/03; retd 31/8/22.

Left: Bandmaster H Borland, 1st Battalion, The Bedfordshire and Hertfordshire Regiment (RMSM)
Top right: Bandmaster K A Elloway 2nd Bn Bedfs & Herts R (RMSM)
Right: Bandmaster H C F Monk 1st Bn Essex R (RMSM)

1922-1933 **COMPTON**, William Cyril. Born 1891 died 19??. Enl 1 DCLI 19/1/09; WO1 (BM) 3 R Fus 22/10/19; WO1 (BM) 4 R Fus 25/11/19; WO1 (BM) Bedfs & Herts R 1/9/22; retd 18/1/33.

1933-1945 **THORPE**, John Bassett Hodgeson ARCM. Born 1903. Enl 1 Hampshire R 15/5/19; WO1 (BM) 2 Bedfs & Herts R 19/1/33; retd 27/8/45.

1945-1948 **ELLOWAY**, Kenneth Albert ARCM psm. Born 1916 Died 1981. Enl 2 Dorset 21/10/32; WO1 (BM) 2 Bedfs & Herts R 28/8/45; att 1 Bedfs & Herts R 25/11/48; WO1 (BM) RA (Wool) 1950; retd 8/3/55; Capt (DoM) Canadian Artillery 1955-1964; Inspector of Bands, Eastern Command, Canada 1964-1965.

BANDMASTERS OF THE 1st BATTALION THE ESSEX REGIMENT

1848-1851 **GASSNER**, Signor Giovanni. Born 1828 died 1884. 2 Lt (DoM) 1st Regt Swiss Guards 1847; Sgt (BM) 44 Ft 1848; Sgt (BM) 1/3 Ft 1851; BM HMS *Bellerophon* 1853; Sgt (BM) 1st Royal Lanark Militia 1855; Sgt (BM) 5 DG 1856; Sgt (BM) 50 Ft 1856; retd 22/7/84.

1851-1864 Bandmaster(s) not known.

1864-1867 **FARRUGID**, G. Enl 44 Ft; Sgt (BM) 44 Ft 19/10/64; retd 9/1/67.

1867-1868 **McELENEY**, A. Enl 44 Ft; Sgt (BM) 44 Ft 10/1/67; Sgt (BM) 78 Ft 1/9/68; BM Duke of York's Royal Military School 1/9/80; retd 10/2/88.

1868-1871 Bandmaster(s) not known.

1871-1880 **BEYERS**, William. Enl 1/24 Ft; Sgt (BM) 44 Ft 11/7/71; retd 17/3/80.

1880-1897 **EDMONDS**, James. Born 1848 died 19??. Enl 48 Ft 7/1/63; Sgt (BM) 44 Ft 18/3/80; retd 17/5/97.

1897-1906 **HARMAN**, Samuel William. Born 1864 died 1933. Enl 41 Ft 12/10/78; WO (BM) 1 Essex R 18/5/97; retd 29/5/06.

1906-1908 **GRIFFITHS**, James. Born 1866 died 1944. Enl Viceroy of India's Band 23/4/78; WO (BM) 2 The Buffs 8/12/92; WO (BM) 1 R Gar R 1/3/02; WO (BM) 1 Essex R 30/5/06; retd 22/4/08.

1908-1929 **FACER**, Henry Edward. Born 1876 died 1948. Enl 1 Devon R 21/12/91; WO (BM) 1 Essex R 23/4/08; retd 20/12/29.

1929-1938 **HOWE**, Benjamin ARCM. Born 1898 died 19??. Enl 2 Rifle Bde 24/10/14; WO1 (BM) 1 Essex R 21/12/29; retd 4/1/38.

1938-1954 **MONK**, Horace Charles Frederick ARCM. Born 1901 died 1985. Enl 2 Ox & Bucks LI 28/12/17; WO1 (BM) 1 Essex R 5/1/38; retd 3/5/54.

1954-1958 **BROWN**, Reginald William. Born 1917. Enl RA (Mtd) 9/9/32; WO1 (BM) 1 Essex R 4/5/54; WO1 (BM) 3 R Anglian R 2/6/58; retd 20/5/62.

BANDMASTERS OF THE 2nd BATTALION THE ESSEX REGIMENT

18??-1853 **THOMPSON**, J. H. BM 56 Ft; died in service 1853.

1853-1870 Bandmaster(s) not known.

1870-1879 **McNERNEY**, G. Sgt (BM) 56 Ft 14/1/70; retd 31/7/78.

1879-1883 **HANSEN**, John P. Born 18?? died 1883. Enl 56 Ft; Sgt (BM) 56 Ft 16/1/79; WO (BM) 1/7/81; died whilst serving 1/11/83.

1883-1890 **GODFREY**, William. Born 1855 died 1890. Enl 94 Ft 15/7/70; WO (BM) 2 Essex R 2/11/83; retd 31/8/90.

1890-1899 **HILL**, Robert John. Born 1853 died 1917. Enl 1/60 Ft 13/2/68; WO (BM) 2 Essex R 25/1/90; retd 25/4/99.

1899-1913 **WINGROVE**, Charles. Born 1862 died 1914. Enl 3 H 13/1/79; WO (BM) 2 Essex R 26/4/99; retd 14/10/13.

1913-1925 **RICKETTS**, Randolph Robjent. Born 1884 died 1967. Enl 2 R Ir R 30/8/1900; WO (BM) 2 Essex R 15/10/13; retd 7/12/25; Civ BM R Signals 1/1/26; retd 31/12/38.

1925-1947 **BOTTING**, Ronald DCM MM ARCM. Born 1895 died 19??. Enl 1 R Fus 27/4/09; WO1 (BM) 2 Essex R 8/12/25; 26/11/47.

Bandsmen of 3rd Battalion The Royal Anglian Regiment on active service in the Gulf War, 1991
(R Anglians)

BANDMASTERS OF THE 3rd BATTALION THE ROYAL ANGLIAN REGIMENT

1958-1962 **BROWN**, Reginald William. Born 1917. For full details see The Essex Regiment.

1962-1968 **COCKCROFT**, Frank AmusTCL. Born 1931. Enl 15/19 H 4/11/46; WO1 (BM) 3 E Anglian 21/5/62; WO1 (BM) 3 R Anglian 1/9/64; retd 5/6/68.

1968-1974 **BOWNESS-SMITH**, Robert A ARCM. Born 1939. Enl Worc R 9/8/54; WO1 (BM) 3 R Anglian 6/6/68; WO1 (BM) RA (Wool) 14/1/74; retd 29/5/79.

1974-1980 **WATTS**, Stuart Alastair LRAM psm. Born 1945. Enl RHG/D 6/9/60; WO1 (BM) 3 R Anglian 14/1/74; WO1 (BM) Queen's Div 1980; Capt (DoM) Para 1/11/82; Capt (DoM) Guards Depot (badged RHG/D) 8/7/85; Capt (DoM) Gurkhas 16/3/87; Capt (DoM) Gren Gds 18/7/88; Maj Snr Instr RMSM 31/8/92; Maj (DoM) WG 7/94.

1980-1982 **LEASK**, Gordon Hankins LTCL. Born 1943. Enl 2 RGJ 6/2/61; WO1 (BM) QLR 8/1/73; WO1 (BM) King's Div Depot 27/6/78; WO1 (BM) 3 R Anglian 1980; Capt (DoM) JLR badged RTR 12/5/82; Capt (DoM) Light Div 12/10/83; retd 17/4/86.

1982-1987 **BYRNE**, Patrick H. Born 1947. Enl 2 Para 14/10/65; WO1 (BM) JLR badged RTR 26/2/80; WO1 (BM) 3 R Anglian 1882; retd 30/11/87.

1987-1993 **PARKINSON**, Timothy John ARCM ALCM. Born 1955. Enl WG 4/5/71; WO1 (BM) 3 R Anglian 6/2/87; WO1 (BM) 1 R Anglian 10/92; WO1 (BM) Queens (Minden) 1/8/94.

THE ROYAL LEICESTERSHIRE REGIMENT

1688	Richard's Regiment of Foot
1751	17th Foot
1782	17th (Leicestershire) Foot
1881	The Leicestershire Regiment
1946	The Royal Leicestershire Regiment
1964	4th (Leicestershire) Battalion, The Royal Anglian Regiment

The accounts of many regimental bands prior to the mid-19th century are very patchy, but nowhere is this more so than in the case of the 17th Foot. A letter written in 1931 by Major-General Sir Edward Woodward, then Colonel of The Leicestershire Regiment, to the Under Secretary of State for War, explains the difficulties:

The records of The Leicestershire Regiment prior to 1840 are believed to have been lost when the transport ship Hannah *in which the Regiment was being conveyed from Kurrachee in March of that year, was wrecked off the Indian coast, and the men barely escaped with their lives.*

A clue to the early nature of the band comes from the regimental slow march, 'General Monckton, 1762'. Monckton was the Colonel Commandant of the 17th Foot from 1759 to 1782, and is reputed to have written the march himself. The inclusion of the date '1762' probably indicates that this was when it was adopted by the Regiment, and the fact therefore that it was originally scored for just seven instruments would suggest that this was the size of the Band at the time.

It is likely, however, that this was still essentially a fife and drum ensemble, and that the military band was formed later. A possible date is given in a 1950s edition of the regimental journal; a report of a concert given in an old people's home states that 'one lady who attended was the grand-daughter of the very first man to form a band in the Regiment in 1804.'

Though uncorroborated, this date is plausible. Certainly by 1828, when Mr E Hull produced his famous series of paintings of British military uniforms, the Band was sufficiently established to be included. A bandsman of the 17th Foot is shown resplendent in pink trousers (as distinct from the

BANDS OF THE

4TH BATTALION

THE ROYAL ANGLIAN REGIMENT

1st Battalion The Leicestershire Regiment, Leicester 1909, Bandmaster C Witt (Eagles/Ogilby)

more normal scarlet favoured by most other regiments), white coatees with gold braid facings and a pink-plumed helmet.

In 1858 a 2nd Battalion was raised, and we can assume that, in common with other infantry battalions of the era, it had a band from the outset, though its first known bandmaster, Mr F Brim, did not arrive until 1865. The following year saw the Battalion undertake its first overseas posting with a visit to St Andrews in Canada.

Official records of the 1st Battalion begin in 1866 with the appointment of Mr Sommer as Bandmaster. Undoubtedly, however, he would have had predecessors, amongst them a Mr Wickels (or Wickells), about whom little is known save that he had previously served with the 64th Foot; when that regiment was posted to India in January 1849, he transferred to the 17th, then stationed at Chatham.

In the 1890s the 1st Battalion, together with its Band, spent two years in Barbados, followed by a spell in South Africa, where it fought in the Boer War. During the retreat to Ladysmith, several instruments were lost; though most were never recovered, a side drum fell into the hands of an enemy soldier, who eventually returned it to the Regiment in 1934.

From South Africa the Battalion moved to India, before finally coming home in 1908. Stationed in the South-East, the Band played regularly in Folkestone and in Herne Bay. Illustrative of its repertoire is this programme from a concert given in Herne Bay on Easter Monday 1910:

March	Ma Petite Bretonne	Bosc
	(the Parisian success)	
Ethiopian Selection	By The Mississippi	Knowles
Descriptive Piece	The Phantom	Myddleton
Glockenspiel Solo	The Bohemian's Polka	Waldteufel
Grand National		
Fantasia	The Flying Squadron	Kappey
Valse	Venus on Earth	Lincke
Idyll	An Evening Breeze	Langey
Grand Overture		
Solenelle	1812	Tchaikovsky
Two Step	Starland	Connor
	(the rage of New York)	
Regimental Marches	A Hunting We Will Go &c.	
	God Save The King	

The Bandmaster at this time was Mr Witt, who was held in high regard within the Battalion. Between 1902 and 1910, he received a series of glowing reports from his Commanding Officer, which give some indication of the qualities most cherished in bandmasters at the turn of the century: 'Temperate, zealous, hard-working; a teetotaler [sic], all that could be desired; general deportment and bearing an excellent example to Band.'

These annual reports – though they are simply brief, hand-written notes – give an insight into the lot of bandmasters at the highpoint of the Empire, and can even provide a sketch of human tragedy. John Hayward, for example, served with the 2nd Battalion for less than a year, having arrived from the 3rd Warwicks; his only report read: 'Exemplary, most satisfactory, invalided tuberculosis.'

Mr Hayward's truncated tenure was an exception, and during the first half of this century, the 2nd Battalion was fortunate to have the services of two long-serving bandmasters with impressive academic records. Mr James Denman, who took the Band through the Great War, was a Bachelor of Music, whilst J A G Mantz, who served during the Second World War, was awarded the Doctorate of Music. Mr Mantz later became Director of Music of the Royal Artillery (Salisbury Plain).

While the inter-war years were ones of relative tranquillity for most of the Army, both battalions of The Leicestershire Regiment were actively engaged in policing the fringes of the Empire, and the musicians were often called upon in a military capacity.

The 1st Battalion was stationed in India from 1927 onwards and was involved in the perennial problems of the North-West Frontier, with the bandsmen employed as medical orderlies and on guard duties. In one incident in the late '30s, just before the wider hostilities broke out, a day-long

The Royal Leicestershire Regiment, Leicester, Bandmaster D Walker   (Jean Walker)

skirmish with tribesmen resulted in six fatalities, including Private Thurman, an ex-bandsman, and Lance-Corporal Sibley, a former band boy.

Closer to home, but still in danger, the 2nd Leicesters sailed for Palestine in 1938, where the Band was soon acting as a scout company, patrolling the hills and exchanging fire with local brigands.

With the coming of the Second World War, both bands converted to stretcher platoons. The 2nd Battalion spent most of its time in the Mediterranean theatre, winning a battle honour at Sidi Barrani on 11 December 1940. Amongst the wounded that day were the twin Scully brothers, both former band boys, serving as stretcher bearers.

The 1st Battalion, meanwhile, faced the horror of the retreat through Malaya and the subsequent fall of Singapore. So depleted were the ranks after even the initial encounters with the Japanese, that on 20 December 1941 a composite unit, The British Battalion, was formed with the 2nd East Surreys. Further terrible casualties were sustained, such that the new battalion was reduced from a strength of 786 all ranks to just 265 by the time of the surrender of Singapore. After the war a tradition was established in the two regiments of commemorating the temporary amalgamation every 20 December with a toast to 'The British Battalion', and the playing in both Officers' Messes of the other's regimental march.

In common with other infantry regiments, the Leicesters lost their 2nd Battalion in the late '40s. The Band of the 1st Battalion, on the other hand, was kept extremely busy with a variety of postings as far apart as Germany, Hong Kong, Khartoum and Cyprus. Its tasks were as diverse as the locations and included massed band performances in Kowloon, playing with Professor Jimmy Edwards on his 1956 tour of Cyprus, and acting as a pit orchestra for a production of *The Pirates of Penzance*.

The foreign travel, however, also gave opportunities for forms of relaxation not generally available at home; the Band Notes in the regimental journal in 1955 talk of 'a sing song stimulated by lager, hashish and a few reefers secreted into the camp by the "gone" element in the Band.'

In 1963 The Leicestershire Regiment was redesignated the 4th Battalion of The East Anglian Regiment.

Regimental Music

The quick march of the 1st Battalion was for a while a piece known simply as '1772', presumably referring to the date it was adopted. Some time around 1848-50 'Romaika' (also spelt 'Roumika' and 'Ramauka') was introduced to the Regiment from the 64th Foot – possibly by Bandmaster Wickels, or possibly by a surgeon, William Smith, who also came from the 64th – and in 1882 it officially became the march past. The title is believed to derive from a Greek dance, and the words were probably written by Thomas Moore (1779-1852).

In 1933 this too was supplanted, this time by 'A Hunting Call (We'll All Go A-Hunting Today)', which had originally been the quickstep of the 3rd Militia Battalion. An old Leicestershire hunting song, it had the advantage of being associated with the County. It had been adopted by the 2nd Battalion in 1858.

The 1st Battalion used the aforementioned 'General Monckton, 1762' as its slow march, though for a short period in the mid-19th century it was replaced by 'Robin Adair' and later by 'The Bird in the Desert'. The 2nd Battalion used a slow march entitled 'The Grenadiers'.

4th BATTALION, THE ROYAL ANGLIAN REGIMENT

1964	4th (Leicestershire) Battalion, The Royal Anglian Regiment
1968	4th Battalion, The Royal Anglian Regiment
1970	disbanded as 4th Battalion

Save for the change in title and regimental march, the Band was scarcely affected by the amalgamation of 1964: James Battye remained in command, and all the NCOs and instrumentalists were the same.

In 1968 Bandmaster Battye accepted a regimental commission and was succeeded by Tom Cooper, who proved to be the last bandmaster of the old 17th Foot. Further cuts were made throughout the Army and the 4th Battalion was disbanded in 1970. Bandmaster Cooper then moved to the Queen's Division Depot until his retirement in 1972.

The county name returned in 1980, when territorial associations were restored to The Royal Anglian Regiment, and the 2nd Battalion was renamed the 2nd Battalion (Lincolnshire, Leicestershire and Northamptonshire).

Regimental Music

The quick march was a combination of 'Rule Britannia' and 'Speed the Plough'. (For further details see 1st Battalion The Royal Anglian Regiment).

The slow march was 'The Devonshire Rose'. (For further details see The Northamptonshire Regiment.)

The quick and slow marches of The Royal Leicestershire Regiment were also used.

BANDMASTERS OF THE 1st BATTALION THE ROYAL LEICESTERSHIRE REGIMENT

1849-185? **WICKELS** (or **WICKELLS**). Civ BM 64 Ft 1845; Civ BM 1/17 Ft 1849; retirement date not known but probably mid-50s.

185?-1866 Bandmaster(s) not known.

1866-1874 **SOMMER**, Josef MVO. Born 1843 died 19??. Enl 65 Ft or 84 Ft 5/4/64 (there is some doubt which regiment he enlisted into, as in 1881 they became respectively the 1st & 2nd Bn York & Lanc R); Sgt (BM) 1/17 Ft 8/1? ?6; Sgt (BM) 26 Ft 31/7/74; Sgt (BM) Hyderabad Contingent 30/1/90; Lt (BM) RE 1/3/91; retd 8/1/05.

1874-1891 **PLANT**, Stephen John. Born 1847 died 1910. Enl 1/7 Ft 23/9/61; Sgt (BM) 1/17 Ft 1/2/74; WO (BM) 1/7/81; retd 21/5/91.

1891-1902 **HUGHES**, Edward. Born 1866 died 19??. Enl 1 KSLI 12/3/81; WO (BM) 1 Leicester R 22/5/91; retd 20/5/02.

1902-1919 **WITT**, Charles Stokes. Born 1873 died 19??. Enl 2 Loyal R 28/10/89; WO (BM) 1 Leicester R 21/5/02; retd 27/3/19.

1919-1934 **HEDGES**, Ernest Henry. Born 1887 died 19??. Enl 4 DG 30/11/01; WO1 (BM) 1 Leicester R 28/3/19; retd 2/4/34.

1934-1948 **NEALE**, Albert Edwin ARCM. Born 1906 died 1970. Enl 12 L 21/12/21; WO1 (BM) 1 Leicester R 3/4/34; retd 1948.

1948-1952 **PURCELL**, Joseph ARCM. Born 1912. For full details see 2nd Battalion The Royal Leicestershire Regiment.

1952-1959 **WALKER**, Desmond Kiernan ARCM psm. Born 1924 died 1974. Enl RECCE 5/11/42; trans 12L 1/46; WO1 (BM) 1 R Leicester R 17/5/52; WO1 (BM) Forester Bde 10/6/59; Lt (DoM) RTR (Rhine) 26/1/62; Lt (DoM) RASC 15/7/63; Capt (DoM) RCT 15/7/65; Capt (DoM) WG 14/10/69; died whilst serving 26/7/74 rank of Maj.

1959-1964 **BATTYE**, James Edgar ARCM. Born 1929. Enl 16/5 L 22/11/45; WO1 (BM) R Leicester R 10/6/59; WO1 (BM) 4 R Anglian 1/9/64; Lt (regt duty) 14/6/68; retd 1/10/74 rank of Capt.

Bandmaster C Witt, 1st Battalion The Leicestershire Regiment (RMSM)

BANDMASTERS OF THE 2nd BATTALION THE ROYAL LEICESTERSHIRE REGIMENT

1865-1871 **BRIM**, F. Sgt (BM) or Civ BM 2/17 Ft 1865; retd 30/4/71.

1871-1876 **HOLT**, James. Enl 2/17 Ft; Sgt (BM) 2/17 Ft 1/5/71; Sgt (BM) 36 Ft 1/5/76; WO (BM) 1/7/81; retd 15/11/81.

1876-1884 **STEVENIGHT**, James George. Born 1846 died 1929. Enl 32 Ft 17/10/59; Sgt (BM) 2/17 Ft 1/5/76; WO (BM) 1/7/81; retd 9/12/84.

1884-1891 **JOHNSON**, Arthur. Born 1855 died 19??. Enl 2/11 Ft 24/11/69; WO (BM) 2 Leicester R 10/12/84; retd 18/3/91.

1891-1907 THOMPSON, William. Born 1863 died 1927. Enl 2/1 Ft 20/3/77; WO (BM) 2 Leicester R 19/3/91; retd 19/3/07.

1907-1908 HAYWARD, Joseph Henry. Born 1864 died 1912. For full details see The Royal Warwickshire Regiment.

1908-1913 OWEN, William Henry. Born 1975 died 19??. Enl 14 H 26/4/90; WO (BM) 2 Leicester R 19/2/08; retd 18/2/13.

1913-1919 DENMAN Walter James Mus Bac ARCO. Born 1885 died 19??. Enl 2 HLI 3/5/09; WO (BM) 2 Leicester R 19/2/13; retd 14/5/19.

1919-1924 GROUT, Henry. Born 1888 died 19??. Enl 2 Rifle Bde 5/4/02; WO1 (BM) 2 Leicester R 15/5/19; retd 4/4/24; BM 2 BB & CL Rly Regt.

1924-1933 PAY, Louis James LRAM ARCM. Born 1890 died 19??. Enl 1 W York R 11/9/05; WO1 (BM) 2 Leicester R 5/4/24; retd 4/4/33.

1933-1942 MANTZ, James Alfred George Mus Doc LRAM ARCM. Born 1905. Enl 12 L 9/8/21; WO1 (BM) 2 Leicester R 5/4/33; WO1 (BM) RA (Sal Pl) 20/1/42; retd 18/3/46.

1942-1948 PURCELL, Joseph ARCM. Born 1912. Enl 1 Border R 26/12/26; WO1 (BM) 2 R Leicester R 20/1/42; WO1 (BM) 1 R Leicester R 1948; retd 16/5/52; BM Canadian Army 17/5/52.

1919-1924 GROUT, Henry. Born 1888 died 19??. Enl 2 Rifle Bde 5/4/02; WO1 (BM) 2 Leicester R 15/5/19; retd 4/4/24; BM 2nd Bombay, Baroda and Central India Railway Regt.

BANDMASTERS OF THE 4th BATTALION THE ROYAL ANGLIAN REGIMENT

1964-1968 BATTYE, James Edgar ARCM. Born 1929. For full details see The Royal Leicestershire Regiment.

1968-1970 COOPER, Thomas George. Born 1932. Enl RHG 6/2/50; WO1 (BM) 4 R Anglian 3/5/68; WO1 (BM) Queen's Division Depot 1/3/71; retd 1972.

Opposite page: Entertaining the troops: Royal Army Service Corps near the front line in Italy 1944, Bandmaster D Pope (RMSM)

Below: 1st Battalion The Leicestershire Regiment, Aldershot 1910 (Eagles/Ogilby)

MUSICIANS AT WAR

MUSICIANS AT WAR

One of the key arguments advanced over the years by supporters of British Army bands is that musicians have a secondary military role which they are called upon to fulfil during wartime; bandsmen are in effect soldiers who also play music when the country is at peace. It is certainly an argument that has the weight of recent history on its side: bandsmen have served in the ranks and, more particularly, in a medical capacity from the Crimea through to the Gulf War of 1990. Even more recently, the Band of The Cheshire Regiment has worked with the United Nations peace-keeping forces in the Bosnian conflict.

It was not always thus. The origins of British military music are on the battlefield, believed to date from the battle of Halidon Hill in 1333 when drums were first used in the English Army. Drums, pipes and later trumpets were the only viable means of communication, used to signal orders to the combatant soldiers. The musician's task was thus to play music, albeit of a primitive form, not to fight.

In some instances, this was considered military enough. When the Highlanders who had fought for Charles Stuart in 1745 were being tried, one of those charged was a piper, James Reid. The court rejected his defence that he was simply a musician, not a combatant, and instead ruled that since Highlanders would not fight without pipers being present, the bagpipes had legally to be considered an instrument of warfare. Sadly, such an acknowledgement of the pipes' supreme importance can have been of little comfort to Mr Reid, who was executed for his music.

In general, however, it was the non-combatant nature of the drummer that opened up greater responsibilities; Robert Ward, in his *Animadversions of Warre*, written in 1639, saw the drum-major as an important member of the military staff, acting almost as an ambassador in conflict:

> *A drumme is one of the necessariest officers to a Company . . . for many times they are sent to Parlie with the Enemie, and to redeeme Prisoners from the Enemy; therefore hee ought to be a man of personage, faithful, secret and trusty; He ought to speak several languages.*

Even in the mid-18th century, when the concept of military music evolved beyond the basic function of signalling and wind bands began to emerge, there was still an important place for musicians. Simes' *Military History*, published in 1768, explained that the position of 'Musik, drummers and fifers' was in the centre of the infantry square alongside the colours, where they should play suitably martial

11th (Service) Battalion The Queen's Own Royal West Kent Regiment during the Great War   (RMSM)

music to strengthen the resolve of the front line troops. Prefiguring their later duties, Simes also noted that they should be prepared to help the wounded and, in emergencies, to constitute the last line of defence of the colours.

There were, of course, problems attached to the introduction of more sophisticated instruments to the field of war. When damaged, the early drums and trumpets could be repaired, after a fashion, by the farriers and pioneers who accompanied the Army. With oboes, clarinets and flutes, this was no longer possible; damage to a mouthpiece could effectively write off an instrument.

Similarly, the ebb and flow of war, which frequently saw the loss of some instruments and the capture of others, began to take a heavier toll as bands developed. When it was simply a question of exchanging drums, this was a matter of regimental prestige – drums enjoyed a status only slightly below that of the colours – but of little musical significance. The wind instruments of the late 18th century, however, did not conform to any standardized tuning; a band whose musical stores were an ad hoc collection of the spoils of war could not even therefore be counted upon to play in a uniform pitch.

There was also the problem of the unpredictability of the line-up at the end of a campaign. Phillipe Girault, in his book *Les Campaignes d'un Musicien d'Etat-Major pendant 1791-1810* (1901), describes a parade to celebrate the capture of Dusseldorf by the French; the vicissitudes of combat had reduced the French band to just one clarinet, a bassoon and a pair of cymbals. 'Jugez quelle musique!' exclaims M. Girault.

The growth of bands thus presented new questions for the Army. By the early years of the 19th century, a huge gulf was opening up between the logistics of, say, a Scottish infantry battalion taking a piper to war to inspire the men, and the presence in the front line of a fully-fledged wind band. There was also the perennial problem of how to justify the existence of musicians within the ranks of the nation's armed forces. The result was an order issued by Horse Guards in 1803 that bandsmen 'are to be drilled in their exercise and in case of actual service are to fall in with their companies completely armed and accoutred.'

The effect of this order was not immediately apparent. Although many foreign bandsmen were dismissed during the Napoleonic wars in deference to patriotic sentiments back home, several bands

5th Battalion The Royal Irish Regiment in a prisoner of war camp, Sennelager 1915   (RMSM)

– including, for example, that of the 48th Foot mentioned elsewhere – were involved in the campaigns in a musical capacity. And there are photographs from as late as the end of the century that still show an infantry square forming up in training with the band in the centre (see *Volume One*, p.179).

The major problem with implementing the new order was that – with the exception of the Royal Artillery – bands in the first half of the 19th century were funded directly by their regiments. Officers paid for their bandmasters and musicians by voluntary subscription, and tended to regard their bands almost as private institutions, accountable only to themselves. (A similarly proprietorial attitude can be seen in an incident during the Netherlands campaign of 1799, when the Duke of York ordered his band to play loud marches to drown out the sounds of the enemy firing; it appears that the French muskets were disturbing the ladies in his party, particularly Elizabeth, Lady Holland.)

For much of the 19th century, too, most regiments had foreign bandmasters (an exception again being the Artillery, who appointed a British Master of the Band as early as 1810). These musicians were employed as civilians and had no intention of serving abroad, let alone in the ranks. The same was also true for many bandsmen.

By the time of the Crimean War, there had been some concession made to the wishes of the authorities, and a large number of bandsmen joined the ranks to fight. Nonetheless, several civilian bandmasters did resign their posts, and even at this late stage the Band of the Scots Greys took instruments to war.

These qualifications notwithstanding, the Crimean War ushered in a new era in military music. For the first time substantial casualties were sustained by bands: the 4th Light Dragoons lost ten musicians killed, wounded or captured at the charge of the Light Brigade, whilst The Rifle Brigade ended with just 16 bandsmen from an original complement of 45. Here too, the first Victoria Cross was won by a musician, awarded to Andrew Henry, who was the principal keyed bugle player of the Royal Artillery. From the same Regiment came John McLaren, a flugel horn player who won the French Military Medal.

Even more significant, in terms of the evolution of military music, was the founding in the aftermath of the Crimea of Kneller Hall. Though it took some time to complete, a process of bringing bands under central control was now under way, and the old days of regimental independence began to recede into history. With them disappeared civilian bandmasters and bandsmen, who regarded themselves simply as musicians rather than soldiers.

Between the Crimean and Boer Wars, a number of Victoria Crosses were awarded to musicians, though in all the cases these were not to bandsmen as such, but to trumpeters, drummers and pipers. Amongst those whose bravery was so honoured were Bugler Frederick Whirlpool (of The Leinster Regiment), Trumpeter Thomas Monaghan (2nd Dragoon Guards), Lance Corporal – later Trumpet Major – Robert Kells (9th Lancers), Bugler W Sutton (60th Rifles), Bugler R Hawthorne (52nd Foot), Drummer M Ryan (1st Bengal Fusiliers) and Drummer T Flinn (64th Foot). All were honoured for services during the Indian Mutiny.

These awards were for medical and military duties; in the case of Bugler Whirlpool, for example, it was for both, as the citation indicates:

For gallantly volunteering on the 3rd April 1858, in the attack on Jhansi, to return and carry away several killed and wounded, which he did twice under a very heavy fire from the wall; also for devoted bravery at the assault of Lohari, on the 2nd May 1858, in rushing to the rescue of Lieutenant Doune, of the Regiment, who was dangerously wounded. In this service Private Whirlpool received seventeen desperate wounds, one of which nearly severed his head from his body. The gallant example shown by this man is considered to have greatly contributed to the success of the day.

Similarly, Victoria Crosses were won during the Maori Wars by Drummer Stagpoole of the 57th Regiment (recipient of the Distinguished Conduct Medal the week before he won the VC), in Abyssinia by Drummer M Magner of the 33rd Regiment, and in India in 1897 by Piper G Findlater of The Gordon Highlanders.

After nearly a century of pressure from above, the Boer War finally saw the full implementation of the 1803 order, with the bandsmen of all the regiments involved in that conflict laying down their instruments in favour of military tasks. It was a move that was to be repeated in the Great War, when the need for trained soldiers vastly outweighed the requirement for music, at least in the minds of those in central government responsible for such decisions.

Exempted from such wartime duties were bandmasters, who for the most part returned to their regimental depots with the bandboys to form new bands. A distinguished exception was Mr William Dunn of the 2nd Battalion, 60th Rifles. At the outbreak of war 'Paddy' Dunn ignored orders and secretly joined the draft as a rifleman. When discovered in France, he was initially threatened by his Commanding Officer with a court martial, but argued his case strongly enough to be appointed Commander of the 2nd Infantry Brigade Ammunition Column. He was awarded the Military Cross for taking small arms to the 3rd Infantry Brigade, but was later wounded at Neuve Chapelle in 1915 and subsequently returned to take charge of the bands at the Rifle Depot, Winchester.

Six Victoria Crosses were won by musicians during the Great War, including one by a bandsman, Thomas Edward Rendle of the 1st Duke of Cornwall's Light Infantry. A contemporary newspaper report paid tribute to his bravery and modesty:

When it was thought to obtain an interview with [Private] Rendle he first refused point blank to be seen, much less interviewed. This was because he

Sergeant T Rendle VC, Duke of Cornwall's Light Infantry (Ernest Trotter)

1st Battalion The Buffs on stretcher drill c1922   (Buffs)

has been embarrassed by the fuss which has been made of him in consequence of the honour he has earned . . . . His impression of the events of Nov 20th [1914] was not at all clear and as he modestly put it, 'there is really nothing in it.' Sights he had seen in the trenches, he said were 'enough to move the heart of a stone.' Near Wolverghem he was in the trenches eight days and he made up his mind to assist in the removal of the wounded at whatever cost. In the midst of shell and rifle fire, he took his wounded comrades out of the trench one after the other. He was warned again and again to come down, but paid no heed to the danger.

Despite these, and many other, tales of individual heroism, and despite the honourable service rendered by bandsmen in the ranks through the ages, the need for military music remained as strong as ever, and by 1916 bands were reappearing both at home and abroad.

The Second World War saw a virtual repeat of the experience of the Great War – bands were disbanded on the outbreak of hostilities, only to be rebuilt back at regimental depots soon after, as their value became apparent to even the most blinkered politician. At a time when the civilian population of Britain was labouring under the twin onslaughts of the U-boat campaign and the Luftwaffe, the boost to morale that sometimes only music can provide was an urgent priority. So urgent, indeed, that where bands did not exist, unofficial combinations sprang up to fill the gap. 167 Company of the Pioneer Corps had a volunteer band, whose members – after working all day to clear the bomb damage in London – spent their evenings touring the bomb shelters.

Quite apart from these formal and informal bands, there were also the musical initiatives launched by the Army Education Corps. In association with ENSA, the AEC sought to provide activities for the vast army of conscripts training in the UK in anticipation of future offensives. At one point in 1942 there were three symphony orchestras functioning in Britain, comprised entirely of men on National Service. Their performances helped slake the public thirst for entertainment.

Similarly the value of music within the Army was even greater in times of war than in peace, an issue addressed by Rudyard Kipling in a speech delivered to the Recruiting Bands Committee in 1915:

No one, not even the adjutant can say for certain where the soul of the battalion lives, but the expression of that soul is most often found in the band . . . . A wise and sympathetic bandmaster – and the masters I have met have been that – can lift a battalion out of depression, cheer it up in sickness, and steady and recall it to itself in times of almost unendurable stress.

In both world wars, there were bands touring occupied areas to entertain the troops within a couple of years of regimental bands being dismantled. Again irregular bands were formed where necessary, often from the newly mobilized territorial battalions which brought many civilian musicians into the Army. Typical of many was the 30th Battalion of the Somerset Light Infantry, which spent much of 1944 in Italy engaged in the mundane and tedious task of guarding the railways. Under Captain R B Holder, a Dance Orchestra was formed, proving a hit not just with its own Battalion, but on a six-day tour of the Allied bases and on local radio.

Many of the territorial battalion bands in fact continued to operate throughout the war, both at home and abroad. The 1/4th Essex Regiment, for example, took its band to Sierra Leone in 1940, where a changing of the guard ceremony was mounted at Government House in Freetown; thus was British imperial tradition kept alive even in Africa and even in the midst of war.

Music also had an important part to play in captivity. The experiences of Lance-Corporal Howe of The Royal Scots in a prisoner of war camp have been recounted elsewhere in this volume, but his is by no means a unique story; many bandsmen and amateur musicians formed impromptu bands after capture, partly to keep spirits high, and partly as a simple exercise in relieving boredom.

In the half century since 1945, bandsmen and other musicians have given active service throughout the world, mostly as stretcher-bearers. Time and again, in the conflicts that accompanied the shrugging off of Empire, from Guyana to Ireland to Cyprus, men laid down their instruments to come to the assistance of their regiments.

The position of musicians in an army has often seemed paradoxical to outsiders, their relationship to a force with twin objectives of deterrence and defence not always being obvious. But a modern army, as the Second World War amply demonstrated, is not simply a body of armed men; it requires too the services of clergymen, teachers, dentists and a whole panoply of support systems in order that the men called upon to fight – still in this technological age more than likely to be the 'poor bloody infantry' – can operate successfully. Acknowledging the fact that an army, however efficient, is still composed of human beings, Montgomery once remarked:

The most important people in the Army are the Nursing Sisters and the Padres – the Sisters because they tell the men they matter to us – and the Padres because they tell the men they matter to God.

If musicians cannot quite compete on these exalted levels, their contribution is nonetheless highly significant in human terms. A band raises morale both within the service and in the country generally, acts as an intermediary between the sometimes faceless Army and the world of the civilian and keeps alive the traditions of the past. It also – in the words of Kipling – 'aids recruiting perhaps more than any other agency.' All these contributions are enhanced, not diminished, during wartime.

Drums of The Northumberland Fusiliers lost in France in 1940 and subsequently recovered
(Northumberland Fusiliers)

And in the modern era, as memories of National Service recede into distant history, the need for a medium through which the Army can communicate to the country, and through which a nation at arms can speak to itself, is greater than ever. Notwithstanding the medical endeavours of bandsmen in the Gulf and in the former Yugoslavia, it is worth noting that the most potent images of British military bands in the '90s have come from musical events: specifically from the performance of the Coldstream Guards at a football match in Bosnia, and from the 50th anniversary commemorations of the Second World War. The unique musical contribution of bands remains their greatest strength and one of the greatest assets of the British Army.

Above:
Entertaining the populace: Scots Guards at Tower Hill 1942, Director of Music Maj S Rhodes   (RMSM)
Top right: Dance Band Stalag VIIIb, leader LCpl J Howe   (J Howe)

APPENDIX

CORRECTIONS TO *VOLUME ONE*

CORRECTIONS TO *VOLUME ONE*

We are grateful to all those who wrote to us following the publication of *Volume One* of this series with encouragement and comments, including many who pointed out errors. We would, of course, like to apologize to those whose details were incorrectly published. In an undertaking of this nature, mistakes are perhaps inevitable, but we are happy that with the assistance of our readers we are able to make the following corrections.

page

4 & 5   Captions to photographs should be reversed.

7   Caption to photograph on page 6 should read 1993, not 1933.

22   Anthony Richards should read Antony Richards.

23   Charles Boosé should read Carl Boosé.

24   Captions to photographs should be reversed.

28   D H Mackay retired 1984, not 1982.

28   Joseph Albert Thornburrow – though this is given as his name in the *Army List*, the Registry of Births and Deaths records him as Albert Joseph.

33   W Jackson was appointed DoM Junior Musicians Wing (Pirbright) 8/70, not 8/80.

39   Royal Scots Dragoon Guards were formed 1971, not 1671.

41   Douglas Wawick Turner should read Douglas Warnock Turner.

47   M S Cammack – first name is Melvin.

58   C Zoeller died whilst serving 1886.

64   C H Jaeger died 1970, not 1960.

69   The 9th/12th Royal Lancers were not amalgamated in 1993.

70   A Lemoine appointed to Life Guards 1938, not 1926 (also page 114).

70   Initials after B T Keeling's name should read: MBE LRAM ARCM psm (also pages 28 and 114).

70   M J Peagram should read Pegram.

105   R B Bashford appointed Ass DoM RMSM 18/6/74 not 1970.

105   T Griffiths appointed DoM JMW Pirbright 1981 not 1979.

114   R A Hunt retired 1982, not 1983 (also page 142).

114   W G Lemon appointed Maj (DoM) RE (Chatham) 23/4/61.

115   D K Walker – full name Desmond Kiernan Walker.

Right: Major J Howe, Scots Guards c1970   (Howe)
Above: Bandmasters V Webster and D Pope of 1st and 2nd Battalions, The Queen's Own Cameron Highlanders
(Webster)

115   K Boulding – full name Keith Ronald Rex Boulding.
129   B E Hicks took over from T A J Kenney 1978, not 1977.
131   W Allen was Captain when appointed DoM RCT 1969; promoted to Major 1973.
131   P E Hills enlisted RA, then transferred to Welsh Guards.
142   Roy Arthur Hunt's first names have been omitted.
144   F E Hays was Captain when appointed DoM REME in 1961.
144   D E Pryce was promoted to Major in 1980, not 1984.
155   L Sharpe's first name is Leigh, not Lee.
159   Photograph is of the Royal Hong Kong Police, not the Brigade of Gurkhas.
159   J P C Bailey's MBE has been omitted. Retired in the rank of Major.

159   William Henry Moore should read Ernest James Houghton Moore.
163   J F Dean was WO1 (BM) when appointed to RCT; commissioned as Lieutenant 1947.
168   G H J Hurst retired 1977, not 1974.
172   H C Jarman retired 1954, not 1952.
172   In details of D Beat's career, Capt (DoM) SG 28/8/74 was omitted.
176   C J Ross was appointed DoM REME 1986 not 1989.
186   Captain Zara Bowness enlisted in 1962, not 1946.
187   M G Lane died 1989, not 1991.
195   Frederick Vivian Dunn should read Francis Vivian Dunn.

Undoubtedly there are further errors in this volume; we will again be grateful to learn of any mistakes so that we can rectify them in *Volume Three*.

REGIMENT AND CORPS ABBREVIATIONS

All abbreviations are taken from the official Army Lists that were in use at the time.

1 Ft	1st, or The Royal Regiment	21 Ft	21st (Royal North British) Regiment
1 RTR	Ist Royal Tank Regiment	21 Fus	The Royal Scots Fusiliers
2 Ft	2nd, or Queen's Royal Regiment	21 L	21st Lancers (Empress of India's)
2 LI	2nd Battalion, The Light Infantry	22 Dns	22nd Dragoons
2 RTR	2nd Royal Tank Regiment	22 Ft	22nd (Cheshire) Regiment
2 Wessex	Berkshire, Buckinghamshire and Oxfordshire (Wessex) Band (TA). The	23 Ft	23rd (Royal Welsh) Fusiliers
		23 H	23rd Hussars
3 DG	3rd Dragoon Guards (Prince of Wales's) before 1922. 3rd Carabiniers (Prince of Wales's Dragoon Guards) after 1922	24 Ft	24th (2nd Warwickshire) Regiment
		24 L	24th Lancers
		25 Dns	25th Dragoons
3 Ft	3rd (East Kent – The Buffs) Regiment	25 Ft	25th (King's Own Borderers) Regiment
3 H	3rd Hussars	26 Ft	26th Cameronian Regiment
3 RTR	3rd Royal Tank Regiment	26 H	26th Hussars
4 Ft	4th, or The King's Own Regiment	27 Ft	27th (Inniskilling) Regiment
4 H	4th Hussars	27 L	27th Lancers
5 Ft	5th, or Northumberland Fusiliers	28 Ft	28th (North Gloucestershire) Regiment
5 Innis DG	5th Royal Inniskilling Dragoon Guards	29 Ft	29th (Worcestershire) Regiment
5 L	5th (Royal Irish) Lancers	30 Ft	30th (Cambridgeshire) Regiment
6 DG	Carabiniers (6th Dragoon Guards), The	31 Ft	31st (Huntingdonshire) Regiment
6 Ft	6th (Royal 1st Warwickshire) Regiment	32 Ft	32nd (Cornwall) Light Infantry
7 Ft	7th (Royal Fusiliers)	33 Ft	33rd (Duke of Wellington's) Regiment
7 H	7th Hussars	34 Ft	34th (Cumberland) Regiment
8 Ft	8th (The King's) Regiment	35 Ft	35th (Royal Sussex) Regiment
8 H	8th Hussars	36 Ft	36th (Herefordshire) Regiment
9 Ft	9th (East Norfolk) Regiment	37 Ft	37th (North Hampshire) Regiment
9 L	9th Lancers	38 Ft	38th (1st Staffordshire) Regiment
9/12 L	9th/12th Royal Lancers (Prince of Wales's)	39 Ft	39th (Dorsetshire) Regiment
10 Ft	10th (North Lincolnshire) Regiment	40 Ft	40th (2nd Somersetshire) Regiment
10 H	10th Hussars	41 Ft	41st (The Welsh) Regiment
11 Ft	11th (North Devonshire) Regiment	42 Ft	42nd (The Royal Highland) Foot
11 H	11th Hussars	43 Ft	43rd (Monmouthshire Light Infantry) Regiment
12 Ft	12th (East Suffolk) Regiment		
12 L	12th Lancers	44 Ft	44th (East Essex) Regiment
13 Ft	13th Ft (1st Somerset)(Prince Albert's Light Infantry) Regiment	45 Ft	45th (Nottinghamshire Regiment) Sherwood Foresters
13/18 H	13th/18th Royal Hussars (Queen Mary's Own)	46 Ft	46th (South Devonshire) Regiment
		47 Ft	47th (Lancashire) Regiment
14 Ft	14th (Buckinghamshire) Regiment	48 Ft	48th (Northamptonshire) Regiment
15 Ft	15th (Yorkshire, East Riding) Regiment	49 Ft	49th Princess Charlotte of Wales's Hertfordshire Regiment
15 H	15th The King's Hussars		
15/19 H	15th/19th The King's Royal Hussars	50 Ft	50th (The Queen's Own) Regiment
16 Ft	16th (Bedfordshire) Regiment	51 Ft	51st (2nd Yorkshire, West Riding, The King's Own Light Infantry) Regiment
16/5 L	16th/5th The Queen's Royal Lancers		
17 Ft	17th (Leicestershire) Regiment	52 Ft	52nd (Oxfordshire Light Infantry) Regiment
17/21 L	17th/21st Lancers		
18 Ft	18th (The Royal Irish) Regiment	53 Ft	53rd (Shropshire) Regiment
19 Ft	19th (1st Yorkshire, North Riding) Regiment	54 Ft	54th (West Norfolk) Regiment
		55 Ft	55th (Westmorland) Regiment
19 H	19th Royal Hussars (Queen Alexandra's Own)	56 Ft	56th (West Essex) Regiment
		57 Ft	57th (West Middlesex) Regiment
20 Ft	20th (East Devonshire) Regiment	58 Ft	58th (Rutlandshire) Regiment

59 Ft	59th (2nd Nottinghamshire) Regiment	AJSM (Bov)	Army Junior School of Music (Bovington)
60 Ft	60th, or The King's Royal Rifle Corps	AJSM (Pir)	Army Junior School of Music (Pirbright)
61 Ft	61st (South Gloucestershire) Regiment	Albuhera	Albuhera Band, The Queen's Regiment
62 Ft	62nd (Wiltshire) Regiment	ASC	Army Service Corps
63 Ft	63rd (West Suffolk) Regiment		
64 Ft	64th (2nd Staffordshire) Regiment	Bays, The	Queen's Bays, The
65 Ft	65th (2nd Yorkshire, North Riding) Regiment	Bedf R	Bedfordshire Regiment, The
		Bedfs & Herts R	Bedfordshire and Hertfordshire Regiment, The
66 Ft	66th (Berkshire) Regiment		
67 Ft	67th (South Hampshire) Regiment	Border R	Border Regiment, The
68 Ft	68th (Durham – Light Infantry) Regiment	BAOR	British Army Of The Rhine
69 Ft	69th (South Lincolnshire) Regiment	Buffs, The	Buffs, The
70 Ft	70th (Surrey) Regiment	BW	Black Watch (Royal Highland Regiment), The
71 Ft	71st (Highland) Light Infantry		
72 Ft	72nd (Duke of Albany's Own Highlanders) Regiment	Cameronians	Cameronians, The
		Camerons	Queen's Own Cameron Highlanders, The
73 Ft	73rd (Perthshire) Regiment	Cheshire	Cheshire Regiment, The
74 Ft	74th (Highlanders) Regiment	Coldm Gds	Coldstream Guards
75 Ft	75th (Stirlingshire) Regiment	Conn Rang	Connaught Rangers, The
76 Ft	76th Regiment		
77 Ft	77th (East Middlesex) Regiment	D and D	Devonshire and Dorset Regiment, The
78 Ft	78th (Highland) Regiment, or Ross-shire Buffs	DCLI	Duke of Cornwall's Light Infantry, The
		Derby R	Derbyshire Regiment, The
79 Ft	79th Regiment, or Cameron Highlanders	DERR	Duke of Edinburgh's Royal Regiment (Berkshire and Wiltshire), The
80 Ft	80th (Staffordshire Volunteers) Regiment		
81 Ft	81st (Royal Lincoln Volunteers) Regiment	Devon R	Devonshire Regiment, The
82 Ft	82nd (The Prince of Wales's Volunteers) Regiment	Dorset R	Dorsetshire Regiment, The
		Durham LI	Durham Light Infantry, The
83 Ft	83rd (County of Dublin) Regiment	DWR	Duke of Wellington's Regiment, The
84 Ft	84th (York and Lancaster) Regiment		
85 Ft	85th (Bucks Volunteers)(The King's Light Infantry) Regiment	E Kent R	East Kent Regiment, The
		E Lan R	East Lancashire Regiment, The
86 Ft	86th (Royal County Down) Regiment	Essex R	Essex Regiment, The
87 Ft	87th (The Royal Irish Fusiliers) Regiment	E Surr R	East Surrey Regiment, The
88 Ft	88th (Connaught Rangers) Regiment	E York R	East Yorkshire Regiment, The
89 Ft	89th Regiment		
90 Ft	90th Perthshire Light Infantry	Foresters	Sherwood Foresters, The
91 Ft	91st (Argyllshire) Regiment		
92 Ft	92nd (Gordon Highlanders) Regiment	Gds Depot (Pir)	Guards Depot Pirbright
93 Ft	93rd (Sutherland Highlanders) Regiment	GJ	Green Jackets, The
94 Ft	94th Regiment	Glosters	Gloucestershire Regiment, The
95 Ft	95th, or Derbyshire Regiment	Gordons	Gordon Highlanders, The
96 Ft	96th Regiment	Green Howards	Green Howards (Alexandra Princess of Wales's Own Yorkshire Regiment), The
97 Ft	97th (The Earl of Ulster's) Regiment		
98 Ft	98th Regiment	Gren Gds	Grenadier Guards
99 Ft	99th (Lanarkshire) Regiment	Greys, The	Scots Greys, The
100 Ft	100th (Prince of Wales's Royal Canadian) Regiment		
		HAC	Honourable Artillery Company, The
101 Ft	101st Royal Bengal Fusiliers	Hampshire R	Hampshire Regiment, The
102 Ft	102nd Royal Madras Fusiliers	Highland Bde	Highland Brigade, The
103 Ft	103rd Royal Bombay Fusiliers	Highland R	Highland Regiment, The
104 Ft	104th Bengal Fusiliers	HLI	Highland Light Regiment, The
105 Ft	105th Madras Light Infantry		
106 Ft	106th Bombay Light Infantry	IG	Irish Guards
107 Ft	107th Bengal Light Infantry	Inniskilling Fus	Royal Inniskilling Fusiliers, The
108 Ft	108th Madras Light Infantry		
109 Ft	109th Bombay Infantry Regiment	JLR	Junior Leaders Regiment (Bovington)
		JMW	Junior Musicians Wing (Pirbright)
AAC	Army Air Corps		
A&SH	Argyll and Sutherland Highlanders, The	KDG	1st King's Dragoon Guards
ACC	Army Catering Corps	KH	Kneller Hall (Royal Military School of Music)
AGC	Adjutant General's Corps		

Kings	King's Regiment, The	QRL	Queen's Royal Lancers, The
Kings (Norm)	Normandy Band, The King's Division	QR Surr	Queen's Royal Surrey Regiment, The
Kings Own Border	King's Own Royal Border Regiment, The	RA	Royal Artillery
King's Own R	King's Own Royal Regiment, The	RA(Alan)	Royal Artillery (Alanbrooke)
Kings (Water)	Waterloo Band, The King's Division	RA(BAOR)	Royal Artillery (BAOR)
KOSB	King's Own Scottish Borderers, The	RA(Gib)	Royal Artillery (Gibraltar)
KRH	King's Royal Hussars, The	RA(Mtd)	Royal Artillery (Mounted)
KRRC	King's Royal Rifle Corps	RA(N Cmd)	Royal Artillery (Northern Command)
KSLI	King's Shropshire Light Infantry	RA(Plym)	Royal Artillery (Plymouth)
		RA(Port)	Royal Artillery (Portsmouth)
Lan Fus	Lancashire Fusiliers, The	RA(Sal Pl)	Royal Artillery (Salisbury Plain)
LD	Light Dragoons, The	RA(Wool)	Royal Artillery (Woolwich)
Leicester R	Leicestershire Regiment, The	RAC	Royal Armoured Corps
Leins R	Leinster Regiment, The	RAC Jnr Ldrs	Royal Armoured Corps, Junior Leaders Regiment
LG	Life Guards, The	RAEC	Royal Army Education Corps
LI	Light Infantry, The	RAF	Royal Air Force
Lincoln R	Lincolnshire Regiment, The	RAMC	Royal Army Medical Corps
Lowland Bde	Lowland Brigade	R Anglian	Royal Anglian Regiment, The
Lowland R	Lowland Regiment, The	RAPC	Royal Army Pay Corps
Loyal R	Loyal Regiment, The	RASC	Royal Army Service Corps
L'pool R	Liverpool Regiment, The	RAVC	Royal Army Veterinary Corps
		R Berks R	Royal Berkshire Regiment, The
Manch R	Manchester Regiment, The	RCT	Royal Corps of Transport
Midd'x R	Middlesex Regiment, The	RDG	Royal Dragoon Guards, The
MSC	Medical Staff Corps	R Dub Fus	Royal Dublin Fusiliers, The
		RE(Ald)	Royal Engineers (Aldershot)
N Lan R	North Lancashire Regiment, The	RE(Chat)	Royal Engineers (Chatham)
Norf R	Norfolk Regiment, The	Recce	Reconnaissance Corps, The
North'd Fus	Northumberland Fusiliers, The	REME	Corps of Royal Electrical and Mechanical Engineers
North'n R	Northamptonshire Regiment, The	RFC	Royal Flying Corps, The
N Stafford R	North Staffordshire Regiment, The	R Fus	Royal Fusiliers, The
		RGA	Royal Garrison Artillery
Ox & Bucks LI	Oxfordshire and Buckinghamshire Light Infantry, The	R Gar R	Royal Garrison Regiment, The
Ox LI	Oxfordshire Light Infantry, The	RGJ	Royal Green Jackets, The
		RH	Royal Hussars (Prince of Wales's Own), The
Para	Parachute Regiment, The	RHA	Royal Horse Artillery
PoW (Clive)	Clive Band, The Prince of Wales's Division	R Hamps	Royal Hampshire Regiment, The
PoW Div	Prince of Wales's Division Depot	RHF	Royal Highland Fusiliers (Princess Margaret's Own Glasgow and Ayrshire Regiment), The
PoW (Luck)	Lucknow Band, The Prince of Wales's Division	RHG	Royal Horse Guards
PPLI	Princess Patricia's Light Infantry of Canada	RHG/D	Blues and Royals (Royal Horse Guards and 1st Dragoons), The
PWO	Prince of Wales's Own Regiment of Yorkshire, The	R Highrs	Royal Highlanders, The
PWRR	Princess of Wales's Royal Regiment	Rifle Bde	Rifle Brigade, The
		R Innis Fus	Royal Inniskilling Fusiliers, The
QDG	1st The Queen's Dragoon Guards	R Ir Constab	Royal Irish Constabulary
QLR	Queen's Lancashire Regiment, The	R Ir Fus	Royal Irish Fusiliers, The
QO Buffs	The Queen's Own Buffs, The Royal Kent Regiment	R Irish	Royal Irish Regiment, The (after 1992)
QOH	Queen's Own Hussars, The	R Irish Rang	Royal Irish Rangers, The
QO Hldrs	Queen's Own Highlanders (Seaforth and Camerons)	R Ir R	Royal Irish Regiment, The (before 1922)
Queens	Queen's Regiment, The	R Ir Rif	Royal Irish Rifles, The
Queens (Alb)	Albuhera Band, The Queen's Regiment	R Lanc R	Royal Lancaster Regiment, The
Queens (Mind)	Minden Band, The Queen's Division	RLC	Royal Logistic Corps
Queens (Norm)	Normandy Band, The Queen's Division	R Leic	Royal Leicestershire Regiment, The
Queens (Queb)	Quebec Band, The Queen's Regiment	RM	Royal Marines
Queen's R	Queen's Royal Regiment, The	RM(Chat)	Royal Marines (Chatham)
QRH	Queen's Royal Hussars, The	RM(Plym)	Royal Marines (Plymouth)
QRIH	Queen's Royal Irish Hussars, The		

RM(Port)	Royal Marines (Portsmouth)	Sco Rif	Scottish Rifles, The
RM(Wool)	Royal Marines (Woolwich)	Scots DG	Royal Scots Dragoon Guards
RMA(Sand)	Royal Military Academy (Sandhurst)		(Carabiniers and Greys), The
RM Art	Royal Marine Artillery	Scots Fus Gds	Scots Fusilier Guards
RMC(Sand)	Royal Military College (Sandhurst)	Seaforth	Seaforth Highlanders, The
RMLI	Royal Marine Light Infantry	SG	Scots Guards
RMSM	Royal Military School of Music, Kneller Hall	Shrops LI	Shropshire Light Infantry, The
R Mun Fus	Royal Munster Fusiliers, The	S Lan R	South Lancashire Regiment, The
		Somerset LI	Somerset Light Infantry, The
R Norfolk R	Royal Norfolk Regiment, The	S Stafford R	South Staffordshire Regiment, The
R North'd Fus	Royal Northumberland Fusiliers, The	Staffords	Staffordshire Regiment (The Prince of
RNSM	Royal Naval School of Music		Wales's), The
		Suffolk R	Suffolk Regiment, The
Royals, The	Royal Dragoons, The	S Wales Bord	South Wales Borderers, The
RRF	Royal Regiment of Fusiliers, The	S Yorks	South Yorkshire Regiment, The
RRW	Royal Regiment of Wales, The		
RS	Royal Scots (The Royal Regiment), The	Welsh R	Welsh Regiment, The
R S Fus	Royal Scots Fusiliers, The	WFR	Worcestershire and Sherwood Foresters
R Signals	Royal Corps of Signals		Regiment, The
R Sussex R	Royal Sussex Regiment, The	WG	Welsh Guards
RTR	Royal Tank Regiment	Wilts R	Wiltshire Regiment, The
RTR (Alamein)	Alamein Band of the Royal Tank Regiment	Worc R	Worcestershire Regiment, The
RTR (Cambrai)	Cambrai Band of the Royal Tank Regiment	WRAC	Women's Royal Army Corps
RTR (Rhine)	Rhine Band of the Royal Tank Regiment	W Rid R	West Riding Regiment, The
R U Rifles	Royal Ulster Rifles, The	W York R	West Yorkshire Regiment, The
RWAFF	Royal West African Frontier Force		
R War R	Royal Warwickshire Regiment, The	York & Lanc R	York and Lancaster Regiment, The
RWF	Royal Welsh Fusiliers, The	York R	Yorkshire Regiment, The
R W Kent R	Royal West Kent Regiment, The		
R W Surr R	Royal West Surrey Regiment, The		

The Black Watch marching through Belfast, Bandmaster N Rogerson   (RMSM)

GENERAL ABBREVIATIONS

AmusLCM	Associate in music, London College of Music
AmusTCL	Associate in music, Trinity College of Music
ARCM	Associate Royal College of Music
att	attached
BA	Bachelor of Arts
Bdmn	Bandsman
BM	Bandmaster
BMus	Bachelor of Music
Bn	Battalion
BSgt	Band Sergeant
BSM	Band Sergeant Major
Capt	Captain
Civ BM	Civilian Bandmaster
Cmdr	Commander
Cpl	Corporal
CVO	Commander of the Royal Victorian Order
DMjr	Drum Major
DMus	Doctor of Music
DoM	Director of Music
FLCM	Fellow London College of Music
Flt Lt	Flight Lieutenant
FRAM	Fellow Royal Academy of Music
FRSA	Fellow Royal Society of Arts
FTCL	Fellow Trinity College of Music
FVCM	Fellow Victoria College of Music
Instr	Instructor
LCpl	Lance Corporal
LGSM	Licentiate Guildhall School of Music
L/Maj	Local Major
LmusLCM	Licentiate in music, London College of Music

LmusTCL	Licentiate in music, Trinity College of Music
LRAM	Licentiate Royal Academy of Music
Lt	Lieutenant
Lt-Col	Lieutenant-Colonel
LTCL	Licentiate Trinity College of Music
LVO	Lieutenant of the Royal Victorian Order
Maj	Major
MBE	Member of the British Empire
MoB	Master of Band
MSM	Meritorious Service Medal
Mus Bac	Bachelor of Music
Mus Doc	Doctor of Music
Musn	Musician
MVO	Member of the Royal Victorian Order
OBE	Order of the British Empire
PMajor	Pipe Major
psm	passed school of music (RMSM)
RO	Retired Officer
Sgt	Sergeant
SSgt	Staff Sergeant
Std BM	Student Bandmaster (Kneller Hall)
(sub)	substantive rank
TDT	Training and Development Team
TMjr	Trumpet Major
WO	Warrant Officer
WO1	Warrant Officer Class One

Top right: Church service in Keijo Camp, Korea, for prisoners of war 1943   (RMSM)

Right: 1st Battalion The Queen's Own Cameron Highlanders, Bandmaster W Babbs, Dover 1958

4TH FOOT 1751.

FOOT GUARDS, 1742.

1ST FOOT GUARDS. 1792.

SCOTS GUARDS. 1893.

9TH FOOT, 1814.

24TH FOOT, 1843.

57TH FOOT, 1852.

18TH FOOT, 1863.

LINE INFANTRY, 1893.

R SIMKIN

BIBLIOGRAPHY

Books

Ascoli, David *A Companion to the British Army 1660-1983* (London, Harrap, 1983)

Barclay, Brigadier C N *The History of The Cameronians (Scottish Rifles) Vol III: 1933-1946* (London, Sifton Praed, undated)

Barthorp, Michael *The Armies of Britain 1485-1980* (London, National Army Museum, c.1980)

Bart-King, Hugh *The Drum* (London, The Royal Tournament, 1988)

Binns, Lieutenant-Colonel P L *A Hundred Years of Military Music: Being the Story of the Royal Military School of Music, Kneller Hall* (Dorset, Blackmore Press, 1959)

Buchan, John *The History of The Royal Scots Fusiliers*

Dean, Colin *Directors of Music of the British Army* (private publication, 1993)

Edwards, Major T J *Military Customs* (Aldershot, Gale and Polden)

Edwards, Major T J *Regimental Badges* (Aldershot, Gale and Polden, 1951)

Edwards, Major T J *Regimental Nicknames and Traditions* (Aldershot, Gale and Polden)

Farmer, Henry George *British Bands in Battle* (London, Hinrichsen)

Farmer, Henry George *Handel's Kettledrums and Other Papers on Military Music* (London, Hinrichsen, 1945)

Farmer, Henry George *Military Music* (London, Parrish and Co, 1950)

Farmer, Henry George *The Rise & Development of Military Music* (London, Wm Reeves, 1912)

Flood, Wm H Grattan *The Story of the Bagpipe* (London, Walter Scott Publishing Company, 1911)

Fredrikkson, Björn *Directors of Music of the British Army* (Sweden, The International Military Music Society, 1987)

Gardyne, Lieutenant-Colonel C Greenhill *The Life of a Regiment: The History of The Gordon Highlanders from 1816 to 1898* (London, Medici Society, 1903)

Godfrey, Sir Dan *Memories and Music* (London, Hutchinson, 1924)

Henderson, Diana M *Highland Soldier 1820-1920* (Edinburgh, John Donald, 1989)

Kappey, Jacob Adam *Military Music; A history of wind-instrumental bands* (London, Boosey & Co)

Lenman, Bruce *The Jacobite Risings in Britain 1689-1746* (London, Eyre Methuen, 1980)

Mackenzie-Rogan, Lieutenant-Colonel J *Fifty Years of Army Music* (London, Methuen, 1926)

Marr, Robert A *Music and Musicians at the Edinburgh International Exhibition 1886* (Edinburgh, Constable, 1887)

Martin, Colonel T A *The Essex Regiment 1929-1950* (1952, regimental publication)

Morris, Eric *Circles of Hell: The War in Italy 1943-1945* (London, Random House, 1993)

Murray, David *Music of the Scottish Regiments* (Durham, Pentland Press, 1994)

Palmer, Roy *The Rambling Soldier* (Harmondsworth Middlesex, Kestrel Books, 1977)

Pertwee, Bill *Stars in Battledress* (London, Hodder & Stoughton, 1992)

Trendell, John *Colonel Bogey To The Fore* (Deal, Blue Band Magazine, 1991)

Turner, Alwyn W, *Tribute, a Salute to The British Armed Forces of the Second World War* (Harpenden, Lennard, 1995)

Verney, Peter *The Micks: The Story of the Irish Guards* (London, Peter Davies, 1970)

Wilson, Lieutenant-Colonel L M B. *Regimental Music of The Queen's Regiment* (private publication, 1980)

Winstock, Lewis *Songs & Music of the Redcoats* (London, Lee Cooper, 1970)

Wood, Walter *The Romance of Regimental Marches* (London, William Clowes and Sons Ltd, 1932)

Zealley, Alfred Edward & Ord Hume, James *Famous Bands of the British Empire* (London, J P Hull, 1926)

Journals

The Antelope

The Army List (HMSO)

Band International, Journal of the International Military Music Society

The British Bandsman

Cabar Feidh

The Covenanter

The Die-Hards

The Essex Regimental Gazette

The Eagle

Fanfare (RMSM, Kneller Hall)

The Green Tiger

Invicta: Journal of The Queen's Own Buffs

The Lancashire Fusiliers' Annual

Leading Note 1929-1938 (RMSM, Kneller Hall)

The Red Hackle

St George's Gazette

Tiger and Sphinx

The Wasp

INDEX

Main entries indicated in bold. Illustrations are indicated in brackets.